# Blue
# Sisters

## Coco Mellors

*Coco*
14

4th ESTATE • *London*

4th Estate
An imprint of HarperCollins*Publishers*
1 London Bridge Street
London SE1 9GF

www.4thestate.co.uk

HarperCollins*Publishers*
Macken House, 39/40 Mayor Street Upper
Dublin 1, D01 C9W8, Ireland

First published in Great Britain in 2024 by 4th Estate
First published in the US in 2024 by Ballantine Books
This 4th Estate paperback published in 2025

1

Book design by Sara Bereta

A catalogue record for this book is
available from the British Library

ISBN 978-0-00-862303-6

Set in Bembo MT Pro
Printed and bound in the UK using 100%
renewable electricity at CPI Group (UK) Ltd

*For Daisy, for being there from the beginning.*

*And for Henry, for promising to stay until the end.*

COCO MELLORS grew up in London and New York, where she received her MFA in fiction from New York University. Her first novel, *Cleopatra and Frankenstein*, was a *Sunday Times* bestseller, has been translated into over twenty-five languages and is currently being adapted for television. She lives in New York with her husband and son.

Praise for *Blue Sisters*:

'In *Blue Sisters*, grief is rendered with gorgeous particularity'
RAVEN LEILANI, author of *Luster*

'Think *Little Women* but for the contemporary female experience'
*Evening Standard*

'Deeply poignant and written in Mellors' emotional, textured prose'
*Harper's Bazaar*

'A beautiful, messy, love and grief-filled book. It is a breathtaking novel, and I found great comfort in reading it. This book is so expertly crafted, it moved me deeply'     LIV LITTLE, author of *Rosewater*

'Even better than *Cleopatra and Frankenstein*, this is emotional heft meets page-turner'     *Grazia*

'It will make you laugh, cry deeply and want to call your siblings'
*Cosmopolitan*

'A stunning exploration of sisterhood and grief, addiction and recovery, pain and pleasure. At once contemporary and timeless, *Blue Sisters* is captivating'     TESS GUNTY, author of *The Rabbit Hutch*

'Mellors' emotionally charged second novel courses with shame and sorrow ... but it also glows with love and sisterly loyalty'

*Mail on Sunday*

'Compulsively readable'

*Telegraph*

'A compulsive page-turner about beautiful young Americans and slightly broken lives – expect it to be just as popular as *Cleopatra and Frankenstein*'

*Independent*

'Instantly compelling'

*Stylist*

'A healing balm. *Blue Sisters* will unearth tenderness and heartache from spectacular depths within you'

XOCHITL GONZALEZ, author of *Olga Dies Dreaming*

'In prose that is at times transcendently beautiful, Mellors has painted a portrait of sisterhood in all its pettiness and messiness and beauty and grace'    RUFI THORPE, author of *Margo's Got Money Troubles*

'A poignant and visceral exploration of sisterhood and grief'    *Red*

'A top contender for book of the year. A stunning story of siblings, family, struggling and belonging'

*Prima*

'A richly textured tale of love, loss and addiction in all its complexities. When I made it to the final page, I had tears in my eyes. I will be thinking about the Blue sisters for a long time'

ISABEL KAPLAN, author of *NSFW*

'An expansive novel about the individuality of addiction and the nature of family connection. *Blue Sisters* examines the complications and beauty of siblinghood with a sensitivity that will be familiar to readers of Mellors' huge debut, *Cleopatra and Frankenstein*'    *GQ*

'Coco Mellors delivers a resounding follow up to her smash hit debut *Cleopatra and Frankenstein* with *Blue Sisters*, a tale of grief, humour and sisterhood that will keep you reading until the early hours. With an intricate narrative and tender vulnerability, this is a gripping, heart-wrenching and utterly addictive read'                    *Glamour*

'This heartbreaking, gripping book is all about human vulnerability in a violent world. A novel of intense relationships and evocative city scenes. Wildly addictive'                    *iNEWS*

## BY COCO MELLORS

*Blue Sisters*

*Cleopatra and Frankenstein*

# Blue
# Sisters

# PROLOGUE

A SISTER IS NOT A FRIEND. WHO CAN EXPLAIN THE URGE TO TAKE A relationship as primal and complex as a sibling and reduce it to something as replaceable, as banal as a friend? Yet this status is used again and again to connote the highest intimacy. *My mother is my best friend. My husband is my best friend.* No. True sisterhood, the kind where you grew fingernails in the same womb, were pushed screaming through identical birth canals, is not the same as friendship. You don't choose each other, and there's no furtive period of getting to know the other. You're part of each other, right from the start. Look at an umbilical cord—tough, sinuous, unlovely, yet essential—and compare it to a friendship bracelet of brightly woven thread. *That* is the difference between a sister and a friend.

The eldest of the Blue sisters, their leader, is Avery. She was born wise and world-weary. At four years old, she returned to their parents' Upper West Side apartment after walking herself home from kindergarten and declared herself *too tired to go on*. But she did go on, she always has. Avery taught all the sisters how to swim the front crawl, how to make friends with the bodega cats by tickling them under the chin, how to shuffle cards without bending the corners. She hates authority but loves structure. She has a photographic memory; in high school she broke into their school's records and memorized her entire grade's Social Security numbers, then spent the remainder of the semester freaking kids out by referring to them by their nine digits.

She graduated from high school at sixteen and completed undergrad at Columbia University in three years. Then, she ran away to join an "anarchic, nonhierarchical, consensus-driven community," otherwise known as a commune, before briefly living on the streets of San Francisco, where she smoked and, eventually, shot heroin. Unbeknownst to anyone in her family, she checked herself into detox a year later and has stayed clean ever since. Afterward, she enrolled herself in law school, where she finally put that memory to good use.

They say you don't know your principles until they become inconvenient to you, and Avery is proof of this. She is deeply principled and often inconvenienced. She might have liked to be a poet or a documentary filmmaker, but she is a lawyer. Now thirty-three, she lives in London with her wife, Chiti, a therapist seven years her senior. She has paid off all her college loans and owns furniture that cost almost as much as her tuition. She does not know it yet, but in a few weeks, she will implode her life and marriage in ways she didn't think possible. Avery would like to be all backbone, but she is tender flesh too.

Two years after Avery was born, their parents had Bonnie. Bonnie is soft-spoken and strong-willed. Her language is the language of the body. By six, she could walk on her hands. By ten, she could juggle five tangerines at a time. She tried both ballet and gymnastics, but she never fit in among that flock of flexible, feminine girls. When she was fifteen, their father bought her a pair of boxing gloves after she punched a hole in her bedroom wall, and she found her true form.

Bonnie discovering boxing is probably how other people felt when they discovered sex. So, *this* is what all the fuss is about.

Bonnie worships at the altar of discipline. After silently watching her older sister's adolescent decline, she vowed never to touch a drop of alcohol. Her drugs of choice are sweat and violence. This got her all the way to the IBA Women's World Boxing Championships, the highest level of amateur competition in the sport alongside the Olympics, where she won silver in the lightweight division before turning pro. Unexpectedly, given her sport of choice, Bonnie is the gentlest of her sisters. She can get ice out of the tray without bashing it on the counter. Babies and dogs trust her instinctively. She is a terrible liar. Though her body is like a vaulted oak door, her nature is transparent as a window. Now thirty-one years old and in what should be her fighting prime, Bonnie has quit both New York and boxing after a devastating defeat in her last fight. She fled to Venice Beach, Los Angeles, where she took a job as the bouncer of a dive bar.

Most people go through life never knowing what it's like to have a calling, one that asks you to sacrifice the pleasure of the moment for the potential of a dream that may not be realized for years, if at all. It sets you apart from others, whether you want it to or not. It can be grueling, lonely, and punishing, but, if it is really your calling, it is not a choice. This is how boxing felt to Bonnie. And yet, right now, you can find her in some backstreet of Venice, collecting empty pint glasses, helping tipsy women into the back of cars, and sweeping up cigarette butts, with no trace at all of the anarchic, ironhearted warrior she was trained to be.

Their parents wanted a son next but, after two miscarriages never spoken of again, they had Nicole, known always as Nicky. Of all the girls, Nicky was the *most* girl. She could blow a bubble as big as her head. She listened to teen pop into adulthood without irony. Her favorite hobby as a child was raising caterpillars to become butterflies by feeding them tiny pieces of squash. When she was ten, she bought her first underwire bra, just so she'd be ready. She'd had five boyfriends by the time she graduated from high school. She liked to pick out a week's worth of outfits in advance, including underwear to match. She could apply a perfect cat eye with liquid liner in a moving taxi without smudging the flicks. Nicky was always popular with boys, but she had a knack for female friendship. She joined a sorority in college, a fact her sisters ruthlessly teased her for, but she didn't care. Her sisters were often busy with their own careers, and she missed them, so she made a family of her friends.

If Avery was sensible and Bonnie was stoic, Nicky was sensitive. She was a carnival of feelings she never tried to hide. Sometimes she was the ecstatic swirl of a carousel, sometimes she was a bumper car collision, sometimes she was the still target waiting in the shooting gallery. She was born to be a mother, but her body had other ideas. After years of agonizing periods, she was diagnosed with endometriosis in her twenties. Though she died at twenty-seven, she was not a natural member of that club; she wasn't the lead singer of a band, and she didn't live particularly fast to die young. If you'd asked Nicky, she would have said she lived an extraordinarily ordinary life as a tenth-grade English teacher at a charter school on the Upper West Side, ten blocks from where she grew up. If it seemed a smaller existence than her sisters', she never saw it that way. She loved her students and dreamed of one day having a family. Nothing about her life portended her death, except for the fact she was in pain.

A year after Nicky's birth, their parents tried one last time for the long-awaited son. They got Lucky. Born at home by mistake in only fifteen minutes, Lucky wasted no time establishing her place in the family. No matter how old Lucky gets, she will always be the baby. In fact, once Nicky could speak, she quickly proclaimed Lucky *my baby* and insisted on lugging her tiny form with her everywhere. They remained inseparable, but Lucky did not stay small. She is five foot eleven. Their parents got four shots to create that so-sought-after thing: female beauty. With Lucky, they succeeded. Even her teeth, which are crooked with unusually sharp canines, give her smile a sensual, wolfish quality. Recently, without the approval of her agency, she chopped off most of her hair and bleached it white. Now, she looks like a combination of Barbie, Billy Idol, and a Siberian husky. Lucky became a model when she was fifteen and has worked all over the world, which is another way of saying she has been lonely all over the world.

When Lucky enters a room, it is like an electric eel slipping into a bowl of goldfish. She is sharp-witted and secretly shy. She taught herself to play the guitar while living in Tokyo and is pretty good but too self-conscious to ever perform in front of anyone. She still loves playing video games, loves any form of escape, in fact. Right now, she is living alone in Paris. She has said the words *I need a drink* one hundred and thirty-two times so far this year. That's more than she's said *I love you* in her entire life. In her apartment in Montmartre, she has the framed blue butterflies Nicky gave her before she died hanging above her bed, but she rarely sleeps. Lucky is twenty-six years old, and she is lost. In fact, all the remaining sisters are.

But what they don't know is this: As long as you are alive, it is never too late to be found.

# CHAPTER ONE

# Lucky

LUCKY WAS LATE. IRRESPONSIBLY, IRREVERSIBLY, IN–DANGER–OF–LOSING– this-job late. She had a fitting for a couture show in the Marais at noon, but that was ten minutes ago, and she was still miles away on the metro. She had spent the night before at a fashion week party enjoying the open bar (the only kind Lucky cared for), where she'd met a pair of corporate-employed graffiti artists who were anxious to restore their reputations as creatives on the fringe of society. They'd offered to take her on the back of one of their motorcycles to an abandoned mansion, a former diplomat's home in the 16th Arrondissement, that they'd set their sights on tagging. Lucky wasn't particularly into the concept of defacing a historical building with spray paint, but she was always happy to delay the night ending.

The building had been more tightly secured than expected, dotted with security cameras and encircled by an intimidating pronged fence, so they'd settled for spraying the metal shutters of a nearby tabac instead, the graffiti artists opting for libertarian slogans popularized by the Paris protests of 1968—*It is forbidden to forbid!*—while Lucky went for a classic rendering of a penis and balls. They'd watched the sun come up from the steps of Palais de Tokyo while drinking bottles of pink Veuve Clicquot they'd swiped from the party, then returned to Lucky's place to smoke a joint. After a predictable attempt by the two men to initiate a threesome, Lucky suggested they skip the middle woman and just do each other before passing out fully dressed on top of her bed, awakening several hours later in her empty and, thankfully, unransacked apartment to a perky reminder from her booker to wash her hair before the fitting today.

It was also the one-year anniversary of Nicky's death.

As the metro surged on, Lucky checked her phone to find a missed call and voicemail from Avery, who was no doubt on a mission to get her to "process" her feelings about this day, plus a formal-looking email from their mother she promptly ignored. She missed the New York subway with its filth, reliable unreliability, and lack of cell service; the Paris metro was almost aggressively efficient and fully accessible by cell phone, even underground. Here, there was nowhere to hide. Without listening to Avery's message, Lucky slid the phone back into her pocket. She had not seen any member of her family since Nicky's funeral a year ago. That night, a strong, hot wind blew through the city; it upturned restaurant tables and sent garbage cans tumbling down avenues, it broke power lines and snapped tree branches in Central Park. And it scattered Lucky and her sisters to their corners of the world, without any intention of returning home.

She was now fifteen minutes late. In her hurry to leave, she'd forgotten her headphones, an oversight guaranteed to throw off her entire day. Lucky usually couldn't walk more than one block without digging them into her ears, building a musical buffer between herself and the world. But she'd gotten out of the door in record time, helped by the fact she'd forgone her usual breakfast of a Marlboro Red and an ibuprofen and left the house in the clothes she'd woken up in. Surreptitiously, she gave her T-shirt a sniff. A bit smoky, a bit sweaty, but, overall, not too bad.

"*Je voudrais te sentir.*"

Lucky's eyes jumped to the man sitting across from her, who had just spoken. He had the tense, rodentlike face of prey, but his eyes were all predator. In his hands, he clutched a large Volvic water bottle over his crotch, pointing it toward her. He was smiling.

"What?" she asked, though she had no desire to know what this man had said, to speak to him at all.

"Ah! You are American!"

He pronounced it the typical French way—emphasis on the *can*.

"Yup."

Lucky nodded and reached for her phone again, trying to radiate uninterest.

"You are beautiful," he said, leaning toward her.

"Mmm, thanks."

She kept her eyes glued to her phone. She considered shooting off a text to her booker to say she was running behind, then decided against it. That would only make the lateness real. Better to enjoy the comfort of this limbo period while she could, before anyone knew she was messing up yet again.

"And so tall," the man continued.

In dark vintage Levi's and a black cropped tee, Lucky was, indeed, as straight and long as an exclamation point. She hunched her shoulders forward, so he could see less of her, and she became a question mark.

"*Mon dieu!*" he exclaimed softly to himself. "*T'es trop* sexy."

She should get up and leave. She should tell him to go fuck himself. She should take his water bottle—his big, stupid, blue imaginary phallus—and crush it between her hands. Instead, she pointed to her phone.

"Look, I'm just—"

She frowned and pointed at her screen to indicate that she was making a call. She scrolled quickly through her contacts. But who could she call? She didn't actually want to talk to anyone. Out of habit, she searched Nicky's name and hit the Dial button. They were all part of a family phone plan that Avery paid for; she guessed Avery had decided to spare herself the anguish of canceling Nicky's number by simply continuing to pay her share. Lucky didn't know where Nicky's phone was now, dead in a drawer somewhere she imagined, but she was grateful to still have this. Her sister's voice filled her ear.

*You've reached Nicky's phone, leave a message after the tone. Have fun!*

She was giggling, self-conscious about being recorded. Just faintly in the background, Lucky could hear herself, several years younger and oblivious to the loss her future held, laughing.

"I would love to know you," the man persisted.

"I'm on the phone," said Lucky.

"Ah, *d'accord.*" The man leaned back, palms open in a ridiculous gesture of gallantry. "We speak after."

It wasn't the first time she'd phoned Nicky since she died; the urge to speak to her sister and tell her what life was like without her was constant. Calling her felt like being an amputee who, believing she still has legs, keeps trying to stand.

"Hi, it's me," began Lucky as the tone sounded. "I . . . Well, I'm just calling to say hi."

She glanced at the man, who made no attempt to pretend he wasn't listening to her.

"It's fashion week here so things are kind of hectic, as always, but I wanted to call because . . . Um, it's a big day for you, I guess. One year! I can't believe it. So yeah, I just wanted to call and say . . . Not congratulations, obviously. It's not, like, a goddamn celebration. But I wanted you to know I'm thinking about you. I'm always thinking about you. And I miss you. Obviously." Lucky cleared her throat. "So that's it. I love you." Lucky waited to see if she would feel anything, some energetic shift in the cosmos to let her know her sister was listening. Nothing. "Also, Avery's being annoying. Bye."

She hung up and glanced out the window. They were almost at Saint Paul, her stop. As she unfurled herself to stand, the man reached to touch her arm. She jumped as though he had held a lit match to her skin.

"Can I take your number?"

The train slowed into the station and Lucky stumbled. He grinned up at her as she faltered. His teeth were stained brown from tobacco.

"You are so sexy," he said.

Lucky looked at the man eyeing her with possessive joy, as though picking out his pastry from a glass display case. The water bottle still protruded toward her from his crotch.

"Can I?" she asked, pointing to it. The train came to a halt.

"This?" he asked, baffled. He handed her the plastic tube. "*Mais bien sûr.*"

She took the bottle from his hands, unscrewed the cap, and tipped the remaining water into his lap. The man shot up with a yelp as a dark patch spread across his jeans. Lucky darted toward the exit and pulled the silver lever, that curious object of agency unique to Paris's metro, and the train doors sprang apart. From the platform, she could hear him calling her a bitch as passengers streamed onto the train between them. She took the stairs two at a time and emerged into the sunlight.

On Place des Vosges, stone archways swooped overhead as Lucky raced toward the address her booker had sent her. Two old men smoking in matching olive trench coats turned to watch her as she passed. She rang the bell and passed through the chipped blue wooden doorway that led to the courtyard. At the other end was a tall, spiral stairway; her heavy boots reverberated off the stone walls as she climbed each floor, stopping on each landing to catch her breath. A pack-a-day smoking habit, started when she was a teenager, had left her ill-suited to this sort of activity. Finally, she dragged herself by the banister to the very top. A woman with her hair scraped into a tight dark bun and a tape measure snaked around her neck was standing in the doorway waiting for her.

"I'm late, I know," Lucky panted. "*Je suis désolée.*"

"And you are?" asked the woman in a sharp voice.

"Lucky—" she heaved. "Blue."

"Loo-key?" the woman repeated, looking down at her clipboard. Behind her, Lucky could hear the industrious hum of sewing machines. "You are not late. In fact, you are quite early. Your fitting is at two."

Lucky placed her hands on her knees and exhaled.

"I thought it was twelve?"

"You are mistaken. Please return at two. Ciao!"

With an authoritative *click,* the door was shut in her face. Lucky resisted the urge to collapse right there and sleep in the doorway like a neighborhood cat until it was her turn to be seen. Slowly, she carried herself back down the stairs.

With nothing else to do, Lucky wandered through the sun-dappled streets of the Marais in search of a place to get a drink. The adrenaline from her Volvic vengeance and ensuing race to the fitting was wearing off, revealing the start of what promised to be a brutal hangover if she didn't nip it in the bud. It was early July and despite the clement weather, an air of restlessness had pervaded Paris that summer. A general strike and the resulting congestion had filled the air with a hazy smog, and a flurry of stabbings in subways and residential neighborhoods had led to a heavy police presence on the streets. Yet the Marais, with its boutiques, packed bars, and bustling cafés, felt cheerfully removed from all that.

Lucky heard a woman's voice calling her name from across the street and turned to see her friend Sabina, a French redhead and fellow model whose body Lucky had once heard a designer describe as *like a hundred miles of good road,* sitting outside a café with two male models. She beckoned Lucky over.

"If it isn't punk Pollyanna," said the taller of the men, Cliff, as she approached.

Cliff was an Australian former pro surfer enjoying some notoriety that season for walking a Milan runway in nothing but a gold thong. Despite this, it was impossible to objectify him; the sheer force of his ego would not allow it. That, and the knowledge that he could always quit fashion and go back to his life of chasing surf and living out of his van, meant that he appeared completely unconflicted about his current choice of career, unlike Lucky, whose beauty was a source of both income and shame for her. Lucky had never done anything but model, which made her feel like she had never done anything. She would not admit it aloud, but she envied Cliff his freedom.

"Ciao, Golden Balls," she said, taking a cigarette from the pack in front of him and pinching it between her lips. "I didn't recognize you with your clothes on."

The other model, a baby-faced American Lucky didn't recognize, laughed and leaned over to light her. He had the coloring of a golden retriever and the same seemingly indiscriminate desire to please. The men each had a large beer in front of them, while Sabina twirled a small glass of white wine without sipping from it. Lucky beckoned for the server and ordered a beer before she took a seat.

"Hey, I'm Riley," said the younger man.

"I need a drink," said Lucky and leaned back to expose a pale slice of stomach.

"This is Lucky," said Sabina. "*Ma soeur.*"

Lucky acknowledged this with a vague nod. Sabina had the only child's tendency of recruiting friends as family members; in truth, the two didn't know much about each other beyond their most recent campaigns and drink of choice.

"You're American!" said Riley. He had a soft southern accent that made each vowel sound like it was wrapped in cotton wool. "I've been waiting to see an American today." He raised his beer. "Happy Fourth of July."

Lucky exhaled smoke in a narrow column toward the sky.

"I don't celebrate that," she said.

This year, next year, every year for the rest of her life, the Fourth would only ever be the day that Nicky died. Riley frowned at her.

"But you're American, right?" he asked.

"New York," she said. "So, barely."

"But today you live in Paris," said Sabina. "Which means you will have to celebrate Bastille Day."

"When's that?" asked Cliff.

"In fact, only next week," said Sabina.

"July is *the* month to wrestle back control from tyranny," said Cliff.

"Well, I miss it," said Riley. "I've never been out of the country on the Fourth before. My folks always throw a big barbecue."

"Sorry to say," said Sabina, "the French do not barbecue." She set down her glass with a flick of her hand. "I can't drink this. I still have a headache from this morning. Why do they insist on serving champagne before breakfast backstage?"

"Because it's the only thing you girls will eat," said Cliff. "What's the saying? Champagne, cocaine, and casual sex, baby."

Sabina simply ignored him. She glanced up at the sky, which was turning an anemic shade of gray.

"It's looking to rain, *non*?"

"Ah, man," said Riley. "My next show's outdoors."

"Mine too," said Lucky.

"My first fashion week and it rains," he said glumly.

Cliff began singing the chorus of Alanis Morissette's "Ironic" in a surprisingly tuneful voice. *It's like raaaaain on your wedding day.*

"This is *haute couture*," said Sabina. "La crème de la crème. Trust me, they won't let you get wet."

"By you she means the clothes," said Lucky, then turned back to Cliff. "Anyway, what you were saying about female models? It's not like you guys are paradigms of health and moderation." She tapped Cliff's near-empty beer glass.

"We can handle our booze, unlike you lot." He pointed a finger at her. "If you don't eat, you shouldn't drink."

"I eat," said Lucky, picking up the beer that had just been placed before her. "*So* I can drink."

Cliff laughed and ordered another round.

"Anything you can do I can do better," he sang.

"I bet I can hold my own better than you," said Lucky.

Cliff raised his drink and downed the last gulp.

"Wanna see about that?"

An hour later, Lucky was five drinks in and about to tell the most hilarious story she'd ever told. The sadness from the morning that had covered her like grime was being washed away with each new round.

"So I'm nineteen and I'm living in Tokyo for the year," she said. "It was fun, but I was also maybe being a little bit irresponsible, you know, staying out late, missing appointments, basically everything you should *not* do when you're starting out."

Here, Lucky gestured to young Riley and raised an eyebrow in warning.

"This seems like a do-as-I-say-not-as-I-do teaching moment," said Cliff. "Since I'm pretty sure you still do all that, Lucky."

"Hey, you don't need to teach me," Riley said. "I'm twenty-three. I know what I'm doing."

"Me too!" exclaimed Sabina. "In fact, I have been twenty-three for the past three years."

Lucky laughed and took another gulp of her drink.

"My agency was threatening to drop me, but then, out of no-where, I booked a campaign. It was for a cheesy commercial brand but still, money, money, money. My agent calls and says to me, 'Lucky, if you are even one minute late to this shoot, we will fire you. One minute.'"

"I know what happens," said Riley. "You were late, and they fire you, but you still end up becoming a big, famous model anyway."

"You think she's famous?" Sabina gasped. "More famous than me?"

Riley looked back and forth between them.

"No, I mean y-yes," he stammered. "I mean, I don't know. You're both beautiful."

"She's kidding," said Lucky.

"She's really not," said Cliff. "Anyway, I'm more famous than the both of them."

Sabina wrinkled her nose at Cliff.

"None of us are famous," said Lucky. "Anyway, back to the story. The night before the shoot, I go to bed early, determined to wake up on time. But I was living in a model apartment in Shibuya that was pretty much one degree removed from a brothel. So I'm lying there in bed, trying to be good, when a troop of girls storm in and are, like, 'There's an opening ceremony party in Harajuku, that crazy hot actor who played the cowboy astronaut whatever in last year's Oscar winner is there, one of us has to fuck him, put your shoes on, we're going out.' And, I don't know, I have no willpower, so I go, I swear to God, to have only one drink."

Lucky paused to down the remainder of her beer, then turned to signal the server to bring another.

"So what happened?" asked Cliff. "Please tell me you got fired."

Lucky emitted a satisfied burp, then grinned.

"Worse. I party all night—"

"And the actor?" asked Sabina.

"Snapped up by a Russian."

Sabina sniffed.

"Typical."

"I wake up the next morning and, of course, I have missed the call time by an hour. Have you ever overslept for a job?"

"I almost missed my SATs because my mom didn't wake me up in time," said Riley seriously.

Lucky nodded.

"Then you know the feeling."

She decided to leave out the fact she was also coming down off a combination of ecstasy, angel dust, and cocaine, all of which were notoriously hard to procure in Japan. Of course, Lucky, who was like a truffle pig for party drugs, had managed it.

"My agent had already called me like fifteen times by the time I woke up," she continued. "I call her back and she's demanding to know where I am, why I didn't answer. In a flash, I tell her I've woken up with conjunctivitis. I didn't answer the phone because I couldn't *see* anything. Idiotic, I know, but I wasn't exactly firing on all cylinders."

Cliff scoffed.

"Did she believe you?"

"Of course not. She told me I needed to get a letter from a doctor confirming I had an infection or the agency would drop me, and I'd have to go back to New York. I mean, fuck that! But, yeah, I was panicking. I decided there is only one thing to do: *give* myself conjunctivitis, then go see the doctor."

"Wait a minute," interrupted Sabina. "What is this conjunctivitis? You get it from sex?"

Riley, who had been taking a sip of his drink, quietly choked.

"Only if the guy misses," said Cliff.

Lucky swatted him across the table and tapped her eyes to show Sabina what she meant.

"Ah, *conjonctivite*!" said Sabina. "*Je comprends.*"

"You couldn't make that leap?" said Cliff. "They're like the same word."

"Shhh," said Sabina. "Stop flirting with me."

"So," Lucky said, "my plan was to touch every dirty thing I could see and then touch my eye. Of course, since Tokyo is notoriously clean, this was no easy feat. Luckily, I was living with twelve absolutely disgusting models. The greasy kitchen counter? Great. The toilet seat? Perfect! One of their ugly tiny dogs' butts? Okay, let me give it a pat."

"Gross!" yelled Riley, clearly delighted.

"I get to the doctor and my eyes are, as you can imagine, pretty red from all this activity. The doctor barely even looks at me. 'What do you need?' I tell him I need a note for my job. He hands me a slip of paper and I'm on my way. So easy. I call my agent to tell her I have the note. 'That's great,' she says. 'But I always knew you were lying so I told the client you were traveling and your flight got delayed. They said you can come in tomorrow.' So, a happy ending, right? That night I go to bed on time. I wake up bright and early and . . . I have an eye infection."

"*Mais non!*" squealed Sabina.

"*Mais oui,* motherfucker!" yelled Lucky.

A table of two middle-aged Frenchwomen looked over at her and frowned. Lucky waved at them cheerily.

"So basically," said Cliff, "you're fucked."

"Exactly. My eyes are totally red and swollen. I miss the shoot. I lose the client."

"Did your agency drop you?" asked Riley.

"Almost." Lucky nodded. "They put me on probation. But a few weeks later, I ran into the editor of *Vogue Japan* at a party. You know he has the best sense of humor, so I told him the story. He loved it so much he ended up booking me a few weeks later. It kind of launched my editorial career."

"You're fucking lucky," said Cliff, shaking his head.

"Lucky's like a cat," said Sabina. "She has nine lives."

"Your parents obviously knew what they were doing when they named you," said Riley.

"My parents didn't know shit," said Lucky and lit another cigarette. "Still don't."

Silence descended on the table. With the end of the story the dark tide of sadness that threatened each moment to pull her under returned. She didn't want to think about her parents, about Nicky, about anything outside this small café table, but her family was always there, ready to push themselves to the front of her mind.

Her sisters were more forgiving, but Lucky knew they had a bad dad. They certainly weren't the only ones. In her whole life, she'd probably only met a handful of people who had good dads. All of them were weird. Kids who grew up with loving fathers had the same starry-eyed softness as kids raised in places like Malibu, those homes of eternal sunshine. They never had to toughen up. Lucky had this theory that having a bad dad was like growing up in a place with a long, rough winter. It hardens you. It also prepares you for reality, which is that summer is a season, not a lifestyle, and most men will hurt you if they get the chance. Or maybe it was only the people who grew up with bad dads who believed that.

The funny thing about their father was that he wasn't cold, or at least not always. *Mercurial* was how she would describe him. Changeable as the weather. And like the weather, he had to be regularly checked to work out what kind of day they were going to have. Lucky and her sisters could tell his mood by the way he closed the front door. Just like you wouldn't have a picnic in a hailstorm, you couldn't do certain things around an angry dad. No bickering over the remote, no chatting loudly with friends on the phone, no crying over a bad grade, no laughing over a silly joke, no whining to their mom that they were hungry. He was the only man in the house, but he also *was* the house. They lived inside his moods.

Lucky inherited his blue eyes and light hair, though she liked to believe their similarities ended there. He was a third-generation Scottish American with the kind of Catholic nun–riddled childhood that, as he put it, would make a good atheist out of anyone. He loved to read, maintaining a book-a-week habit well into his drinking years, but his real religion was sports. Football, boxing, golf, cycling—he'd watch anything. Like Bonnie, he was more at home in his body than in his mind. He should have been a professional athlete, and he even went to college on a football scholarship, but a torn hamstring meant he ended up taking a job at a regional bank after graduation, which he worked at for the rest of his life. No matter how drunk he got, or how often, he always went to work on time. That was why their mother could never admit he had a problem. What kind of alcoholic keeps his job all those years? Theirs, it turned out.

It was easy for Lucky to say they had a bad father. Harder for her to admit was that their mother wasn't all that great either. She grew up in a crumbling estate in Sussex, the only daughter of a depressive mother and vicious drunk of a father, who were that peculiarly British combination of upper class and totally broke, "posh but not flush" as their mother put it. Her father squandered most of his inheritance by the time their mother reached adolescence. Even after meeting and marrying their dad, their mother maintained a deep and abiding contempt for the British class system she had escaped from.

There was a lot about their mom's life she didn't know, but what Lucky did know was that her mother hightailed it out of that unhappy house she grew up in, that whole wretched country, as she called it, as soon as she could. She landed in New York and started working at a gallery downtown. At that time, she had silky auburn hair down to her waist and a beautiful, tulip-shaped face. She claims she was hired primarily to stand in the window in a miniskirt and lure rich men into the gallery, but she had a canny eye for young artists too, convincing her superiors to buy a number of early pieces of painters who were world-famous today.

If her mother hadn't had kids, Lucky was sure she could have become a gallery director or a celebrated curator, but she left the gallery after Avery was born. Then, when Avery was fifteen and Lucky was eight, their mother went back to working as a museum docent, charging her eldest to look after the rest of them. She claimed they needed the money, which was true, but she probably earned less an hour than one of them could babysitting. Mostly, she was just done being a mom, a mantle Avery stoically took up in her place. Lucky hated to admit it, but Avery was a better mom than most people ever got, which still didn't mean she had any plans to call her back that day.

She flicked the ash of her cigarette into the scalloped tray and exhaled. She wanted to find a trapdoor in her mind and disappear down it, to the place where memories couldn't reach her anymore, and there was only one way she knew to do that. She pushed her empty pint glass away and shot her wolflike grin toward her friends.

"Shall we get something stronger?"

LUCKY WOVE HER WAY BACK to the atelier through dove-gray streets smearing like impressionist paintings before her eyes. She had vaguely considered fucking Riley in the bathroom, but he seemed the type to get attached, so she made the extremely responsible decision to head to the fitting on time instead. She sidestepped a dog and stumbled, her fingertips stroking the sidewalk, then righted herself. She was only a tiny bit drunk. She could hold her alcohol better than any man, she thought with satisfaction. Certainly better than Cliff, who she had left singing an emotional a capella rendition of John Lennon's "Imagine" to a bemused Sabina.

When Lucky opened the blue wooden door, the previously quiet courtyard was a flurry of activity. A long white runway had been erected through the center of the cobblestone patio, around which workers were busy unstacking chairs, laying down cables, and setting up the photographers' pit. Lucky felt the odd collision of worlds that combined to create the fashion business; this industrious crowd of stagehands would perform Herculean feats in the next hours, then melt into the background, as if they had never been there at all, so silk-clad Lucky and her ilk could float above a sea of spectators on their handiwork.

She circumnavigated a man carrying a wobbling tower of chairs so tall it could have been a circus act and climbed back up the dizzying coil of the spiral staircase. Everything was spinning as she entered the stuffy atelier. A hot wave of human perspiration hit her nostrils. Overhead, a wooden ceiling fan turned ineffectually, swirling, but not disbanding, the heat of the room. A woman pushing an overflowing rack of sherbet-colored taffeta dresses trundled past without looking over.

Lucky felt her head whooshing in time with the fan. She went over to the window and leaned out, breathing deeply. The atelier looked onto the courtyard below and Lucky focused her attention on the bald spot of the man polishing the gleaming white runway beneath her. She tried to still her rushing head as she stared at his.

"Does it appear to rain?"

Lucky turned to find the stylist from earlier with the tight bun and the tape measure bustling over.

"We are all very worried for rain," the stylist clarified, removing a silver pin from her mouth.

Lucky stuck her head back out the window to inspect the sky. It was gray to her left and pale blue to her right.

"Fifty-fifty," she said.

The words felt like fuzzy pieces of fruit in her mouth. The stylist gave a tiny frown.

"*Alors,* come this way, please."

Lucky was ushered to an even hotter corner of the room, where her outfit was suspended on a velvet hanger with a Polaroid of her taped to the hook. It was a halter-neck ball gown with a flared skirt the shape of an upside-down martini glass. The fabric was the palest confectionary pink, like the underside of a kitten's paw. Across the artfully draped bodice, a network of silver beaded branches sprang heavy with sparkling cherry blossoms. The stylist looked at Lucky expectantly.

"The appliqué alone took three hundred hours," she said.

But Lucky was too busy trying to strip her jeans off without keeling over to respond. She succeeded in removing them and her T-shirt, then stood swaying in her underwear with the unselfconsciousness drilled into her early in her modeling years. Whatever reaction of cooing delight the stylist was hoping to get from Lucky, it wasn't going to happen. Still wearing her dirty socks, she stepped into the stiff gown. She felt herself being hooked in from behind, the bodice crunching her ribs and pinching her waist.

"Beautiful, no?" a seamstress at her workstation said with a sigh. "Just like a princess."

Lucky emitted a soft belch.

"The designers will be here soon to look it over," said the stylist. "But first, let me check the fit."

"Could I have some water?" Lucky croaked.

With a puzzled look, the stylist produced a sparkling strawberry-flavored Volvic. Lucky took a tentative sip. She hated strawberries. As soon as the saccharine bubbles hit her stomach, she knew she was in trouble. She ran to the open window as a brown flume of beer and vodka erupted out of her, the bodice acting as a kind of stomach pump. Foul liquid gushed forth in waves. Lucky stared down at the fluid and bile that had just evacuated her, splattered like a Rorschach test against the white runway below. The man with the bald spot she had observed just minutes before was staring up at her in horror, having narrowly missed the deluge. Behind her, she could hear the shrieks of the seamstress and stylist begging her not to get vomit on the dress. Lucky was half inside and half outside the room, her torso dangling over the window ledge. She thought briefly how good it would be to stay like this, in between, neither here nor there, forever, then wiped a sour tendril of saliva from her lips. In front of her, the slanting Paris rooftops shimmered in the light. The sun, at least, was coming out.

# CHAPTER TWO

# Bonnie

BONNIE WOKE BEFORE DAWN TO THE SOUND OF INVASION. SOMEONE was rattling her front door, trying to get in. Within seconds, she had grabbed the baseball bat she kept by her bed and launched herself into the small living room. The room was dark and still, empty but for a stack of cardboard boxes in the corner and a foldout beach chair. Sulfur-yellow patches of light from the streetlamps outside streaked the bare floor. She stood still, listening. Once again, the door rattled in its frame. Bonnie held her breath and padded stealthily across the space until she was close enough to unlock the latch with a soft click. In one swift movement, she yanked the door open and slashed the bat through the air in front of her. It struck the ground at her feet with a metallic thud. She looked out onto the empty landing, lined with the wet towels her neighbor's kids left hanging on the railings overnight to dry, and shook her head. She was fighting with herself again.

These days, Bonnie usually slept until noon. Her job as the bouncer for Peachy's, a nearby bar, meant she often didn't return home until three or four in the morning. It was the exact opposite of her schedule the years prior, during which she rose before sunrise each day to begin training, completing more vigorous physical activity by the time most people woke for breakfast than they could hope to achieve in a week. She still worked out, but with nowhere near the intensity of a prefight program, in which it would be more accurate to call training simply living, as there was nothing else to her life in those periods.

Bonnie went back to bed and slipped into shallow, feverish sleep. She was awoken by the sound of her phone ringing somewhere in the apartment. She used it so infrequently, often leaving it on top of the fridge or the lip of the tub for days at a time, that she could not immediately remember where she'd left it. She staggered from the bed and found it perched on one of the unopened boxes in the living room, Avery's name flashing on the screen. It was early afternoon, a late wake-up, even for her.

"Aves," she rasped.

She heard her sister exhale.

"Bon Bon, *finally*. Can you believe this fucking email from Mom?"

Bonnie frowned.

"What email?"

"You haven't seen it yet? Have you just gotten up?"

Bonnie walked to the kitchen and turned on the tap, leaning to drink straight from the faucet.

"I have a flip phone now," she said, wiping her mouth. "No email. What does it say?"

"Oh, well, buckle up," said Avery. "Let me just find it, hold on . . . Here it is . . . *Dear girls, Hard to believe it's already been one year without our beloved Nicky. I am writing to you because, as you know, the flat has lain empty these past twelve months and your father and I have made the difficult decision to sell it. If you would like to collect any of Nicky's things, please do so by the end of the month. The movers will clear out the rest. I remain, with love, your mother.*"

Bonnie exhaled involuntarily. She had not expected that. Their six-person family had lived in a two-bedroom apartment in a prewar building on the Upper West Side that their parents bought below market value decades ago. Avery had shared one bedroom with Bonnie, with Lucky and Nicky in the smaller one. Their parents slept in what would have been a small dining area, partitioned off from the living room by a painted screen.

Bonnie had once heard that a shark in a tank will grow eight inches, while a shark in the wild will grow eight feet. But their childhood home seemed to have had the opposite effect. Bonnie and her sisters grew and grew until they could not be contained by that apartment. She moved out shortly before her seventeenth birthday to start her amateur career, a few years later Nicky left for college out of state, and Lucky, scouted at fifteen, started modeling all over the world around the same time. Finally, once they were all gone, Avery ran away, reappearing a year later newly clean and determined to go to law school. After their father retired, their parents moved upstate, ostensibly because the city was bad for his health, which really meant it was bad for his drinking. She and Nicky moved back in and did their part to cover the mortgage while Nicky taught English at a high school nearby and Bonnie continued honing her skills at Pavel's gym, dipping in and out of the apartment between tours and training camps. It had been a happy arrangement, while it lasted.

"What does she mean *I remain your mother*?" asked Avery, her voice rising. "Like there was some question of her *not* remaining our mom?"

"It's cold," agreed Bonnie. "Even for her."

Immediately, she felt guilty. She tried never to bad-mouth their mom, but the truth was, they weren't close. Avery and Nicky had always been the ones to bridge the gap between the sisters and their mother. It was Nicky their mother took the most interest in, though she didn't share much of herself with any of her children. Since their mother hated sports and, unlike Nicky, Bonnie had not shown much appreciation for the arts, they maintained a respectful distance from each other. Avery, meanwhile, took on the role of dutiful daughter in adulthood, ostensibly as a living amends for her absence during her addiction, visiting their parents upstate every few years and calling on major holidays and birthdays. But Bonnie could feel the hot fury

Avery secretly harbored toward them roiling like magma beneath the surface of her solicitousness. Both Lucky and Bonnie had essentially outsourced their parental needs since adolescence, Lucky with a rotating team of bookers and agents, and Bonnie with her boxing trainer, Pavel Petrovich. And for what little maternal advice and encouragement they needed, they had Avery. Who Avery had to turn to before she met Chiti, Bonnie still did not know.

"Do you think we should call her?" asked Bonnie, already dreading it.

"Oh, I did," said Avery briskly. "Immediately upon receipt."

Bonnie suppressed a smile. Avery was such a lawyer.

"And?" she asked.

"And they're selling it all right. They already have an interested buyer."

"Wow," Bonnie mustered. She didn't know what else to say. Avery seemed indignant enough for the both of them.

"Then she spent the remainder of the call telling me about the new fertilizer she's using in the garden," said Avery, her voice rising even higher with annoyance. "It was so typical. We barely speak and when we do, she literally wants to talk about shit."

Their mother always fed them, and she never hit them—Bonnie always liked to remind herself of that. But she was overwhelmed by them. She wasn't the kind of mom who derived satisfaction from cooking or domestic work, but she never asked for help. Each evening, she launched herself at the task of feeding the four of them like an explorer on a particularly grueling leg of a solo mission she regretted starting but had resigned herself to completing. In Bonnie's opinion, their mother was afraid of Avery, baffled by Bonnie, intermittently charmed by Nicky, and oblivious to Lucky. None of which, obviously, were ideal.

Bonnie's feelings about their father were more complicated. To both her pride and embarrassment, he had shown more interest in her than in any of his other daughters, often joking that she was the son he never had. Growing up, he took her to Central Park in the evenings, the two of them wordlessly pitching a ball back and forth across the Great Lawn as the last light receded across the grass, the only sound the soft slap of leather against their palms and the occasional murmur of acknowledgment after a particularly good catch. On the walk home, he would place his heavy hand on the back of her neck, urging her forward, and she would feel the competing sensations of pleasure and claustrophobia, the desire to keep his attention coupled with an equally powerful desire to escape it, escape *him,* and run, free and unencumbered, back to the safety of her sisters. By the time Bonnie turned fifteen and discovered boxing, his drinking, previously relegated to outside the house or after they went to bed, had seeped into the early evening hours when they used to play together. Though she worried about him, it was the sense of relief at no longer having that hand on her neck she remembered most clearly.

"So what do you think?" prompted Avery. "Should we try to stop them?"

Bonnie didn't know what she thought. That apartment was the only home she'd ever known, both an albatross around her neck and an anchor. For the past year, Avery had been covering the mortgage and monthly maintenance fee, thereby allowing the place to remain empty, but they all knew that arrangement couldn't last forever. The best approach with her family, she'd found, was neutrality.

"Do *you* think we should?" she asked.

"I do," said Avery decisively. "It's our home, too, and they have no right."

"Except for the fact they own it," mumbled Bonnie.

"Whatever!" Avery replied, exasperated. She sounded just like when they were teenagers. "You seriously don't care if they sell it?"

Bonnie had loved that apartment, but after what happened there, she knew she couldn't step foot in it again.

"I guess it's their apartment and I . . . I can respect their wishes," she offered.

"God, I would kill to be as imperturbable as you," said Avery.

Bonnie laughed shyly.

"I don't even know what that means."

"It means you, unlike me, aren't destined to die of a stress-induced heart attack."

"But what about all of Nicky's stuff?" asked Bonnie.

*That* she was not imperturbable about. Avery made a low hum down the phone.

"I know," she said. "One of us is going to have to go back and claim it all."

"I know I'm the closest . . ." began Bonnie, her heart sinking.

"It's okay," said Avery quickly. "No one would expect you to go back in there. I'll figure something out."

Bonnie exhaled with relief. She hated that Avery was the one who always had to fix everything in their family and relieved by it in equal measure.

"Thank you," she said softly.

"I can't believe it's already been a year," said Avery, her voice low.

"I know . . ." Bonnie smiled sadly to herself. "Time's a trip, man."

"You sound so L.A. How is it out there?"

Bonnie padded across the living room and let herself out onto the landing, wincing slightly at the sunshine.

"Great. I'm looking at the ocean right now."

In fact, all Bonnie could see was the alley below, where a seagull was wrestling a pizza crust from a garbage bag. She lived on a somewhat squalid street a block from the beach, in one of a number of ramshackle buildings that still offered cheap month-to-month rentals and were therefore viable homes to an itinerant community of surfers, students, seasonal workers, aging hippies, and functioning drug addicts—the kind of people who gave Venice what real estate agents called its "local color" but who would never use a real estate agent themselves.

"That's nice," said Avery. "I'm looking at a brief."

"Still? Isn't it late there now?"

"You know me," said Avery.

Bonnie did. Avery used work the way she used to use drugs: to drown out the world.

"Did you do anything to, you know, commemorate the day?" Avery asked.

"Not yet. Have you?"

"Just calling all of you. If we did want to start a tradition, now would be the time."

Bonnie blew a strand of hair out of her eyes.

"What would Nicky have liked? It's not like there's a how-to for grieving."

Avery's voice took on the brisk, efficient quality she usually reserved for her clients.

"Hold on, I'm looking it up now." Bonnie could hear her begin typing. "How . . . to . . . acknowledge . . . death . . . anniversary."

Bonnie shook her head and snorted softly. She directed her attention back to the seagull's ferocious efforts as it pierced the trash bag in search of more prizes.

"I think it's just meant to be a gut thing, Aves. The internet can't tell us what to do here."

"The internet can *always* tell us what to do. See, I have a list right here." Avery began reciting. "Number one, visit their final resting place . . . Okay, well we're not in New York so we can't do that. Number two, release butterflies—"

Bonnie scoffed.

"Sure, let me just grab my net."

Avery laughed.

"Number three is more reasonable. Write a letter, poem, or blog."

"Poem? *Blog?* Who are these people?"

"Okay, okay. Number four is play their favorite song."

"Do you know what it is?"

"No, but Lucky would," said Avery.

"Lucky will probably tell us it's some death metal track just to mess with us."

"I guess if she ever answers her phone, we can find out."

Now Avery's voice took on the flinty edge she used to conceal when her feelings had been hurt, though she would never admit it. Bonnie knew how hard she tried to connect with their youngest sis-

ter, elusive as any butterfly herself. The trick to loving Lucky, Bonnie
wanted to tell Avery, was to respect her need to be free. Let her come
and go as she pleased and eventually, she would land on you. But, as
per usual, Bonnie decided not to get involved.

"Moving on," said Avery. "Five, we can hold a special remem-
brance ceremony. Six, express loving sentiments with flowers . . ."

"None of these sound like Nicky."

"I know. Okay, the last suggestion on the list is to take a seat."

"That's it?" Bonnie frowned to herself. "That's the whole suggestion? To sit down?"

"That's all it says. *Take a seat.*"

"I guess we can do that."

"I'm already sitting at my desk. Should I change seats?"

"Yeah, take a different seat. Sit on the floor."

"Okay, you sit on the floor too."

Bonnie crawled down to the landing floor and leaned her back
against the wall, closing her eyes. She could hear the seagulls and her
neighbors quietly arguing, the man repeating *I told you, I told you,*
and, beyond that, the slow crashing of waves. The sun glowed golden
through the skin of her eyelids. The air smelled of salt and garbage
and light.

"Do you feel like this is doing anything?" she asked.

"I don't think it's meant to *do* anything," said Avery. "It's just
meant to be an opportunity for us to remember her and feel, you
know, our grief."

"Fun," said Bonnie.

"Are you feeling it?"

"My grief? I guess so. I might also just be hungry." She had intended it to be funny, but Avery was silent on the other end. "Are
you?" she asked tentatively. "Feeling it?"

She heard Avery breathing shallowly down the phone.

"I'm so angry with her," Avery whispered. "Isn't that fucked-up?
I know I should feel sad, but mostly I just feel angry at her."

"I think that's . . . normal? Right? You should ask Chiti, she
would know."

"It doesn't feel normal. I could *hurt* her, you know? If she was here, I'd punch her in the neck."

Bonnie smiled.

"That's a pretty weird place to punch someone."

"Well, I wouldn't want to hit her face. Just get close to it, so she'd know I was really, really mad at her."

"I get that. I'd punch her in the neck too."

"Yeah, but you'd probably kill her if you did that."

"Too late."

The words hung between them, vibrating.

"How are you really, Bon Bon?" asked Avery. "How's the . . . nightclub thingy?"

"It's fine." Bonnie shrugged. "I'm working tonight."

Far away in London, Avery gave a little hum of dissatisfaction. "What are you doing there? We're so *not* L.A. people."

"Maybe I am," said Bonnie.

But Bonnie didn't think of herself as any kind of person, L.A. or otherwise. She had been a boxer for so long she'd forgotten to become a person. She'd chosen the city because it was far away from where she'd been training in New York and seemed like an easy enough place to get a job. She didn't care if she liked it. She was only there to escape.

"Living in L.A. is like dating a really beautiful person who has nothing to say," said Avery. "It's fine for a while because, you know, *look* at them, but eventually you're going to realize you need to be around people who read books and have their real noses."

Bonnie frowned. Had Avery even been to L.A. in the past decade? How could she know what it was like to live there?

"I don't know how long I'll be here," she said noncommittally.

The only place she had any fighting spirit was in the ring. Outside the ropes, it was easier to capitulate, especially with Avery, whose self-assuredness was like an anvil anchoring every conversation they had.

"You could come stay with us!" Avery exclaimed. "I know Chiti would love it. And there's got to be a good boxing gym in north London."

"I'm not training anymore. I told you that."

"Fine, fine, forget the gym. You don't have to fight if you really don't want to. You could coach, you could become a sports manager, you could start a charity. Just remember who you *are*, Bonnie."

Bonnie closed her eyes again. She suddenly felt very tired.

"And who is that?" she asked.

"Well, for starters, you're a women's world champion. I can't even remember half the competitions you've won, but I know it's a lot. You're the strongest person I know, inside and out. And you're my sister. Please note that none of the aforementioned descriptors include being a bouncer."

"Except I *am* a bouncer. That's exactly what I am."

Avery was quiet. Bonnie could practically hear the machinations of her mind whirring, testing out which tack to try next.

"Nicky wouldn't want this for you, you know," Avery said eventually.

So, thought Bonnie, she had landed on invoking the wishes of the dead. A classic.

"She would want you to be doing what you love," Avery continued.

Bonnie bounced her head softly against the wall behind her.

"Sometimes I hate what I love," she said.

A beat on the other end.

"Even me?" Avery asked.

"Never you," said Bonnie, though she knew perfectly well Avery would take her remark that way. That was, she supposed, why she said it. Avery made a noise between a hum and a growl.

"Well, I *just* love you," she said. "That's why I'm pushing you."

"I know," said Bonnie. "I love you too. Without the too." It was what Nicky used to say to them. No *too*. Just love. "Look, I gotta go for my run. I'll call you next week?"

"Mmm," hummed Avery. "You can't run forever."


BONNIE CHANGED INTO HER SHORTS and sports bra and set off toward the beach. She ran five miles in the sand a day, then did a series of calisthenic exercises on the bars at Muscle Beach. It was hardly the grueling training regimen she was used to, but it kept her from going completely soft. She didn't particularly enjoy having an audience of tourists milling around watching the bodybuilders who frequented the place, but it was cheaper than a gym, and she garnered far less attention than the bulging, bronzed men, pumped up as inflatable pool toys, who spent their days peacocking around the bench presses. She was often the only woman on the bars, certainly the only one who could do one hundred pull-ups in under five minutes, but she was used to that from the boxing gym. She hadn't played team sports since middle school and had rarely gone beyond surface banter with her sparring partners. She had, she felt, all the social grace of a grizzly bear. On the bars, as in life, she was left to herself—which, she told herself, was exactly how she liked it.

Except since she started training at fifteen, she had never been alone, not really. A boxer in a ring may seem as if they are on their own, but pan back a few feet and their trainer will always be there in the corner, taking every blow with them. A truly great trainer sees as their fighter sees, feels as their fighter feels. And the fighter needs that support, relies on it as completely as a child does a mother. It's the secret vulnerability at the heart of the sport, that intimate dependence. And yet from this surrender to reliance comes a capacity for individual resilience that's almost inhuman. Boxers are trained to be all fight, no flight. Bonnie had seen many a boxer knocked flat on her back, but she had never seen one run from the ring. Despite the referee's instruction at the beginning of every fight to "protect yourself at all times," boxing required an overriding of one's deepest natural instincts to protect oneself at all costs. Inevitably, you had to take pain to deliver it.

The first time Bonnie entered a boxing gym, Nicky had been by her side. She was fifteen and Nicky was twelve; their parents had entrusted her to walk Nicky home across the park from school each afternoon while they were at work. Avery had graduated from high school early and was already killing herself with a double course load at Columbia, and ten-year-old Lucky was put in an after-school program while their mom was at work. One afternoon, instead of continuing west from the park to their apartment, Bonnie guided Nicky south with her toward Midtown without a word.

By that time, Bonnie had been watching nothing but boxing movies for weeks, forcing them all to reenact scenes from *Raging Bull* and *Rocky* with her. She was obsessed before she ever stepped foot in a ring, but their mother considered the sport barbaric and refused to pay for lessons. It was their father, an amateur boxer in high school, who had come out of a drunken stupor just long enough to slip Bonnie the money and tell her to go try it out sometime. Bonnie had looked up boxing gyms on the school computer and picked the one nearest their apartment, which was how they found themselves outside of Golden Ring, a storefront boxing gym of no major repute.

It was winter and the gym's big front window was steamed over, the figures sparring and skipping rope on the other side blurred silhouettes. Bonnie stood frozen outside, suddenly too nervous to go in, but Nicky pushed open the door. It was fetid within, steamy and warm. The air was filled with rhythmic hisses, thuds, pops, and staccato slaps. Bonnie stood at the entrance, her eyes racing from person to person. They were all men, all much older than her, all completely absorbed in training; nobody even glanced up as they walked in. Suddenly, a bell rang, and the noise dimmed. Men dropped their jump ropes or broke from sparring to grab water bottles and towels. Now was the time, but Bonnie's nerve was faltering. Nicky must have known this because she walked over to a tall figure who had just finished jumping rope and peered up at him. His body reminded Bonnie of a panther's; she could see his muscles ripple under his skin as he moved.

*Excuse me,* said Nicky. *My sister wants to learn to box. Can you teach her?*

He smiled down at her, his handsome face streaming with sweat. *She'll want to talk to Pavel about that.*

He nodded at a tall white man leaning against the far wall. Nicky thanked him and grabbed Bonnie's hand. She pulled Bonnie after her, repeating the request once they reached him. Pavel dismissed the boxer he had been watching on the heavy bag with a nod, then looked down at them serenely. His face was beautiful in its contradictions. A thick neck and delicate, curled ears, a brutish square nose set below dancing blue eyes lined with long black lashes. To Bonnie at that age, he was firmly in the category of old person, though she would learn later he was not yet thirty. He held Bonnie in his gaze for a long moment.

*You want to fight?* he asked.

His voice, when he spoke, was thickened by a Russian accent. Bonnie nodded without a word. Pavel turned his light eyes toward Nicky.

*And you, little one?*

*I'm going to be a journalist,* she said primly. *So I'll just take notes.*

Pavel smiled.

*You need pen?*

Nicky gave him a knowing look and tapped the side of her temple. *It's all up here.*

Pavel nodded to indicate this was fair enough.

*Okay, you*—he pointed to Nicky. *Take notes.* He turned to Bonnie. *You, come.*

He guided her in front of the big mirror on the back wall, stopping her about six feet away from her reflection. Up close, the glass was coated in a hazy layer of dried sweat, snot, and spit that softened the edges of anyone it reflected. Pavel instructed Bonnie to take a stance. Tentatively, Bonnie separated her feet hips width.

*You feel good?* Pavel asked.

Bonnie nodded. Pavel extended one thick finger and pushed Bonnie's shoulder, knocking her easily off-balance. He shook his head. *Not solid. Try again.*

Bonnie repositioned her feet, so they were at an angle underneath her hips, and locked her knees.

*Solid?* asked Pavel, his index extended.

Bonnie nodded again, more confidently this time. Pavel pressed the tip of his finger to her shoulder blade and sent her staggering without effort.

*Not solid,* he said.

Bonnie glanced over at Nicky nervously. *You got this,* Nicky mouthed at her. Pavel pointed at the wooden floorboards beneath her.

*I want that you place feet shoulder width apart,* he said. *Now—*

He showed her how to relax her muscles, bend her knees, and plant her lead foot flat on the floor, then raise her back heel slightly with her toes planted so she was ready to pivot. At his instruction, Bonnie brought her hands just above her chin and made fists.

*Your knuckles,* said Pavel, tapping her hands and pointing up. *Always to the sky. Now tuck elbows.*

He instructed her to balance her weight equally between her front and back foot, then check her stance in the mirror. She could not know it at the time, but he was giving her a more useful lesson on gravity and the body than she had ever learned in school. When she was set up, he pushed her shoulder with his finger again. She didn't budge. He circled her, nudging from different angles but, with her feet planted as he'd shown her, Bonnie could not be tipped. Pavel crossed his arms and nodded.

*Now, you are solid.*

Bonnie looked over at her sister in delight. She had found, for the first time in her life, her feet.

BONNIE NEVER PUT MUCH STORE in the concept of fate, but she knew that she was meant to meet Pavel. It was Pavel who showed her how to move like water in the ring. In contrast to the plant-and-hook technique many other trainers favored, he taught a long-armed jab-and-move style, encouraging his boxers to flow with liquid agility around the ring. This suited Bonnie, whose earlier dance training and natural energy meant she was happiest when ducking, weaving, and bouncing around her opponent. He schooled her on how to slip punches and hit from a distance, how to plant her feet and dance from the ankles up with swift reflexes that were more protective than steel armor.

She could never have known how small the odds were of finding someone willing to even talk to a girl, let alone train her. There were only a handful of good trainers who worked with women in the whole country at that time, let alone in the city. But Pavel had been taught to box back in Moscow by his father, who insisted on training all his children, including his daughter, so Pavel had seen firsthand what a female fighter was capable of. His sister had been a natural, but she'd gotten pregnant young and remained in Russia to marry and raise a family. Pavel, meanwhile, had become a youth world champion, then moved to America to pursue a respectable but not exceptional professional career before a broken eye socket forced him into early retirement. Pavel molded Bonnie into the fighter she was born to be and remained her trainer for the next fifteen years. Until last year, she had lived her entire adult life with him in her corner.

Here is what she could not admit to anyone, not even, for many years, herself: She wanted more from Pavel. She didn't know when it started, this wanting, but once the seed was planted in her it kept growing until she was like a cracking pot that cannot contain its plant. The truth was that she wanted him everywhere, not just in her corner. The specifics of her wants were not extravagant, but the very fact of them felt enormous. She wanted, for instance, to sit in a dark movie theater beside him and watch something that had nothing to do with boxing, a romantic comedy maybe, or the new Marvel movie. She wanted to prepare her special morning smoothie for him, then sit in silence with him while they drank it. She wanted to watch him brush his teeth. She wanted him to turn in his sleep and reach for her. He had wrapped her hands thousands of times, but what she really wanted was for him to hold hers. Hold her hand! She was like a teenage girl. She sweated even thinking about it.

No one in Bonnie's life would describe her as a romantic. Between her grueling training schedule and natural inclination toward asceticism, almost every part of her life was in service to toughness. But her heart, her heart remained tender. And she was not completely inexperienced in the world of romance; during her twenties she had, if not relationships, then relations with a handful of men, usually other athletes with whom she made arrangements that ensured each got their physical needs met. She had even engaged in an ill-advised fling with a boxing promoter everyone called Knuckle (his name, in retrospect, should have been the first warning sign). Pavel was married for most of that time to Anahid, an Armenian war photographer who was rarely home and usually, it seemed, narrowly avoiding kidnap. Bonnie had met her a few times and was struck by both her beauty and her steeliness; she was scrupulously polite and seemed to treat most interactions as negotiations in which she was primarily concerned with getting out alive. By the time she and Pavel quietly divorced, Pavel had been Bonnie's trainer for over a decade.

If she was honest, the wanting had been there all along, but the *hope* started after his divorce. Hope was the dangerous thing. She didn't think Pavel had met anyone since, although thanks to his notoriously private nature she couldn't be sure. Regardless, one thing was clear: Nothing changed in his treatment of her. He saw Bonnie as his young protégée, nothing else. She may not have had a wealth of romantic experience, but she was woman enough to know when a man wanted her. Pavel simply did not. She was sure she could have lived with it, this ache of longing at the center of her life, this inner hollow in the shape of him—could even convince herself that it was *good* for her boxing, after all a satisfied boxer was a soft boxer—if she had never hoped, and he had never betrayed her.


AT NINE P.M. SHE WALKED over to Peachy's on Windward Avenue. Despite its proximity to the Venice boardwalk, the bar had successfully eschewed becoming a tourist destination thanks to a rigorous door policy established and upheld by Peachy himself. Peachy was the unofficial mayor of Venice who, in his own words, knew everyone worth knowing, had befriended everyone worth befriending, and fucked everyone worth fucking on the Westside.

A British expat, Peachy was the son of a Congolese mother and white English father who had sent him to Eton at the age of eleven, then promptly divorced each other never to speak again. He had the desperate charm of a child who has had to make a family of his friends and a handsome, boyish face, despite being well into middle age. During the day, he could often be spotted cruising around the neighborhood in his vintage sky-blue pickup truck, his beloved pit bull seated by his side, sipping iced coffee, puffing on a Camel Gold, and chatting to anyone who flagged him down.

He'd lived in Venice for decades and started Peachy's a few years back to create a place where his friends could drink and dance for cheap without having to drive to the Eastside. His door policy was notoriously mercurial; artists, surfers, models, bikers, musicians, and anyone, of any gender, who Peachy might like to sleep with were let in. Tourists, suits, most media types, and all Hollywood scumbags were turned away on sight. Famous actors who, priding themselves on their authenticity, made the trip from Malibu or the Hollywood Hills were let in but without ceremony or special treatment. Regulars and old friends of Peachy's were treated as VIPs, regardless of their worldly standing, and were always invited to cut the line and go right on in.

Of course, such a door policy required muscle to back it up, which was where Bonnie came in. Peachy worked side by side with Fuzz, a thick-necked former weight lifter from Jamaica, who had been manning the door since the bar's inception, breaking up fights, ensuring only the best-looking underage girls got in, and generally making sure peace reigned under Peachy's stern but benevolent rule. Peachy proudly claimed Fuzz got his name because the two of them were as close as fuzz on a peach, but Fuzz quickly set Bonnie straight that his mom had given him the nickname at birth after he came out with a full head of hair. Bonnie had shown up looking for a job a little less than a year ago and been hired on sight. Peachy, a boxing fan, recognized her as the promising female fighter who had mysteriously quit after just a few professional bouts. Blue-eyed, blond-haired, and, most importantly, female, Bonnie was not exactly typical bouncer material. But Peachy loved the optics of it, not to mention the fact Bonnie was strong enough to take on ninety-nine percent of the men she encountered without raising her heart rate. And, for the other one percent, there was Fuzz.

When Bonnie arrived at the bar for her shift that night, fireworks for the Fourth were already booming overhead. Peachy was standing outside with a cigarette dangling from his lip as he looked thoughtfully at a large, freshly painted mural on the opposite wall. It depicted two smiling pit bulls on either side of what appeared to be a screaming child with the words *Pitbull Love* emblazoned in cursive above the trio.

"I love it, I love it, I do," he was saying. "It's just, does the kid appear to be a bit . . . I don't know, terrified?"

He was talking to Stella, a local artist known for her surrealist animal murals, which could be spotted on walls from Mar Vista to Santa Monica. In fact, Bonnie walked past two of her pieces—a panther crying rainbow tears and a unicorn smoking a pipe—each evening on her way to the bar. Stella was usually in the midst of either kicking or, as she called it, "recommitting" to a crystal meth habit, a substance she extolled as a powerful artistic conduit or condemned as the bane of her existence depending on where in this cycle you happened to catch her. Today, judging by her twitchy demeanor and roving, wide-eyed stare, Bonnie guessed she was back in a recommittal.

"No, no, no, no, man," Stella said, practically vibrating beside him. "That kiddo's *excited*. These two pups want to play with him. They're his *family* now, you know?"

Peachy nodded, frowning.

"But would he be screaming?" he asked. "If they're just trying to play with him?"

"Nah, man, he laughing! He got a pit for a mom and a pit for a pop and they're going to look after him, like, forever. That's what I was trying to artistically convey."

"Right," said Peachy slowly. "It's just, well, I wanted the mural to communicate that pit bulls are lovable and safe, you know, since they get such a bad rap. But I'm not trying to say that they're a replacement for parents. They're still definitely *pets*. Albeit wonderful, highly intelligent ones. But pets nonetheless."

"Totally, man, totally." Stella hopped from one foot to the other and scratched her stomach with both hands. "How's this? I paint the dogs' eyes red, like love hearts, you know, that way it's superclear they have only love for the kid, you know, and mean him—" Stella gulped seriously. "Not one ounce of harm."

"Right, right, paint the eyes red," repeated Peachy. "Could that look, I don't know, a little demonic?"

Stella threw her head back and cackled. Above her, firework sparks streaked down the face of the night sky like tears.

"Only one way to find out, man!"

"Mmm, why don't we put a pin in this for now," murmured Peachy. "But great work, great work. You go on inside and get yourself a drink."

"Oh, I'm not drinking no more," said Stella. "It's just the crank for me now. Figure that's safer."

"Absolutely," said Peachy soothingly. "Just the crank for you. You run along."

She scurried inside as Peachy turned to spot Bonnie, his handsome face splitting into a grin.

"If it isn't the baddest bitch of Venice Beach. Ready for a big night tonight?"

Bonnie smiled and bumped Peachy's fist with her own. Thursday was usually a busy night for the bar, especially in the summer, but tonight was guaranteed to be slammed for the holiday. They were in the middle of the first real heat wave of the season and the evening was unusually warm for Venice, which stayed cool at night even through the hotter months. It was a sensual heat, laced with a tangy breeze from the sea, and a feeling of expectation and possibility hung in the air.

"Owee!" Peachy exclaimed, clapping his hands together. "We're gonna help some people get laid tonight! I can feel it!"

Bonnie took up her position to the left of the door. Soon, Fuzz came and joined them. He was dressed, as he was every night, in a tight black T-shirt that stretched across his veined biceps and loose black jeans. Around his neck hung a puka shell necklace, a gift, he'd told her, made for him by one of his daughters. Fuzz was kind to Bonnie, but he had warned her against taking this job.

"A lot of people think being a bouncer is like being a customer," he'd explained during her first night on the door. "Only the bar pays *you* instead of the other way around." He narrowed his eyes at her. "It's not. Being a bouncer is the lowest job in the joint. You will be hit. You will be spat on. You will get far more puke and blood and urine on you than you thought possible outside of a career in hospice care."

A reel of Bonnie's time training in the ring had flickered before her eyes. Sweat streaming, spit flying, blood leaking, head spinning, nausea rising, gut churning, light fading . . .

"I can handle it," she said.

And she could. Good boxing required such clear and rapid analytical thought that a cool head was mandatory. A fight could be driven by passion, but never led by it, an attitude Bonnie maintained in everything she did. So she was stoic at the door, present but impenetrable. She could pin a guy's wrists behind his back in one swift movement or quiet a rowdy regular with a look. Bonnie wasn't exactly a household name, but every now and then a boxing fan would recognize her. She acknowledged these fans with a nod but didn't engage. Mostly, they were complimentary. Some tried to prove their manhood by asking her to arm-wrestle. She dismissed them with the same patient impassivity of a mule swatting flies away with its tail. Yet she often marveled inwardly at the hubris of these men, weak-limbed, soft-bellied, half drunk, who earnestly believed that they could equal, in fact overcome, a world-class female athlete purely on the basis of their sex. Because that's what Bonnie had been: world-class.

First, she had been an amateur, but her style had always leaned toward the professional. Still, there were real hurdles to her turning pro. Most fighters attempting the transition quit after only one or two bouts. The rules were not dissimilar, but they were different worlds. For starters, there was no protective headguard. Less padding in the gloves meant you felt the punches more, both when you hit and got hit. It was not just speed that counted on the scorecard, but power. And, of course, you weren't fighting three rounds anymore; you were in it for ten.

But Bonnie had done it. She won her first professional fight by knockout in the first round. She stopped her next opponent in the third round, baffling her with blinding combinations and a fluid in-and-out movement Pavel had himself been known for and was now becoming Bonnie's signature. The following year, she won the light-weight world title by unanimous decision after pulverizing the previous titleholder, a Colombian three-weight world champion previously considered unbeatable. She was gaining a reputation as the new star of women's boxing when, while preparing for a title defense fight against an up-and-coming South African fighter that was widely considered to be a shoo-in victory for her, Bonnie's life fell apart.

Bonnie's home gym was Golden Ring in the city, but in the eight weeks before this fight she and Pavel moved her training camp to a gym in New Jersey, where she ate, slept, and trained on the property, thinking about nothing but the upcoming fight. Her waking hours were filled with shadowboxing; hand mitts with Pavel; work on the heavy bag, double end bag, and speed bag; jump rope and body con-ditioning, as well as sparring sessions three times a week. In the eve-nings, she and Pavel watched videos of her opponent's former fights, designing a game plan that capitalized on her bad habits and used Bonnie's style to her advantage. She went to bed early and woke up before sunrise to run five miles wearing a weighted vest. Camp was grueling, there was no doubt about that, but there was also a freedom in having her life narrowed to one singular purpose. It was the great-est level of devotion possible outside of religion.

She was a week out from the fight when Nicky called her unex-pectedly. Bonnie was in her room, a spartan dormitory with a low single bed, lacing up her boxing boots for the afternoon training ses-sion. Upon seeing Nicky's name on her screen, she dropped the laces immediately and answered. Her sisters knew not to bother her in the week before a fight; whatever it was must be important.

*You okay, Nicks?* she asked.

*I'm good. I'm fine! I'm great! You good?* said Nicky, sounding unchar-
acteristically flustered.

*All good,* said Bonnie. *What's going on?*

*I . . . It's nothing really. I seem to have misplaced my pain meds and I'm
getting my period. I think I left them at a friend's house or something.*

She was straining to sound casual, but Bonnie could hear the effort
behind her words. The thought flashed instinctively across her mind
that she was lying, but she pushed it away. Nicky had no reason to lie
to her.

*You can't get more from the doctor?* she asked.

*It's July Fourth weekend. Everywhere's closed.*

Bonnie sighed. Poor Nicky, it was terrible timing.

*The emergency room?* she offered.

*And lose the whole day? You know it will be a shit show there.* Nicky
took a deep breath down the phone. *Do you think . . . you could get
some from the gym, Bon? I don't need much. Just a few pills to get me through
the weekend.*

Bonnie frowned. Most boxers had some kind of painkiller on
hand. Bonnie herself had gotten a cortisone shot earlier in her camp
after injuring her rotator cuff during a sparring session, but in general
she avoided taking anything that could cloud her mind or slow her
reflexes. She had seen guys exchanging pills before, though she had
always stayed clear of that kind of thing. It was a slippery slope and,
anyway, pain was *part* of boxing. Bonnie could ask, but it would risk
her reputation with the other fighters. What if Pavel got wind of it?

*I don't know if that's a good idea . . .* she began.

*I'm asking for, like, two pills,* Nicky snapped. *Please, Bonnie.*

She hated to disappoint her sister, but she was also surprised by
Nicky's tone. If she was honest, Nicky had been different recently,
peevish and quicker to anger.

*If it's that bad, maybe you should go to the emergency room?* she tried
again.

*It's fine,* said Nicky. *Don't worry about it. Look, don't tell the others I
asked, okay? I don't want them to worry.*

She hung up before Bonnie could say goodbye.

That afternoon, Bonnie was working with Pavel on defense drills. Pavel held a foam pool noodle in each hand and used them to tap Bonnie's shoulders, head, and body while she slipped, rolled, and parried to avoid them. It was a classic exercise used to improve a fighter's head movement and hand speed, but Bonnie's head was elsewhere. *Thwack.* The pool noodle hit her ear as Bonnie reacted too slowly to slip its trajectory.

*Move your head!* called Pavel over the swishing of the foam tubes. *Thwack.* Bonnie took a noodle to the other ear, then to the cheek. *Thwack, thwack.* The blows were soft, but Pavel delivered them in a quick flurry that disoriented Bonnie. *Hello!* he called, hitting her in the head again. *Anyone in there?* Bonnie rolled to miss the deluge, but Pavel intercepted her with a swipe to the body, then back up to the head again.

*Stop!* she shouted suddenly, grabbing the noodles from his hands and tossing them across the floor.

Bonnie never ended drills early. Whatever Pavel asked her to do—another minute of plank, another round on the bag, ten more seconds in the ice bath—she did it. She never quit; that was what made her great. She slumped onto the bench and took a long pull of water. Pavel came and sat beside her. He turned and tapped the side of her head gently with his finger.

*What going on in there, hmm?* he asked. He'd been in America for years by then, but his Russian accent was still as thick as ever.

*It's Nicky,* she said eventually. *She's in pain again.*

Pavel nodded silently and clasped his hands in front of him.

*You know, I did not go home to Moscow for six years?* he said. *Even when my mother died.*

Bonnie glanced at him. She did not know that, but she could have guessed. Pavel rarely mentioned his family.

*Boxing is sacrifice,* he said slowly. *Is pain. Most people, they could never do what we do.*

*I know that,* said Bonnie impatiently. She didn't need him to tell her about sacrifice. What else had she been doing all these years? Why else had she been suffering with these feelings for him in silence?

*There is boxing.* Pavel cut his hand through the air with one hand. *And there is everything else.* He placed his other hand below the first. Bonnie sat quietly for a moment.

*But my sisters are—* She took his second hand and lifted it, so it was parallel to the first. Pavel shook his head and moved the hand back, returning it below the other.

*We are not like other people, Bonnie.* He spoke softly but his voice was firm. *We are the lonely hunters.*

Bonnie looked at Pavel. Was she imagining it, or was he sending her a message? Could it be that he felt the same way for her as she did for him, and this was his way of saying that never admitting their feelings was the sacrifice they both must make for greatness? Or was he simply talking about boxers in general? Pavel always said that the longest distance in boxing was from the dressing room to the ring, not because of the crowds watching or the commentators judging, but because that was how long a boxer had for the belief they could win to travel from their head to their heart. It was one thing to *think* you were a champion, another to *feel* it. The head to the heart, Pavel said, was the greatest journey a boxer could make.

*But what if I'm not like you?* she asked.

*What if I don't want to be lonely forever?* she did not add.

*You not,* he said. He placed his hand on her knee, then quickly removed it again. *You better.*


"HOW YOU DOIN' TONIGHT, SISTER?" asked Fuzz, offering his fist for a bump. "You feel that earthquake this morning?"

"Sure did," intercepted Peachy. "I was with a lady friend. Not the worst timing." He gave Bonnie a quick wink. "Added a bit more rock to my roll, if you know what I mean."

"What time was it?" asked Bonnie.

"'Round five," said Fuzz. "You should have heard my wife. Yelling at me to save the kids. Got all four of them out of bed and then what? Nuttin'. Nightmare to get the little ones back to sleep."

Bonnie smiled ruefully to herself.

"I thought someone was trying to break into my apartment," she said.

Fuzz laughed and spat between his feet.

"Lord help the guy that tries to rob you, Bonnie Blue. He be knockin' on the *wrong* door."

The first revelers began to arrive and within an hour a line was snaked around the block. People tumbled in and out of the doors, growing increasingly vociferous as the night wore on. Though thirty-one years old, Bonnie had never been drunk, never even smoked a cigarette. At the age when the rest of her peers discovered the wonders of inebriation, Bonnie won her first bout and experienced the intoxication of victory. As she grew older, she never felt the tug toward experimentation that seemed to lure others. She had watched drugs almost destroy Avery's life before she got clean and became the faultless perfectionist she presented herself as today. Even glamorous Lucky and her carousel of parties didn't make staying up until four A.M. seem more tempting than waking up at that time to work out. And watching people stumble and swerve out of the bar each night didn't do much to convince her that she was missing out. It always seemed like a waste of time to Bonnie, a person who for years had had no time to waste.

And, of course, there'd been Nicky. Nicky liked a glass of wine every now and then, but she'd never been much of a partyer. She, like Bonnie, preferred a clear head. But the pain of her endometriosis had changed her. At twenty, when she was finally diagnosed, she had laparoscopic surgery to remove the damaged tissue from around her uterus. For a few months, she appeared to be better. But then it came back, even worse this time. The only solution doctors could offer was managing the symptoms with more pain meds or a hysterectomy, a surgery to remove the uterus altogether, thereby ensuring Nicky would never have a child. For Nicky, it wasn't a choice.

For years, she managed. Often, she wouldn't talk about it for months at a time; she looked well, and it was easy to forget. Then Bonnie would get a glimpse into the secret shadow world her sister occupied—a wince when she thought no one was watching, the way her hands would flutter to her stomach as if to catch the pain at the source—and she knew Nicky suffered more than she said. The day after Nicky called her at the training camp, Bonnie had taken the train into the city to see her without telling Pavel. It was July Fourth, and the gym was quiet anyway. Bonnie had done her usual day of training with Pavel, who of course did not believe in taking the holiday off, then snuck out that evening. The gnawing sensation that her sister needed help had not left her all day and, as she sat on the train, she was happy to think they could spend the evening together watching the fireworks.

BONNIE'S MIND SKIPPED FORWARD AWAY from that night to her final fight, a memory almost but not quite as painful. In the footage of it online, she is almost unrecognizable. It's the eighth round and the South African has her in the corner. Bonnie has her gloves up and her head bowed as she gets pummeled from the inside. Her left eyebrow is split open and streaming blood down her mottled cheekbone. One eye is swollen almost shut. Her white gold-trimmed shorts and sports bra are soaked red. Her opponent loads up her right and releases it into Bonnie's exposed ribs. She bows but she does not break. She also does not fight back. The South African looks to her corner to see if she should continue. The referee is stepping forward to stop the fight when slowly, blood running down her face and chest, Bonnie raises her glove and motions for her to keep going. *Come and get me.* Bonnie takes two more jabs to the face, her head snapping back with each blow. A woman ringside hides her face in her seatmate's shoulder. Even hardened boxing viewers cover their eyes. Bonnie has just taken another hook to the head when from her corner comes a fluttering movement. A single white towel sails across the ring, landing in the center. The fight is over.

*Throw in the towel.* Most people forget that phrase comes from boxing. It's often said casually enough, but in the sport, it's the highest humiliation. Many fighters would rather die in the ring than have their corner quit on them. A boxer can recover from a loss, but a surrender marks them for life. As soon as the towel is thrown from Bonnie's corner, Pavel ducks under the ropes and races toward Bonnie, grasping for her shoulders. Still on her feet, her face twisted with agony, she shoves him away. She eschews the cutman and medic, pushing her way out of the ring alone. In the stands above her, the crowd clamors, waves of human noise crashing over her braided head, some carrying insults, others, cries of undying support. She makes the long walk from the center of the stadium to the dressing room without looking back. What no one in that arena except Pavel knew was that one week before that fight, it was Bonnie who found Nicky dead.

AT AROUND ONE A.M., Peachy lit the last in his first pack of Camels for the night and turned to Fuzz.

"Hey, man, can you do me a favor right now? Can you say *bacon*?"

"Bacon?" said Fuzz, the word in his Jamaican accent rhyming with *pecan*. "What you want me saying *bacon* for?"

Peachy doubled over, hooting with laughter. Fuzz rolled his eyes at Bonnie.

"This fool's always laughing at nuttin'," he said. "Must be drunk."

Peachy shot back up, feigning insult.

"I am sober as a judge! Well, almost . . . Now get this, get this. Listen to me say beer can. *Beer can*."

In Peachy's British accent the words sounded almost identical to Fuzz's pronunciation of bacon. Peachy laughed so hard the tendrils of his long, copper-streaked Afro bounced like antennae. Fuzz spat at the ground again, unmoved.

"Oh come on, it's funny!" cried Peachy. "Bonnie, can you explain to this man what funny is?"

But Bonnie was distracted because, for one moment, she could have sworn that she saw Nicky. She was walking toward the bar in a denim dress over a striped shirt, just like the kind her sister had worn when she was still alive. Her hair was tied in a low ponytail and her face was bare but for a streak of dark red lipstick. She was holding the arm of a hefty guy in a blue collared shirt, turning to him and asking him something nervously. She turned to look directly at Bonnie and suddenly the vision was gone; she was just another brown-haired girl in a denim dress.

"Oh boy, here come the last dregs," muttered Peachy as the couple approached. "Sorry, guys, we're closing up for the night," he called as they came closer.

The guy in the blue shirt stopped square in front of Peachy. He had a large round head like a piece of puffed rice and the unnaturally bulging shoulders born of steroids and bad form at the gym. His face registered the surprise and irritation of a person who is not often told no.

"But it's only one," he said. "You're not closing for another hour."

"That may be," said Peachy, reaching into his back pocket to produce a new pack of Camel Golds from his seemingly endless supply. Slowly, he unpeeled the plastic casing and crumpled it in his palm. "But, as I said, we're closing up."

The door flung open, releasing with it the sound of a raucous Motown track and a wave of chatter and laughter; one of Peachy's regulars, a leather-clad biker with a handlebar mustache, strolled out.

"I'll be back," he called over his shoulder. "Just checking on my ride. You need anything, Peach?"

"All good, brother," said Peachy, turning back to the couple with his guileless smile. "As I was saying, have a good night, folks."

"You've got to be fucking kidding me," said Blue Shirt. "That guy's coming back but you're not letting us in? You can't do that."

Peachy wrinkled his nose and popped a cigarette between his lips.

"The funny thing is," he said, lighting it, "I can."

"Babe, let's go," the non-Nicky said, pulling at the guy's bulky arm. "There's a sports bar right over there."

"Nah, babe, nah." Blue Shirt shook her off. "I'm not leaving until this clown lets us in."

"Never gonna happen, mate," said Peachy. "Listen to your girl and trot along 'round the corner to Scores. You'll like it there."

Blue Shirt puffed his chest up.

"You think you can talk to me like that?"

Beside her, Bonnie could feel Fuzz bristle to attention. Peachy chuckled and exhaled a cloud of smoke.

"That's just my accent, mate. I talk to everyone like that."

Blue Shirt stepped closer so his face was inches from Peachy's. Fuzz let out a low hum of warning. But Bonnie was watching the face of the brown-haired girl. She saw now why she had thought it was Nicky. It wasn't her clothes or hair; it was the expression on her face. Or rather, it was the expression beneath her expression, the one she thought she was hiding. This girl was lost. The loneliness around her was palpable. And this man beside her had no idea, was completely oblivious, just as Bonnie had been with Nicky.

By the time Blue Shirt had uttered the second syllable of the word white men have invoked for centuries to degrade Black men, Bonnie was already on him. She hit him first with a crisp, nose-flattening jab. He doubled over, clawing at the center of his face, which was gushing blood, then barreled forward with a roar, attempting to tackle Bonnie around the waist. She caught him with a sharp left uppercut, then socked him in the belly twice with her right. He lunged for her again, his fist whistling past her ear as she slipped him and countered with a blow just below his kidney. His legs crumpled beneath him. By the time he reached the pavement, Bonnie was staggering backward as if just awakened from a dream. The brown-haired girl was screaming in one long high pitch like an air-raid siren.

Bonnie took off down Windward, rounding the corner toward the sea. She could hear Peachy calling her name as she bolted onto the boardwalk, past the novelty T-shirt stores still inexplicably open at this hour, past the skate park where lithe teenage boys sailed between yellow lagoons of light from the streetlamps, past a huddle of ragged figures passing around a small flame, and onto the wide stretch of sand that led to the black sea.

She walked the beach until sunrise, stopping at one point to scrub her hands clean in the surf. When the first pale light appeared on the horizon, she headed home. Back at her apartment, she discovered that the soles of her feet were covered in a thick, sticky black oil. She sat on the edge of the tub and scrubbed each foot with soap and water, but the tar would not budge. She scraped at it with her fingernails but, even once the top layer came off, a black stain remained on her skin. She grabbed a pumice stone hanging on a string from the shower head, a relic of a former resident, and managed to grind and exfoliate the remainder off, leaving her feet raw.

But the tar was like a plague, it had marred everything it touched. She saw it had left track marks across the floor and ruined the bottom of her leather sandals, a gift from Nicky and one of the few nice things Bonnie owned. She grabbed a knife from the kitchen and attempted to scrape the dark muck off the soft leather insoles, but she only succeeded in scratching away the top layer of leather too. When she returned to the bathroom, she found the tub was now stained with a black residue that would not wash off when she turned on the tap. In a panic, she grabbed a bottle of ammonia from under the sink and, without diluting it, sloshed it over the porcelain and began scouring the surface with a wire sponge. She inhaled the chemical fumes until, lightheaded, she staggered from the bathroom and collapsed on the foldout beach chair in her living room.

Only then did she remember what the black tar could be. She'd been warned about it by her neighbors when she first moved to Venice. It usually happened after storms or earthquakes, the result of disrupted oil from the seafloor seeping into the sand on the shore. The easiest way to remove it was to gently wipe your skin and any surfaces it touched with a cloth soaked in olive oil. She would find, her neighbors had promised, that the black tar simply melted away.

In training, she had been taught the difference between reacting and responding. Responding was when you used the tools you'd been taught to clinically counter an attack according to your game plan; reacting was when you acted purely on adrenaline, usually leaving yourself open to further harm. In the early morning light, in her empty living room, Bonnie looked down at her destroyed shoes and feet. For the first time since Nicky died, she let herself cry.

# CHAPTER THREE

# Avery

AT THE END OF THE GARDEN, BEHIND THE SHED, BEHIND THE PINK Queen Elizabeth rosebushes, Avery was preparing to smoke her daily cigarette. She pulled on the oversized Barbour jacket and yellow dishwashing gloves she kept squirreled behind the gardening tools for this express purpose, along with mouthwash, air freshener, and gum. She struck a long cooking match and brought it to the tip of the Winston with a feeling caught somewhere between anticipation and resignation. Long inhale, long exhale. In the pale evening light, the first cloud of smoke floated away from her like thought. She was never more aware of her breath than while smoking, never more present. It would be a great form of meditation if it wasn't also killing her.

The garden was in full summer bloom, violet and fuchsia geraniums turning their pert faces toward the setting sun. Avery looked up the path lined with ink-blue pansies to the house, checking again that no one was coming. Her home was a narrow Victorian just two streets from Hampstead Heath. From the outside, it was ivy covered and charmingly ramshackle, the kind of house one would imagine an artist living in, and probably once did, though few could afford the area's real estate prices today. They'd bought the house together seven years ago with a down payment heavily padded by a surprise sum Chiti inherited from her grandfather in India around the time she and Avery first met, but even Chiti, a psychotherapist with a healthy private practice, would have struggled to pay the mortgage without Avery's corporate lawyer income.

Hampstead was the England Americans liked to imagine, its sprawling heath a taste of country life without the inconvenience of actually having to leave London. Its high street, which boasted an organic tea shop, two bookstores (one used, one new), and an artisanal chocolatier, was a beacon of British good taste. Even its tube station, cast in red brick with handsome half-moon windows, felt sophisticated. In Hampstead it was easy for Americans to ignore the other London, the city of council flats and William Hill betting shops, of evenings spent slumped over a pint and packet of crisps at the pub and belligerent nights out ending with a kebab sloppily polished off on the night bus home. Avery loved saying she lived in Hampstead because of all it instantly communicated about her—togetherness, taste, and wealth.

Growing up, she and her sisters had everything they needed, but not what they wanted, which was space. *Too close for comfort.* A cliché, but it was true. They were too close to be comfortable in that home. There was one bathroom for all six of them; Prufrock may have measured out his life with coffee spoons, she always thought, but Avery measured hers in the hours she spent waiting for that bathroom to be free. At the time, she'd hated it; she and her sisters felt like lobsters packed into a murky tank, each of them jostling and bumping up against the other to reach the light above the water. All through her adolescence she had longed to leave, but she stayed living in that home until Bonnie started training, Nicky went to college, and Lucky began traveling as a model. Once her sisters were all safely out, she allowed herself to flee.

Avery exhaled smoke. For years, she had put her sisters first. By the time she left, she was already sneaking drinks in the morning, leaning out the bathroom window late at night to smoke the heroin-laced joints that she needed to sleep. It was only once she left home that she finally allowed herself to inject. She tipped herself off the high, thin ledge she'd been balancing on for years and let herself fall and fall. For a year while she was in San Francisco, even if her sisters managed to speak to her, they couldn't really reach her. She had gone somewhere they couldn't follow. Even after she got clean and graduated from law school, she left for London soon after, chasing her own success, her own freedom. Avery had abandoned her sisters before, but she would never do it again. It wasn't just that they needed her; she needed them. She was at her best when she was helping them, she realized now. That was the only structure in her life, the only higher power she believed in.

After Nicky's funeral, it was Avery who paid for time to stand still. She had covered the mortgage payments on the New York apartment for the past year, allowing it to lie empty with all of Nicky's belongings untouched inside. But time was more powerful than money; no one knew that better than Avery. It had been a short-term arrangement, yet she still didn't feel ready to face its conclusion. Now, knowing that it would soon be gone, she felt an unfamiliar nostalgia for that cramped apartment. For better or worse, it had been hard to feel alone in a home like that.

Avery unwillingly extinguished the cigarette in the baked beans can she kept tucked behind a spade for this purpose, then swigged mouthwash and spat it into the bush. She shrugged off the Barbour and peeled away the yellow plastic gloves. Finally, she pushed a piece of spearmint gum into her mouth. She felt like a teenager. Avery had started smoking again a few months ago after quitting ten years earlier when she was twenty-three. It wasn't the cigarettes that made her feel young again exactly, it was the return to the hidden self, the Avery only she knew.

She walked up the garden path toward the yellow lights of the house. The French doors were flung open to reveal Chiti and her younger brother, Vish, leaning against the marble kitchen island,

their faces aglow in the blue light of a computer screen. From a distance the siblings could be twins, both resting their narrow chin in a
cup of their long hands, their smooth black hair reflecting the light as
if lacquered. They each had strong noses and imperious, arched fore-
heads, features that suggested intelligence and discernment. Chiti
lifted her face from her hands with a smile as Avery passed through
the door.

"We're watching a livestream of Mum's screening," she said.
"You're just in time for questions from the audience."

"It's brutal," said Vish.

Vish and Chiti's mother, Ganishka, was an award-winning documentary filmmaker and political activist whose scurrilous criticism of
neocolonialism and U.S. foreign policy kept her regularly in the
news. She had raised her children between Delhi and London, then
shipped them off to boarding school as soon as Chiti turned thirteen
and Vish eleven in order to return to India, and her primary love of
filmmaking, full-time. Ganishka had never taken issue with Chiti's
sexuality; her only disappointment, as she reminded her regularly,
was that she had chosen to be with, of all things, an American.

Avery came to stand beside them, and Chiti rested her head against
her shoulder automatically. Avery stiffened. Her method of hiding
the smell of her new habit only worked from a safe distance.

"Since when do you chew gum?" asked Chiti mildly. "I can hear
your jaw clicking."

"I'll spit it out," Avery said quickly, practically leaping away from
her.

"Dude, she doesn't drink or do drugs," said Vish. "Let her at least
have some gum."

"You know I don't either?" said Chiti with a light laugh.

"But that's because you don't like it," he said. "Whereas Avery—"

"Loved it," said Avery as she spat the wad into the bin. "But Chiti's right, it's a bad habit."

Chiti frowned very slightly.

"I didn't say that," she said.

"Hey, Avery, um, Chiti told me what day it is," Vish said, rubbing the back of his neck with visible discomfort. "And I'm really sorry. About Nicky. My, uh, condolences."

"Thanks," said Avery, giving him a soft punch in the arm. "But I'm fine."

Chiti gave her a knowing look.

"You know what I say about *fine*."

"*For therapists, fine is a four-letter word*," intoned Avery. "But I actually am."

"I'm just saying you don't have to be fine with us," said Chiti, her voice soft. "Your family."

"I know," said Avery more forcefully than she'd meant to.

"Uh-oh," said Vish, pointing toward the screen. "A new lamb to the slaughter."

The camera panned through the audience to a young Indian man in glasses. A microphone on a boom was thrust in front of him and he reached to steady it, running his other hand through his hair self-consciously.

"My friends and I often zealously debate the best Oscar-winning docs." He smiled with affected impatience. "Though we have yet to reach a satisfying consensus. I dare to think that you, too, have these kinds of pub conversations." He cleared his throat. "So, my question is, which was your favorite from this year's lineup, and why?"

"Oh shit," said Vish.

The camera returned to Ganishka's face, which was hardening with frustration.

"I don't have these 'pub conversations' as you call them, because I don't think about art in this way. It does films a great disservice to think of them hierarchically. Awards are a capitalist model for cre-ativity; I put zero store in such accolades, though I may have won several of them."

"Couldn't resist slipping that in," murmured Chiti.

"In fact," continued Ganishka, clearly warming up to this line of thought, "I have been asked many times to sit on prize committees and it is my habit to refuse in all cases. They are bad for filmmakers, create bad politics in the industry, and represent entrenched marketing strategies that are outdated. I don't need a committee, in most cases majority male, to *micturate*"—Ganishka paused with satisfaction after enunciating this word—"on my work to prove its value." She concluded, "I strongly question any authority that presents itself as a deciding body in the arts, and I advise you and your friends to do the same."

The squinting young man, visibly chastened, sat back down.

"Aw, man," said Vish.

"She's not wrong," said Avery.

"Yeah, but these are, like, Mum's *fans*. She could be a bit nicer to them."

"I think they like it," said Avery. "She's like their domme."

"Disturbing," said Chiti.

"But accurate," said Vish.

Next, a timid white woman wearing dangly plastic fruit earrings rose and took the microphone.

"Hi. First of all I just wanted to thank you for changing my life."

Groans from Chiti and Vish.

"My question is simple: What moments in your life give you solace?"

Ganishka nodded and gently closed her eyes like a cat who has been tickled in the right spot.

"That is a good question," she purred, and the woman flushed with pleasure.

"Have you ever noticed how much Mum closes her eyes when she speaks?" asked Vish. "It's like what she's saying is *so true* she can hardly stand to bear witness to it with all her senses."

"To be fair, I think she may have just forgotten her glasses," said Chiti.

Sometimes, Avery saw Chiti's desire to love her mother breach the surface of her disdain like a seal cub peeking its head above the ocean. The problem with Ganishka was that you never knew if you were going to get cuddled or clubbed.

"A moment that comes to me now," Ganishka was saying solemnly, "is the sensation of putting my cheek on my dog's tummy. I have two of them, and one has a considerable tummy—"

The audience laughed, in part to relieve the tension from the previous question, in part for the gift of hearing one of the fiercest living cinematic minds say the word *tummy* so seriously.

"Both of them used to be strays," she continued. "One of them, her mother was killed by a car on the road outside my house. She was so small when I found her that I had to feed her with a pipette."

Chiti released an involuntary snort.

"Yet she didn't believe in breastfeeding *us*."

"The other dog I stole," said Ganishka with a proud shrug. "She was tied to a tree night and day near my home, and one day I just took her. I feel it is my duty to liberate the unloved."

A murmur of approval rustled through the crowd as Chiti snapped the laptop shut.

"That's enough of that," she said. Avery checked her face for signs of hurt, but she appeared unruffled. "I'm hungry. You staying for dinner, Vishnoodle?"

He spun around on the island stool and emitted a loud sigh toward the ceiling.

"I'm too heartbroken to eat," he said.

"What's this?" asked Avery.

"The new love of Vish's life," said Chiti, smiling.

Avery turned to inspect the contents of their large fridge.

"Ah! And when did you meet this new love?" she asked.

"Last night."

"So it's serious," she said.

She removed a bunch of wilted cilantro from the top shelf and tossed it in the bin. She had never been much of a cook and, when alone, still considered cereal an adequate dinner.

"It is!" defended Vish. "She's cool, man. She knew all the words to Wu-Tang's 'Bring Da Ruckus.'"

"That *is* cool," conceded Avery. "Should we order from the Italian spot?"

"There's perfectly good food in the fridge," said Chiti. "I'll roast some veggies."

"I like Avery's idea better," said Vish. "Anyway, I fucked it all up. I needed to text her something today that would make an impression."

"So what did you send her?"

Vish hung his head.

"It doesn't get more predictable," he said. "More prosaic."

Chiti inhaled sharply.

"It wasn't a picture of your penis, was it?"

Vish's head snapped back up.

"Woman, no!" he yelled. "Get your mind out of the gutter."

Chiti offered an apologetic chuckle.

"What could be worse than a picture of your penis?" asked Avery.

"Hey!" said Vish, feigning outrage.

Avery raised her hands in apology.

"I was referring to the *nature* of the content, not the quality."

"We're sure your penis is perfect, Noodle," said Chiti.

She looked at Avery and her eyes were dancing with amusement.

"Woman!" cried Vish. "You're my sister! Stop!"

"So what was it?" Avery asked, laughing. "It can't be that bad."

"I said . . . *Happy Thursday.*" He pushed his face back into the crook of his arm. "The banality! I'll never hear from her again."

Chiti rolled her eyes and rubbed Vish's back. This week, her long nails were painted a rhubarb pink.

"It's all right," she murmured. "You'll get another chance. Tomorrow is a new day."

"Exactly." Avery grinned. "You can text her TGIF."

As Vish moaned with despair, Avery turned to pull her buzzing phone from her briefcase.

"Everything okay?" asked Chiti, catching her frown.

"It's from my sister."

"The hot one or the scary one?" asked Vish, visibly perking up.

Chiti swatted at the back of his head.

"Don't be reductive," she said. "You know their names."

"Bonnie Blue could snap me in half like a twiglet," said Vish. "I'm saying *scary* with the utmost respect."

"The hot one and the scary one," repeated Avery. *And the dead one*, she thought. "What does that make me? The boring one."

"*Stable*, darling," said Chiti cheerily. "There's a difference."

But Avery was not stable, not really. She was unraveling. It was just that no one knew it yet—not even, really, her.

"You're also the gay one," said Vish generously. "If we're going purely by generalities."

Chiti grabbed the back of his head and shook it.

"What has gotten into you?" she tutted.

Avery raised an eyebrow.

"Who says my sisters aren't gay too?"

"You're just saying that because you're with this one," said Vish, wrapping his arm around his sister's waist. "Who thinks everyone's gay."

"That's because they *are*," Chiti said. "A little at least."

"Yeah, yeah, Kinsey scale shminzie shmale," he said. "I'm just saying, whatever part of me wants something put in my butt must be buried pretty deep, because I'm certainly not aware of it."

"Much like your prostate!" said Chiti brightly.

"Anyway, the answer to your question is Lucky," said Avery. "She wants to come stay."

"That's fantastic!" exclaimed Chiti. "You're always saying she should come. She's so close, after all."

Avery shook her head.

"Something's not right."

"What makes you say that?"

"She wants to come soon. Like, tomorrow. Something must have happened in Paris."

"Or maybe she just heard about our fabulous guest room, which I have finally gotten around to painting?"

Chiti had been redoing the house a room at a time, each with its own color theme. She understood color like a language, one in which she was fluent, and Avery was still trying to catch the odd word. For instance, she'd told Avery, in Jaipur where her grandparents lived, there were fifty variations of blue and turquoise, each with its own name. Avery, by contrast, struggled to think of one. Chiti had chosen emerald for the walls of the guest room and covered the bed with linen sheets the color of rose quartz for contrast, transforming what had once been a rather poky office into a precious jewel box of a room. Avery felt that it was an apt analogy for Chiti's effect on her own life.

"And why haven't I been invited to stay in this fabulous guest room?" asked Vish.

"Because you live in London, silly boy," said Chiti.

Vish cast his eyes around the kitchen, with its tasteful powder-blue walls and gleaming metal appliances, the polished marble countertops, and large farmhouse sink complete with a separate sparkling water tap Avery had paid to install at great expense.

"Not this London," he said.


LATER THAT NIGHT, AVERY LAY in their deep claw-foot bath listening to the radio. She didn't care what was on; she just needed some noise in the room to prevent her from being alone with her thoughts. This was something she remembered from early sobriety, how unbearable it felt to even brush her teeth without having something to distract her. She would blast the television while she showered, hold a hairdryer in one hand and a book in the other, scroll the news while she ate, and lie in bed with headphones piping music into her ears late into the night. Over time, however, her mind had become a more peaceful place. She had even been on meditation retreats, whole days spent simply being present with herself, paying attention to her breath, letting thoughts drift through her mind like clouds in a clear sky. Not anymore. Now, when she closed her eyes, she saw every mistake she had made leading up to this moment. Her inner weather, once calm, had become stormy again.

Avery sank beneath the surface of the water and listened to the liquid murmurs around her ears. She stayed under for as long as she could, then burst forth gasping for breath. When she opened her eyes, Chiti was standing above her.

"Can I join you or is this one of your solo baths?"

"Of course you can."

Chiti unbuttoned her pants and linen tunic and let them crumple around her feet. Her naked form, once so thrilling to Avery, was now as familiar as the furniture. Chiti unwound her waist-length black braid and twisted it into what she called a bedtime bun, a plump swirl on the top of her head. She had the kind of hair people stopped in the street to admire, its length a perpetual performance and party trick. Chiti was thirty-nine, almost seven years Avery's senior, but from behind her hair gave the impression of someone either very young or very old, which was fitting given one of the earliest things Chiti had told Avery about herself.

The first time they met, Chiti had sat across from her in her old therapy office, a notepad in her hands and her ankles crossed. It was Avery's first therapy session ever and they had been talking for just under an hour. In answer to why she was there, Avery explained that she had kicked a heroin addiction, graduated from law school, and moved to London to join one of the most prestigious firms in the world, but she could not force herself to sleep at night. As they began to wrap up, Avery found, to her surprise, that she did not want the session to end.

*Can I come again next week?* she asked.

*I'd like you to, if you'd like to,* said Chiti.

*So, you can help me?*

Chiti nodded.

*I think so.*

*I'm not beyond help?* Avery clarified.

Chiti sat back in her chair and regarded her.

*Can I tell you something personal? I don't usually talk about myself with clients, and I likely won't again, but I think it might be helpful for me to explain myself this way.*

Avery nodded. She had been intrigued by Chiti immediately and wanted to hear anything she had to say.

*The people I have the hardest time treating are the ones I cannot imagine as a child,* she said. *Because of the circumstances in which I was born and raised, I had to be a pretty adult child and I would like at least some part of me to be a pretty childish adult. I often see the same desire in my patients.*

*And what about me?* Avery asked. *Can you see what kind of child I was?*

Chiti nodded.

*And?* Avery asked.

*You dissembled,* she said. *You still do.*

Avery could have been offended, but she was not. It was true.

*And how do I stop?* she'd asked.

Chiti dropped her notepad into her lap and caught Avery in her cool, still gaze.

*You tell the ugly truth,* she said.

And she had. She had told Chiti the truth for years, long after she stopped being her patient and became her partner. *That* truth, that Chiti had been her therapist first, was harder on Chiti. She didn't see herself as someone who would fall in love with a client, had judged it when teachers had warned of the powerful pull of countertransference during her training course. She had stopped seeing her supervisor because of it, had spent many anguished sessions with her own therapist trying to understand why she was willing to risk her reputation, perhaps even her career, for this young American woman who had come to her office complaining of insomnia. The most unethical thing Chiti had ever done was fall in love with Avery. But she did love her. It wasn't a choice; it was the ugly truth.

For seven years, they were happy together. That first time making love, Avery had lain with her head hanging off the bed as Chiti explored the secrets of her body and let tears run backward down her face. The evening sun stretched lazily across the bed in golden bars; when Avery closed her eyes, it glowed like honey behind her eyelids. *I didn't know,* she kept saying, in wonder, in mourning. *I didn't know.* Chiti's head appeared above her, surrounding her in the swishing, whispering folds of her hair. She was flushed rose gold. *Didn't know what, my darling?* But Avery couldn't explain it in words. She didn't know that love could feel like this, so honeyed, so sweet. That her body deserved such tenderness. They held each other as the light drained from the room, saliva and sweat cooling on their skin, and Avery felt it then, that longed-for sensation, love, yes, but safety too; she was safe at long last.

*Harmony* was the best word she could think of to describe their life together. They had their arguments, like any couple, but their daily life was harmonious. Their natures complemented each other. Chiti, naturally more of a nurturer, did the cooking when they ate in, took care of the garden, and made their house feel like a home. Avery, ever pragmatic, filed their taxes, paid their bills, and planned their holidays. Neither of them particularly enjoyed cleaning, so they hired a cleaning service to come every other week. Avery had previously thought love was built on large, visible gestures, but a marriage turned out to be the accrual of ordinary, almost inconsequential, acts of daily devotion—washing the mugs left in the sink before bed, taking the time to run up or downstairs to kiss each other quickly before one left the house, cutting up an extra piece of fruit to share—acts easy to miss, but if ever gone, deeply missed. For years, Avery and Chiti prided themselves on not missing them.

Then last year Nicky died, and Avery changed. She wouldn't drink over her sister's death; she knew she couldn't do that. But the grief. She didn't know how to handle the grief. It was the surprise that hurt most. She had lived her entire adult life minimizing risk to avoid being caught off guard by pain, yet she had not protected herself from this. Avery had been in recovery for almost a decade when Nicky died; how could she not have known how deeply her sister was struggling? How could she have missed the signs? She was the big sister; it was her *job* not to miss things. A part of her, which she never said aloud, feared it was because she had been so busy noticing Chiti.

At Nicky's funeral in New York, Avery took a book of prayers from the church. It had been years since she had stolen anything, but the feeling was the same. Her heart rate quickening, the sound of blood pumping in her ears. No thoughts but the weight of that book pressed snugly into the waistband of her black pants. When she returned to London, she kept doing it. Nothing big, a chocolate bar from the corner store, a lipstick from Boots, a pair of sneakers from the charity shop next door. Stealing from a charity shop on her salary. It was abhorrent, she knew.

So she moved on to the bigger Bond Street stores, the Burberrys, Guccis, and Chanels. It was so much easier than when she was in her early twenties in San Francisco, stealing to get by. Now, she could use a new strategy. Now, she was a successful woman in her thirties, a corporate lawyer who could afford any of the beautiful goods she trailed her fingers over as she smiled knowingly at the shop assistants. She accepted flutes of champagne without taking a sip, made a show of asking for the glass cases to be opened, inspected herself in the mirror, then feigned an appointment and, in a whirl of thanks and promises to return, made the indiscreet exit of someone with nothing to hide. All the while her purloined prize—a quilted wallet, a gold chain bracelet, an embroidered silk handkerchief—nestled snugly against her skin like an animal searching for warmth.

Above her, Chiti dipped a foot into the water and winced.

"You always make it too hot."

"That's how I like it." Avery shifted to one side to make room for Chiti, who bobbed herself in and out of the water with a yelp. "If I'm not struggling to maintain consciousness by the end, I don't consider it a real bath."

Chiti finally submerged herself and rested her head against the lip of the tub.

"Only you could make something supposedly relaxing a fight for survival. How long have you been stewing in here?"

Avery raised her hand to show her pruned fingers. Chiti took it between her own and stroked along the frills of wrinkled skin.

"You know, they've only *just* proven there's an evolutionary function to why our hands and feet do this?"

"They have?"

"It's to help grip underwater, like treads on a car tire."

"That makes sense." Avery nodded. "If you think about early humans gathering in streams and rivers and things."

"Exactly. Or hunting in the rain. It seems so obvious now, but it's only just been proven. All this time, our bodies have been performing this miracle of intelligent design, and it's been a mystery to us."

Avery smiled.

"But now we know."

Chiti nodded.

"Now we know."

Chiti tilted her head against the lip of the tub and exhaled.

"One whole year," she said. "I'd ask how you're feeling, but I think I know."

"You do?"

Chiti gave a tired smile.

"Two therapists walk into a bar," she said. "*You're good,* says the first therapist. *How am I?*"

Avery attempted to return the smile. It was Chiti's favorite joke; favorite, of course, because it was true. She was preternaturally empathetic, often able to read Avery's mood by how much milk she put in her coffee in the morning. She had made a profession of understanding others. But Avery didn't want to be understood right now, not by her wife, not by anyone.

"Did you go to a meeting today?" Chiti asked tentatively.

Avery had only just returned to AA after almost a year hiatus and Chiti seemed not to want to jinx it. Avery shook her head.

"Tomorrow."

Chiti nodded.

"I miss her, too, you know," Chiti said suddenly. "Right here." Chiti clutched her throat and Avery saw her eyes were glazed with tears. "I know it's important for you to experience your own feelings without competing with mine. But—" Her voice caught. "I loved her, too, and I still love her every day. I just wanted you to know that."

And Nicky had loved Chiti, all of Avery's sisters did. Chiti, who had flown to New York with Avery for Nicky's twenty-first birthday in their first year of dating (if you could call buying a house together within three months of meeting dating) and convinced Avery to stay out dancing and doing karaoke until four in the morning to celebrate.

She had surprised them all by singing Dolly Parton's "Gonna Hurry (As Slow as I Can)" in a voice so tender and full of longing the whole bar gave her a standing ovation. Chiti, who was that rarest of things: a truly great listener. Who remembered the names of her sisters' friends and lovers and asked after them the next time they met, who made every conversation feel like a house of cards you were building together that never fell down. Chiti said things like *I was thinking about what you said last time about trust . . .* and then would deliver some totally brilliant insight while giving the other person credit. She gave beautiful Christmas presents that somehow captured both who the recipient was and who they wanted to be.

She wasn't perfect, of course. Avery had the usual domestic gripes, like how Chiti's long hair clogged the shower drain, leaving Avery with the task of yanking out the nauseating tangle. She had truly terrible taste in television and watched the kind of reality shows Avery considered both stultifying and shockingly exploitative. She had very flat feet, but refused to wear her orthotic inserts, let alone shoes that weren't designed by the patriarchy to cripple women, so she was always insisting on taking cabs because her feet hurt, while Avery loved to walk.

And there was bigger stuff too. Chiti's growing desire for a baby, for one, which Avery still felt ambivalent about. And, if Avery was honest, sometimes Chiti's caretaking felt claustrophobic. In Avery's least generous moments, she saw it as Chiti's way of gaining control and making others dependent on her so she could protect herself from the same abandonment she had experienced with her mother. Even the act of buying a house in the neighborhood Avery wanted to live in so quickly after they first met was a kind of coercion. Avery may pay half the mortgage and have covered much of the renovations since, but she could never have afforded this house back then. By giving Avery what she always wanted—space, security, a place of her own—Chiti made sure she would never leave.

But that was unfair. Avery had been a willing recipient of all of Chiti's nurture. She had convinced Chiti to date her despite Chiti's misgivings about how they met, had delighted at the prospect of moving in together so soon. All her life she had been looking for a love like Chiti's. And Avery's sisters loved Chiti for the same reason Avery did: She was her match. Chiti's keen emotional intelligence acted as a rose to the thorn of Avery's spiky intellect and, together, they bloomed.

"I know you miss her," said Avery, attempting to soften. "It's your loss too."

She wanted to make room in her heart for Chiti's grief, but she struggled. If Vish died, Avery would be devastated, of course, but it could never compare to this. Her life had been reduced to two days, the day Nicky was still alive and the day she died. The rich and subtle patchwork of years and seasons that made up her life before was gone.

"It's Lucky I'm worried about," she continued. "She didn't even mention what day it is today in her message. Could she seriously have forgotten?"

"I'm sure she didn't forget," said Chiti. "Maybe she just didn't know what to say."

Avery could have relented, but she wasn't done with her grievances.

"And how could our mom have sent that email today of all days? You *know* I'm going to end up dealing with that whole apartment," she said, feeling her whole body tighten, despite the relaxing effects of the bath. "It's just so typical."

"You never ask your sisters for help," said Chiti. "If you did, they might be glad to give it."

Avery shook her head.

"Bonnie won't go back there, and I get it, you know, after everything she's been through. Lucky can't be relied on for anything, you know that. But to sell it now? It's only been a year! It's too soon. I told my parents I'd keep paying for it, why won't they just let me?"

"Maybe they want to move on," said Chiti softly.

"Well, *maybe* they should think about us for a change."

"It sounds like your sisters might be ready to let it go too." Avery opened her mouth, but Chiti raised her hand to finish her thought.

"Not because they don't care as much as you do, but because it's too painful to hold on."

Avery was about to dispute this, but she let herself fall slack against the back of the tub instead.

"I wish I saw people the way you do," she said, submerging herself deeper.

"How is that?"

"Generously."

Chiti leaned back, too, and looked down at her body beneath the rippling water. Her face, which before had been content, grew slack. Sadness spread through her features; it was like watching a cloud cast its shadow over a great, wide field. Chiti put a hand wearily across her eyes.

"What is it?" asked Avery.

Instinctively, she raised a hand to cup her left breast. It was a habit she'd had since adolescence to soothe herself, an act so unconscious, she often had to stop herself from doing it during stressful client meetings at work. Beneath her wet fingertips, her heartbeat quickened.

"I hate that I care," said Chiti. "I hate that it bothers me so much."

So this was it. The moment of reckoning. Chiti knew about the smoking, the stealing, everything. Avery squeezed her left breast. But beneath the fear, there was relief too. She could stop, with Chiti's help she could stop.

"Look, I'm embarrassed, but I'm glad you know . . ." she began.

Chiti looked up at her from beneath her hand.

"You've noticed too?" She frowned. "Of course you have."

This was not what she had been expecting. She searched Chiti's face.

"Noticed what?"

"I've gained weight."

"*What?*"

Avery's jaw unclenched with relief. Or disappointment. Or both.

"You don't have to pretend to be surprised," exclaimed Chiti. "Look at me!"

Avery looked at her wife, really looked at her, for the first time in a long time. Two long legs like tapered candlesticks. The soft, dark trail of hair beneath her belly button. How many times had Avery traced that winding path? She looked at Chiti's elegant, narrow hands dipping into the water like cranes. The deep, glossy pink of her painted nails. And yes, if she was honest, her stomach was rounder than when she had first met her, her thighs thicker. But it only made her look more sensual, more womanly.

Avery glanced down at her own pale, flat stomach and felt, as she often did, the lack of loveliness in her when compared to Chiti. Avery was not unattractive, but she was no Venus, she knew that. Her tattoos added some intrigue, at least. The best she could say about herself was that she was *neat* looking. A symmetrical face and economical body; square shoulders, narrow hips, sturdy legs. A body that, to her mind, was about as sensual as a cereal box.

Of course, growing up with a sister who looked like Lucky, Avery had been in proximity to beauty most of her life. But unlike Lucky, whose seraphic good looks complicated and concealed the darkness within her, Chiti looked exactly like who she was. She was soft and burnished, graceful and robust. She was beautiful the way nature is beautiful, eternally.

"Okay, *stop* looking at me," said Chiti.

She slung an arm across her chest and laughed self-consciously. Avery grabbed for her hand.

"You're perfect, Chiti." Chiti frowned and Avery hurried to correct herself. "I know we're not meant to use that word because women use perfectionism as a form of self-harm blah blah. It's just—to *me* you are. I wouldn't change a single thing about you." Was this true? Hadn't she just been sitting here listing Chiti's faults? "You know I don't care what you weigh," she added. This, at least, was entirely true.

"I care! I don't *like* that I care, but I do. My trousers cut into me when I'm sitting in session. Look! Look at these incriminating marks all over me."

"We'll get you new pants."

"But these are my favorite."

"The silk YSL ones?"

Chiti nodded.

"I'll buy you another pair," said Avery.

"They were vintage," Chiti said sadly. She slapped the water in front of her. "I am *not* going to be one of those people who only wears elasticated pants. God *help* me if I become one of those people!"

"No one's going to make you wear elasticated pants."

Chiti let out a little moan.

"I'm almost *forty*. When did that happen?"

"Forty is young."

Chiti looked at her.

"Thirty-four is young."

"I'm thirty-three."

Chiti flicked water at her.

"Even worse!" She picked up the soap and lathered it into her hands. "I thought if my body ever felt unrecognizable to me it would be because I was having a baby. I wasn't prepared for this . . . *rounding* into middle age."

Avery stiffened. Chiti had frozen her eggs shortly after they met, a decision that had seemingly taken the pressure off this type of observation. But it couldn't forever. Avery had always known she didn't want to carry a child, while Chiti knew that she did. Because Chiti was older and Avery wanted to focus on her career, freezing had seemed like the sensible option. But Chiti didn't want to be an old mother. She had started to talk more seriously about finding a donor last year, an idea Avery never overtly rejected, but certainly didn't encourage. Then Nicky died and they had not spoken about anything related to their future, let alone something as life-altering as a child, since.

"I'm too hot," Avery said. "I'm overheating." In one movement, she hauled herself out of the tub and stepped onto the freezing bathroom floor with a gasp. "I knew we should have got those floor heaters installed."

She hopped onto the bath mat and wrapped herself in a towel, watching as Chiti carefully rinsed the soapsuds off her shoulders and chest. When she was finished, Avery opened a large towel and shuffled over. Chiti stepped out of the tub and let Avery wrap her in it. They stood marooned on the tiny island of bath mat as Avery rubbed Chiti's arms to warm her up.

"Have you changed your mind?" Chiti asked quietly. "About the baby?"

She looked up at Avery from beneath wet, black eyelashes clinging together in thick spikes. Her face was completely open, unarmed. The thought of hurting her with the truth—that Avery had never made *up* her mind; Chiti had planned, and she had simply gone along with it—was unbearable.

"Have *you*?" Avery asked, trying not to sound hopeful.

Chiti let out a little sigh.

"No," she said. "I'll never change my mind about this."

Chiti was like Nicky, undeniably maternal. But Avery wasn't sure, she wasn't sure of anything. Maybe only one of you had to know, she thought. Maybe it was okay not to be certain, if one of you was? Was it enough to do it for Chiti and not for the child? Would that make her a bad mother? She was already proving to be a bad wife. Surely she should do anything for Chiti, the only person she loved as much as her sisters?

"Okay," she said.

Chiti's eyes shot to hers.

"Okay, as in you're ready?"

"Okay, as in I don't think I'll ever feel ready, but let's do it. What do you think?"

Chiti held her with her steady, defenseless gaze.

"Darling, I'm almost forty. I want to have a baby and I want it to be yours. I'd have one today if we could."

In spite of the doubt, in spite of the guilt, in spite of everything, Avery smiled.

"Maybe we should start practicing then."

They walked together from the bathroom to the bedroom. Chiti unclasped her bun and let her hair fall in a swishing black wave over her shoulders. She laid herself on the bed, still swaddled in the towel, and looked up at Avery, tentatively, hopefully.

"We've not done this in a little while," she said quietly.

"I know."

Very gently, as though removing the dressing from a wound, Avery unwrapped her. The faint smell of soap wafted off her damp skin. Chiti put her hands to Avery's chest and held her still above her.

"You want me?"

The question could have been seductive, but in Chiti's mouth it was earnest. Avery had not initiated sex in so long, who could blame her for asking? Avery did want her, but what she felt most deeply was her own sense of *being* wanting, the shadow side of that word. As a wife, as a sister, as a woman, she was wanting.

In place of an answer, Avery laid her cheek on Chiti's chest and nestled her hand between her legs. There was that familiar warmth. She stroked her in small, tight circles, first this way, then that, round and round, until she could feel the wetness come. She sank one finger inside of her, then two, filling Chiti up until there was no room for anything else. Chiti let out a single, fluttering sigh.

"Let's make a baby," said Avery, her face buried in Chiti's neck, in a place she could not be seen. "Let me give you a baby."

AFTERWARD, AVERY LAY AWAKE IN the dark staring out the window. They tended to keep the curtains open, both preferring to wake early with the morning light. Just faintly, she could trace the outline of a half-moon hidden behind a fleece of clouds. Beside her, Avery could feel Chiti's body relax into sleep, her breath hot and steady. Chiti had always slept the deep sleep of the innocent, sliding from wakefulness to slumber as easily as slipping her body from a dock into a lake. But Avery remained wide-eyed. The insomnia that had lifted soon after she met Chiti had returned. Back then, she used to dread the nights, but now she found the quiet, undisturbed hours a relief. It was better than dreaming that Nicky was alive, waking up each morning to remember again. She gazed out of the window at the dark flower beds and blooming magnolia tree silhouetted against a deep navy sky. She knew that part of her was still out there, standing alone at the bottom of the garden huffing smoke into the night air, out of sight and out of reach.

## CHAPTER FOUR

# Lucky

LUCKY ARRIVED OUTSIDE THE HOUSE IN HAMPSTEAD AND WONDERED, not for the first time, how Avery had wound up living somewhere so fancy. She lived in a home ten times the size of their family apartment, and she only had to share it with Chiti. Maybe it was because she was the firstborn, so she remembered what it felt like to be alone before her domain was gradually infringed upon by each new addition to their family, but Avery had always seemed to crave more space than the rest of them. *Well,* thought Lucky as she lugged her duffel bags up the steep stone steps, *she got it.*

A ring of the golden doorbell, a rustle, a murmur, a yelp, and there was Chiti. She flung the door open wearing an embroidered apron, her long hair flying around her shoulders.

"Lucky's here!" she cried, pulling her into an embrace.

"Hi, Chiti," said Lucky softly into her hair.

She smelled of citrus and flowers and bread. Lucky had not known how much she had missed her, missed family, until this moment.

"Come in, come in." Chiti ushered her into the hallway. "Now *please* tell me you have not become a vegetarian."

"I couldn't even if I wanted to," said Lucky, dragging her scuffed bags behind her. "If you tell the French you don't eat meat, they just offer you chicken."

"Good, because I've been marinating this lamb leg all day and it is predicted by me to be divine."

Chiti gestured for her to leave her stuff at the foot of the stairs and beckoned Lucky into the kitchen. Everything about this house reflected good taste. The floor of the entranceway was covered in black and white tiles in an intricate herringbone pattern; the hallway walls were a bright blood red, a bold choice that would have looked out of place in any home but this. Lucky followed until she was expelled into the cool blue kitchen with its French doors flung open to the garden beyond, everything gleaming and beautiful and bright.

"Now," said Chiti, wiping her hands on her apron. "Do you want some time to wash up and take a shower?"

Lucky shook her head. Now that she was in the warm presence of someone who actually knew her, she found herself unwilling to leave it so soon.

"Great. Then you can chop those cucumbers for the salad."

Chiti was good at this, giving people small tasks to do so they felt included in the creation of something. It meant, no matter how minor your contribution, you could share some pride in the result. After Lucky washed her hands, Chiti handed her a knife and she began to chop. She glanced tentatively up at Chiti.

"Am I cutting these thin enough?"

Chiti peered over.

"That is exactly perfect," she said.

Lucky smiled.

"So where is Avery? Still at work?"

"Amazingly, no. She's at an AA meeting, but she should be home soon."

"She still goes to those?"

Lucky was hurt that Avery hadn't offered to pick her up from Saint

Pancras or at least arranged to be home when she arrived, though she would never show it.

"Mm-hmm," said Chiti. "Third one this week. It's good for her. She stopped going for a little after last year, you know."

"She never talks to me about AA."

"She doesn't like to beat anyone over the head with her program," said Chiti. "You know how private she is. Anyway, I think she lost a little bit of faith in it for a while."

"I get that," said Lucky quietly.

"So I'm happy she's there," Chiti said with a brightness that Lucky noticed seemed faintly forced. "Though I know she was disappointed not to be here for your long-awaited arrival."

"Oh, I'm not so sure about that," said Lucky. "She's probably avoiding me. I'm the bad sister, remember."

Chiti tutted.

"Nonsense. Good sister, bad sister, no such thing. She loves you girls more than anything."

"Except you," said Lucky.

Lucky had meant for the comment to be kind, but Chiti only frowned. She exhaled a low hum that was neither an agreement nor a denial of this statement. She looked up and smiled, though Lucky could see her eyes weren't joining in.

"Sometimes your sister reminds me of one of those medieval fortresses you can take tours of in Scotland," she said suddenly. "She can be a very . . . private woman."

Lucky nodded, though she was unsure what Chiti was trying to say. She and Avery had always seemed an unassailable unit from the outside. They were the only people Lucky had ever met who made marriage look kind of nice. Her parents certainly hadn't managed that feat.

"I guess it can be hard to live up to Avery's standards," she said.

But this didn't seem to be what Chiti was getting at. Lucky watched her set her face back into an expression of resolute cheerfulness.

"She's had a hard year," she said, reaching over to squeeze Lucky's forearm. "You all have. Now, tell me how *you* are. What precipitated this most welcome visit?"

An image of pink, tulle-clad Lucky projectile vomiting out the window of one of the most famous design houses in Paris flashed like a perverse postcard before her eyes. She had claimed to be suffering from food poisoning, but the stylist must have smelled the booze on her because they sent her home without walking the show, which Lucky considered a ridiculous overreaction. A couple of espressos, a couple of bumps, and she would have been just fine. Her agency had already called her twice that morning. She didn't answer the phone. When she eventually got up the nerve to check their website on the Eurostar that afternoon, all images of her had been removed from their board as if she had never existed at all.

"I just needed a break," she said.

Chiti peered at Lucky from under her dark brows, appeared to want to say something, then thought better of it.

"I can't think where Avery is. The meeting started at six." Chiti frowned with frustration. "I simply will not serve this lamb over-cooked. Let's eat; Avery will just have to join us when she joins us."

They sat at one end of the dining table, the other covered in paperwork from Avery's various legal cases, which Chiti tried to compensate for by lighting two tall candles. Lucky looked around hopefully for a bottle of wine to accompany the food, but of course neither Chiti nor Avery drank anymore. In fact, Avery made a point of not keeping alcohol in the house, even for guests, a fact Lucky found ridiculous. But perhaps it was for the best, she told herself. She wouldn't have wanted to drink in front of Chiti anyway. Trying to make a single glass of wine last for an entire meal, eking out tiny little sips and pretending to enjoy the taste rather than chase the effect, was worse than not drinking at all.

The lamb, as Chiti had predicted, was delicious. It melted off the bone like butter, its softness contrasting perfectly with the fresh crunch of the salad. Lucky's favorite part of any meal was invariably the alcohol, but without that to distract her, she found she was in fact starving. She demolished her first helping in minutes, gladly accepting a second.

"Now *this* is a sexy piece of meat," she said between mouthfuls.

Chiti smiled and touched her throat lightly.

"Sometimes you remind me so much of her. The same mannerisms exactly. I'm sorry if you don't like talking about—"

But Lucky was looking at her with pleasure.

"Really? You think I'm like her?"

Chiti nodded.

"This was her favorite dish too."

Lucky felt the possessive pride of being closer to Nicky than her other sisters were.

"I always made this when she came to visit," said Chiti.

Ever since Nicky started teaching high school and got the summers off, it had become tradition for her to spend at least part of them in London with Avery and Chiti, then visit Lucky in whatever city she happened to be living in at that time. Lucky realized suddenly how unmoored her summer had felt this year without the expectation of Nicky's visit.

"And what about you?" asked Lucky. "How's the therapy business treating you?"

"That's kind of you to ask," said Chiti. "It's different every day. Sometimes I feel like I'm making an impact on people's lives, others I feel . . ." Chiti looked at her hands. "Less convinced."

"Doesn't it get boring listening to people complain about their problems all day?"

Chiti tilted her head and smiled.

"People don't just share their problems with me. I get to hear about a lot of joyful things too. Marriage, babies, people breaking old patterns, surprising themselves in ways they didn't think possible . . ."

"But why would you need to talk to a therapist about good stuff?"

"Most of my clients are what we call the *worried well,* people like you or me who don't have serious underlying mental illness but are looking for someone to talk to who can offer a more objective insight than they might find from a partner or a friend."

"How do you know I'm not seriously mentally ill?" asked Lucky.

She had meant for it to be a joke, but the question came out strangely earnest.

"That's true," said Chiti with a gentle nod. "I don't. None of us really know what another is going through until that person feels able to share the truth of their lived experience."

"But how do you do that?" asked Lucky. "What if you don't even *know* the truth of your, um, lived experience?"

"It takes practice," said Chiti.

"Sounds hard," said Lucky.

Chiti glanced at Lucky and forced a smile.

"*Now* you remind me of Avery," she said.

They finished eating and Chiti began loading the dishwasher, shooing away Lucky's attempts to help. Avery had still not returned from her meeting, and they both kept surreptitiously glancing at the clock.

"Can I get you coffee or tea?" asked Chiti. "We have this fancy espresso maker I'd love an excuse to use."

"Sure, I'll have one if you are."

Chiti turned to pull a tiny coffee cup off one of the high shelves.

"I'm actually not drinking caffeine at the moment, if you can believe it." She emitted a light laugh. "Chinese water torture would be preferable."

Lucky raised her eyebrows in surprise. Chiti was famously addicted to coffee. Lucky had once actually heard her ask what altitude the beans she was drinking were grown at.

"First the booze, now the caffeine. What are you, pregnant?"

Chiti turned around quickly, her face flushed.

"Sorry, that was stupid," said Lucky. She'd spoken without thinking and years of working with mostly female models meant she knew better than to ever ask a woman if she was pregnant.

"No, it's okay," said Chiti. "I'm not, but we've decided to start looking for a donor." She cast her eyes down, unable to contain her smile. "I know the no-caffeine thing is a bit preemptive, but I thought, well, better overprepared than under."

"Oh shit," said Lucky. "I mean wow. That's great."

"I shouldn't have said anything," said Chiti. "It's not my news to tell. Not that we have any news!" She threw up her hands as if releasing something from her grasp, a bird perhaps, or a butterfly. "Silly me, I'm just excited."

Lucky stepped forward and hugged Chiti.

"You're going to be the best mums ever," she said.

But there was a sadness, too, beneath Lucky's words. Life as she knew it was ending yet again. Avery and Chiti would be busy with their baby, and they wouldn't have time to look after her anymore. Even though she hadn't seen Avery in a year, the knowledge that her eldest sister was there, willing to drop everything if she needed her, had been a comfort. But she was twenty-six years old, Lucky reminded herself sternly. She didn't need a mom anymore, and she *especially* didn't need her sister to be her mom. Chiti pulled away, smiling, and clapped her hands together.

"Now, I've laid everything out in the guest room for you," she said. "There are towels folded on the chair if you want to take a shower before bed. Or we could curl up and watch telly. Don't judge me, but I've become addicted to this reality show about young people sequestered on an island together trying to find love. They spend a lot of time getting drunk, then fighting in the hot tub. Mesmerizing stuff." Chiti grinned. "I'd feel a little less sad if I was watching it with company."

"Actually," said Lucky, her face growing hot, "I was going to head out and meet this stylist I know. Her friend's having a party. If that's okay?"

Lucky had met the stylist at a fashion week party back in February. She couldn't remember much about her, but she'd been peppering Lucky with messages ever since and Lucky wasn't one to turn down a party with an open bar. She tried not to notice the look of disappointment Chiti was quickly wiping from her face.

"Of course, of course! We're such homebodies in this house, I can forget it's Friday night. Vish is always mocking me for it."

"How is Vish?" asked Lucky, eager to get off the subject of where she was going.

"Oh, he's well. In love with someone new every week as far as I can tell, but such are the foibles of youth."

"Right . . . You sure you don't mind?"

"Absolutely not," said Chiti resolutely. "Go be young. I'll just get the spare key for you so you can come and go as you please."

LUCKY LET HERSELF OUT OF the house with a wave of guilty relief. The truth was, she was dying for a drink. She shut the door with a soft clunk and turned to find Avery opening the gate at the bottom of the steps. She looked different. Her cheeks were pink and her dark hair, usually pulled back in some kind of sensible ponytail, fell softly around her face. A wrap dress in a pretty print of purple hydrangeas cinched her waist. She looked flushed and girlish, completely unlike the Avery Lucky remembered. Avery turned to see Lucky at the top of the stairs and stopped.

"You're wearing a *dress*," said Lucky.

"It's summer!" said Avery, flustered instantly into defensiveness.

"No, it looks great. I just haven't seen you in one since we were kids, is all."

"That's preposterously untrue," said Avery, shutting the gate behind her with a sharp click. "I wear dresses all the time. You just never see me."

Lucky threw her hands up in surrender. "Okay."

Less than thirty seconds and they were already arguing. Avery's face softened suddenly and she stretched out her arms.

"Sorry. Let's do this properly. Hello, you."

Lucky bounded down the stairs and stood before her. She bowed her head and pressed her forehead to Avery's. They rolled their brows slowly against each other, the way lions in a pride show affection to one another. That was how it felt reuniting with her eldest sister, Lucky thought, like two wild animals yielding to each other.

"It's good to see you, Aves," murmured Lucky.

"You too," said Avery. "Now, let me have a proper look at you."

She held Lucky at arm's length, taking in her tiny cropped T-shirt and lace-up leather trousers, the dark roots and darker circles around her eyes.

"You're too thin," she said.

Lucky shrugged.

"That's what they pay me for."

"Don't be glib. I love your hair like this."

"I love *you,*" said Lucky quickly, before she could think to say something else.

Avery's face split open into a radiant smile. Their family had always been good at hellos and goodbyes, moments ending even as they began. It was easy to love someone in the beginnings and endings; it was all the time in between that was so hard.

"I love you too," Avery said. "Without the too."

Lucky smiled. It was something Nicky used to say. No *too.* Just love.

"I can't believe it's been a year," continued Avery. "And you've been just a train ride away this whole time."

"I know," said Lucky, feeling giddy. "What's *wrong* with us?"

"Too much to catalog in this moment."

"Let's never let it go this long again."

"Never." Avery linked arms with her to walk up the steps to the house. "Did you have a sixth sense I was arriving and rush out to meet me?"

"No, um, I was actually just leaving," Lucky said, disentangling herself awkwardly.

Avery's face fell with disappointment. Lucky hated being the one to cause that expression for the second time in the past few minutes.

"I've been waiting for over an hour for you," she said defensively. "The food was getting cold, so we ate."

"I'm sorry," said Avery. "I got caught up fellowshipping. I should have called."

"What's fellowshipping?"

"Oh, it's what we call hanging out after the meeting."

"So why don't you just call it hanging out?"

"I don't know," said Avery with an impatient flick of her head. "It's just how we say it."

That *we* bristled Lucky. She simultaneously hated feeling excluded from her sister's sober world and relieved not to be part of it.

"You can't come in and talk to me for a little?" asked Avery. "We need to discuss what to do about the New York apartment."

Lucky gave a desperate shrug.

"I made plans, Aves."

"So you don't care that they're selling it?" Avery asked, her voice hardening with indignation. "We can't let that happen!"

Lucky frowned. Selling it? The email their mother sent yesterday flashed, unopened, across her mind. So *that's* what it had been about. On Nicky's anniversary, no less. The timing was cold, even for their mother, though she'd come to expect as much from their ice queen of a matriarch. Avery was staring at her expectantly, waiting for an answer. Lucky rearranged her face to convey thoughtful consideration, as opposed to complete obliviousness. *Did* she care that their parents were selling it? She had no great nostalgia for the home she had stopped living in full-time at fifteen. Ever since she started modeling, New York had always meant Nicky to her, and without her sister there, she had no real reason to return. Also, she couldn't help feeling Avery's desire to hold on to the place was also her way of keeping the family dependent on her. As long as she paid for that apartment, they all had a reason to owe her. But mostly, what Lucky felt right now was a desire to leave.

"I don't know," she settled on noncommittally. "I trust you to do what's best."

Avery looked momentarily taken aback by this unusual display of diplomacy, then immediately annoyed again.

"Where are you even *going* at this hour?" she demanded.

"Just to this thing with a friend," said Lucky.

*Friend* was a generous term for how well she knew this stylist.

Why *couldn't* she just go back inside and be with Avery? Because there was nothing to drink in there and she needed a drink more than she needed anything right now, including her sister.

"I *waited* for you," she said again.

"I get it," snapped Avery. "I'm sorry I was late. I didn't realize you had made plans."

The warmth that had encircled them just a moment ago was gone. It was as though they had stepped from sunshine into shade.

"We can talk tomorrow," said Lucky.

Somewhere buried within, Lucky would have welcomed her sister stopping her. She wanted Avery to take her in her arms and tell her she knew why she wanted to leave, the thirst that drove her, but she would sit with her until it passed, because it *would* pass, it had to. But Avery only gave a tired smile of acquiescence.

"You got the key?" she asked.

Lucky nodded.

"And you have money? You have pounds?"

"I'll get some on the way."

"Here—"

Avery reached into her bag and extracted an expensive-looking quilted wallet. She opened it and pushed three twenty-pound notes into Lucky's hands. Lucky looked down at the purple face of the young queen with her mysterious smirk.

"You really don't need to," she said, immediately crunching the bills into her back pocket.

"Be safe," Avery said. "Take a taxi home."

Lucky was already disappearing out the gate when she remembered.

"Oh hey," she said, turning suddenly. "Don't be mad, but Chiti told me about the baby plans. Congrats, by the way."

Lucky saw a look of panic flash across Avery's face before rearranging it into a taut smile.

"She shouldn't have . . ." she said, then stopped herself. "It's still early days. But thank you."

Was Avery upset that she knew? Why didn't she want to let her into her life? Lucky pushed the thought away and continued trotting backward down the street away from the house.

"You're going to be a sick-ass mom!" she called before disappearing 'round the corner.

Avery only ducked her head, as if avoiding a blow.

AN HOUR LATER AND LUCKY was rolling one of the twenty-pound notes into a tight cylinder. She was in the living room of the stylist, whose name she'd never quite caught. She was small and pink-haired with big eyes and a scrunchy, curious face redolent of the plastic troll dolls Lucky used to play with as kid, which is how she came to be saved in Lucky's phone under the moniker Troll Doll. It felt rude to ask her name now, so Troll Doll she remained in Lucky's phone and in her mind.

It had taken her the length of three back-to-back albums—Nick Cave, Cocteau Twins, and Kate Bush—to get to the stylist's place from Hampstead. Lucky was always amazed by the sheer size of London in comparison to New York or Paris, its seemingly endless capacity to be inconvenient. What other city would require you to take the overground to the tube to the bus just to get to a friend's house on a Friday night? No wonder Hampstead was so sleepy, everyone ostensibly already in bed as she'd walked the dark residential streets to the overground station; it was too much effort to go out. That must be why the impregnably mature and sober Avery loved it, Lucky thought with a hint of bitterness.

London frustrated Lucky, but she loved the English, the way they were always down to get royally and truly fucked-up. They weren't tasteful like the French or puritanical like the Americans; if you suggested going for a drink in London, odds were you were going to get drunk. The desire for inebriation was tacit, no one needed to make a thing of it. Brits wanted oblivion and they wanted it now. Lucky's kind of people. And Troll Doll had proven to be a true patriot by immediately producing two plastic baggies as Lucky walked through the door. But should they start with the ketamine or the cocaine? An age-old conundrum. Lucky picked coke and poured half the bag onto a large coffee table book emblazoned with a glossy picture of a naked Kate Moss. Her hands shook as she tried to get the lines thick and even.

"It's so cool you texted, yah," said Troll Doll. "Since I gave you my number like six years ago." It had been six months. "Good thing I wasn't waiting."

"Yeah, sorry about that." Lucky glanced up at her with a sharp-toothed grin. "I'm not great with texting. Or phones."

"So mysterious," purred Troll Doll's flatmate, who appeared from his room wearing a leather holster over his taut bare chest.

"You look brilliant!" Troll Doll let out a little shriek of delight. "*So* on theme."

"What's the theme?" asked Lucky.

"Oh my gosh, you didn't know?"

Troll Doll shrieked again, then proceeded to breathlessly explain. They were going to the birthday party of a pair of socialite twin sisters who were notorious in London but, like most minor British celebrities, basically unknown anywhere else. Their father, an old Etonian and investment banker, was frequently in the news for his relationships with various actresses and models, most of whom were around his daughters' age. This year, the twins had decided to scandalize the British tabloids by hosting a joint bacchanal at an exclusive London sex club whose parties had been shrouded in mystery for years. The theme was *Pure Smut* and all of London's wealthy and beautiful elite would be attending in their smuttiest best.

"So everyone's dressing as, like, a prozzie or a stripper. Isn't it perfectly scandalous?"

Troll Doll hoovered up a line from Kate Moss's hip with practiced efficiency.

"I'm pretty sure we're meant to say sex workers now," said Lucky.

"Anyway, I thought you knew that's where we're going!" exclaimed Troll Doll, ignoring her. "Isn't that why you're dressed like that?"

Lucky looked down at her threadbare cropped T-shirt, leather pants, and platform boots. She looked back up at Troll Doll.

"This is just how I dress."

"Oops," stage-whispered the flatmate, hiding a giggle behind his hand.

Lucky flushed ever so slightly. She reached for her drink.

"*Love* that," said Troll Doll quickly, motioning for him to stop. "So how come you're back in London anyway?"

"Um, visiting my sister," said Lucky, downing her glass in one gulp.

"Does your sister look like you?" asked Troll Doll quickly.

Lucky shook her head.

"She's seven years older."

"Is she jealous of you?"

Lucky had never considered this.

"I don't think she's jealous of anyone."

"Are you jealous of her?"

"That's a weird question," said Lucky. "Are *you*?"

"Oh god, you're playing the game again," said the leather-clad flatmate, rolling his eyes.

"You're ruining it!" said Troll Doll.

Lucky cocked her head.

"It's this thing she does," he said, affecting a bored drawl. "Where she asks you a ton of personal questions really quickly in a row to see how many she can get to before you ask her one back."

"How'd I do?" asked Lucky without much interest.

She poured out the remainder of the bag and began the satisfying process of cutting new lines.

"You remain a mystery," declared Troll Doll.

"What's the point of it?" Lucky asked, slicing away with the credit card. She could have been speaking about life in general but decided to clarify by adding, "The game?"

"To try to find out as much as you can about the other person without revealing anything about yourself," said the flatmate.

"It's easier with men," Troll Doll said. "I can get to, like, thirty before they think to ask me a single thing."

The doorbell rang and she bounced up to answer it. A cluster of friends, all dressed in revealing or vaguely kinky costumes, stood in the doorway.

"This is Flopsy and my cousins Cressida and Rupes," declared Troll Doll, seemingly for Lucky's benefit, though none of them acknowledged her.

Lucky looked around at the friends gathered and realized with a sinking feeling that she was ensconced in a gathering of the British upper class, a fact no actual member of this class would ever acknowledge. She remembered her mother explaining that truly posh people never talked about class, in the same way they never discussed the cost of private school, knowing members of the Royal family, or having inherited wealth. It was all just assumed. Their mother hated the rigid class system she had come from. Naturally, she was also staunchly antimonarchist. Growing up, they were not even allowed to play at being princesses. On Halloween, their mother went to the Goodwill down the block and cobbled together costumes of famous rebel leaders like Joan of Arc and Che Guevara. One year, she dressed the four of them as peasants from the 1917 Russian revolutions, outfitting them with historically accurate agricultural tools. When a neighbor's kid attempted to make fun of them for being covered in dirt—their mother had rubbed their faces with soil from a houseplant for verisimilitude—Avery had threatened him with her scythe.

Lucky looked around for something else to drink.

"I'm Flopsy," said one of the friends, sitting down on the sofa beside Lucky. She was wearing a white spandex minidress with a matching ivory feather boa draped around her neck. Her chestnut hair was very clean, straight, and shiny, like a horse's.

"Lucky," said Lucky.

"That's a funny name," said Flopsy.

Lucky gave her a sideways look.

"So how do you know . . ."

Lucky gestured toward their host, who was in the process of helping cousin Cressida apply nipple tape.

"From school," she said with a flick of her mane. "I was the year above at Cheltenham. We've known each other forever."

"So just a quickie drinky here and then we'll head over, shall we?" said Troll Doll.

"I'm *literally* so excited," squealed Cressida, whose breasts had just been secured in a shimmering backless halter dress.

"It is quite *literally* going to be the only party anyone talks about for the rest of the year," proclaimed Flopsy.

"Like Sodom and Gomorrah," said the flatmate. "But chic."

"How do you know them?" asked Lucky.

The flatmate barked a high laugh.

"Sodom and Gomorrah aren't *people,* darling."

"I meant the girls throwing the party," said Lucky.

She genuinely had been asking about the sisters, but she knew the flatmate would still think she was covering a mistake. He appeared to be the kind of person who delighted in highlighting other people's weaknesses, mostly, Lucky presumed, to distract from his own. Besides, as a model, Lucky was used to people taking pleasure in proving she was an idiot. It was a kind of protection against inadequacy, she assumed; if she was pretty but dumb, they could still feel superior, even a little righteous, finding, in their own lack of marketable beauty, a confirmation of their higher intelligence. But if the two weren't causal? If it was possible to be both professionally attractive *and* smart? Then their own average looks served no purpose other than to disappoint, with Lucky acting as the hapless reminder. She'd found, in general, it was easier to keep her mouth shut and let people think whatever comforting thoughts they wanted about her. People seemed to hate her less that way.

"From *school,*" said Troll Doll, as if this should already be obvious.

Strong vodka sodas were dispersed among the group, which Lucky downed gratefully. She had finished the glass of dry white wine she'd been handed upon arrival instantly and was relieved to have something stronger. The group set about ingesting the additional bags of coke and ketamine they had brought with impressive speed. Once everyone was on their way to being suitably severed from sobriety, Troll Doll clapped her hands authoritatively.

"Okay, let's play a game," she declared.

Lucky felt her insides shrivel. She hated organized fun; she had spent most of the birthday parties of her youth hiding out under the coats in the bedroom. Plus, she was already feeling that familiar anxious restlessness, an itchiness in her limbs, that came from ingesting amphetamines too quickly without moving around enough. She regretted not going straight for the Special K, small doses of which left her feeling weightless and outside of reality, as opposed to how she felt now, which was all too present.

"Okay, first task. Ruin a first date in four words," declared Troll Doll.

Everyone seemed to already have their answers prepared.

"I forgot my wallet."

"I just got out . . ."

"Is your nose real?"

"I think we're cousins."

Everyone except Lucky screamed with laughter.

"I've got a good one," said cousin Rupes, who was wearing an *Eyes Wide Shut*–style mask. "What do you *do*?"

More laughter from the group.

"Why would that ruin it?" asked Lucky.

"Because it's so *dull,* dear," said Rupes.

"That's just because you don't *do* anything, darling," said Troll Doll. "Go on, you say one, Lucky."

"I can't think of anything," said Lucky.

The flatmate in the holster snickered and tried to catch the others' eyes.

"Yes, you can," said Troll Doll exasperatedly. "Just say anything that comes into your head."

"My sister just died," said Lucky.

"Oooh, dark, I like it." Troll Doll giggled. "Now, let's do the *best* thing to hear on a first date in four words."

"I'm over nine inches."

"Daddy owns this place."

"The Château Lafite, please."

"Screaming!" said Troll Doll.

"You want a pinger?" asked Flopsy quietly, turning to look at Lucky.

"Is that . . . one of the four-word answers?" Lucky asked.

"No." Flopsy laughed. "Though it could be."

Lucky shrugged.

"Sure."

She didn't know what a pinger was and she didn't really care. Safe to assume she wanted it. Flopsy removed two white pills from her tiny white crocodile bag and stuck out her tongue, motioning for Lucky to do the same. Her eyelids sparkled with silver glitter in the light.

"Fizz pop bang," said Flopsy, and they both swallowed.

*WHOOOOOSH* WENT LUCKY OUT OF the flat into the shiny black SUV someone had ordered, through the dark sleepy streets of London, down the King's Road, past rows of expensive shops that stayed lit all night, up the stairs of a large townhouse, down a long corridor, through a door hidden in a bookcase, down a narrow staircase, and into a thumping, throbbing, shifting, swirling party in full swing.

Everyone was dressed on theme. There were guests lounging on velvet sofas in lingerie and carnival masks and others dancing stiffly in leather bondage gear. There was a hairy-chested man in frilly bloomers tickling a large-breasted woman in an unbuttoned tuxedo shirt and Y-fronts. There was an old Lord in a diamanté thong and opera-length gloves surrounded by dominatrix types swinging their whips and cat-o'-nine-tails in time to the music. A tall brunette wearing crotchless latex briefs stroked Lucky's cheek with a peacock feather as she passed.

Their hosts rushed over to greet the group with a chorus of squeals and coos. The twins were dressed in matching monochrome looks, one clad entirely in black and the other in shocking pink. Their outfits consisted of thigh-high boots, tiny pairs of silk underwear, and fur coats. Across one of their bare chests, large newsprint letters spelled *Pure,* while the other's read *Smut.* Lucky had to hand it to them, they looked good.

"You're here!" cried Pure, embracing each of them in turn. "Isn't it all perfectly ridiculous?"

"Perfectly!" said Flopsy.

"Daddy's here dressed as a naughty nun," said Smut. "You must get a picky with him before he's too drunk to function."

"Scream!" declared Troll Doll.

She grabbed Lucky's hand and rushed her headfirst into the night.

No matter how prestigious the guest list, private the location, or pricey the bar, Lucky had found that, in the end, all parties boiled down to this: dancing, drinking, and shouting over the music. And going to the bathroom to do drugs, which was exactly where she found herself an hour later.

"So you and Flopsy?" asked Troll Doll. "I saw you dancing together. You like her?"

Lucky shrugged, which was, perhaps, becoming her signature move.

"Don't know her," she said.

They were leaning on a pink marble sink with a golden faucet. The walls were pink, too, the color of the inside of a throat. Outside, the bass boomed steadily. All around them glittering mirrors reflected their faces back at them in an infinite loop.

"I wish I looked like you," said Troll Doll suddenly. "Really badly. Like, I'd kill someone to look like you. Not anyone important or good or anything. But some normal-to-bad man? I'd definitely murder him just to have your face. Or your stomach. Your belly button is so sexy, it looks like a cat's eye."

Lucky looked down at her bare torso. At some point in the last hour, she had thrown off her shirt and let someone smear her nipples with black, glittering Xs.

"Does it?" she asked blearily.

"But I mean, how fucked-up is that? About the killing-someone part?"

"Pretty fucked-up," acknowledged Lucky. She proffered a loaded key toward Troll Doll. "This is you."

Troll Doll narrowed her eyes at Lucky.

"You don't even care."

"No, I do," said Lucky unconvincingly.

"Do you want to kiss me, yah?"

She hopped off the counter and launched onto Lucky. Lucky let the stylist suck on her mouth hungrily; it felt like having a small koala bear clinging to her front. What did it matter? She opened her eyes and saw a hundred different versions of them locked in a repeated embrace.

"Let's go back out," she said eventually. "Find your friends."

"I don't care about them," whispered Troll Doll breathlessly, but Lucky was already sliding out the door.

Sniff of coke. Bump of ket. Get a drink. Have a smoke. Sniffy cokey. Bump o' keto. Getta drinka. Hava smoke. Shniffml coke. Bumpbumpket. Getaaaa dreeenk. Hashasnoke . . . The room was bending, the walls relaxing to a wompy softness. Lucky lost track of where her body ended and everyone else's began. The floor kept giving way beneath her like a bouncy castle. Everything was hilarious and mushy and deeply synergistic. She was moving to the music in a way that was both intricate and reflective, and profoundly, purely carnal. She felt like she knew what every note was going to be before it hit. She was in the moment and just a few seconds ahead. Her hands felt huge.

Now she was in the bathroom with the old Lord and his very young friend, a tiny woman wearing golden nipple tassels. Now she was in a private side room where every surface was velvet. She was kissing a tall guy wearing a pair of angel wings. His tongue tasted like lime. Now he was guiding her face toward another girl's, a redhead covered in glitter who looked like a strawberry but tasted like cigarettes and Red Bull. Now the man was kissing them both. It felt good, Lucky guessed, or at least not bad. It felt better than nothing. Actually, it would be better to feel nothing—to *be* nothing. That's what Lucky wanted most, to find a nick in the fabric of the room, tear it open, and disappear into the black hole behind it.

She snorted something, she wasn't sure what, off the back of the hand of a woman dressed as Sailor Moon, then she was back on the dance floor. She'd lost everyone, Troll Doll, Flopsy, Rupes, Angel Wings, Strawberry Glitter, the lot. She was falling forward, the palms of her hands kissing the sticky vinyl floor. She was bouncing back up. She was all good, guys, all good. Among the crowd of bodies, a huge smiling man was making his way toward her. People parted around him like drops of oil in water. He was bald as a baby, wide as a horizon, tall as a cathedral. He was a massive, massive man.

"Lucky," he said, coming toward her. "You're Lucky."

Lucky couldn't stop nodding. Her whole body was juddering. She was dancing, she was falling, she was shaking, she was shedding herself.

"I know your sister," he said.

"Avery?" Lucky mumbled, her head vibrating from side to side. Every time she closed her eyes, she could see black splotches of light haloed in yellow like sunflowers. She opened her eyes again and his face was huge above her.

"Nicky's baby." He beamed down at her. "You're Nicky's baby."

"You knew Nicky?" she tried to ask, but found she could no longer speak.

Lucky grabbed his shoulders and hung the weight of her body from him. He was wearing a plastic tag that said SECURITY. Security, she had never had any security, she thought. He looked down at her and his face blocked out all others. He was the night sky. He was the moon. He was a disco ball reflecting back a thousand versions of herself. She was refracting like light in his gaze. She was a million little particles falling all over the dance floor. She was the air the dancers inhaled. She was the music moving on that air. She was thump, thump, thumping. The man smiled down at her with his ginormous, friendly face. Rays of light were shooting out of his head. His smile was a thousand suns. He was the eclipse.

"You'll always be Nicky's baby," he boomed. His words popped against her skin like bubbles.

Lucky didn't remember letting him go. She didn't remember falling down. She didn't remember wrapping a white feather boa around her bare chest; it would leave tiny red scratches all over her breasts for her to find the next morning. She didn't remember hailing the black cab, tumbling headfirst onto its floor as it stopped outside the quiet Hampstead house, the driver pressing his body to hers, the pinch of his hands on her chest as he carried her out, the relief of him driving off without doing more. She didn't remember crawling up the steps and slumping on the bristled doormat, unable to scrape her key into the lock. She didn't remember looking up to find Avery silhouetted in a rectangle of light above her or being carried into the house and up the stairs, one arm slung around her sister's neck. She didn't remember crumpling, still partially dressed, into the empty bathtub, nor did she remember Avery turning on the shower, the wet feathers dislocating from her body and clogging the drain.

The next thing she did remember was Avery's face above her, a curtain of her wet hair swinging as she straddled her in the tub, shaking her awake. A steady stream of water beat down on them. Avery's face was contorted with effort as she dragged Lucky back to consciousness. She looked like their mother. Lucky tried to say this, but she found she couldn't speak. Avery was saying something over and over again that she could barely make out over the water, over the ringing in her ears. It sounded like, *Not you. Not you too. Not you.*

# CHAPTER FIVE

# Bonnie

BONNIE WAS AT HOME LYING ON HER MATTRESS ON THE FLOOR WHEN she heard the knock at the door. She crouched down and shuffled from the bedroom to the living room silently. Her heart was hammering. She'd spent the last twenty-four hours cycling through periods of frenzied activity and total inertia, manically working out to the point of paralyzing physical exhaustion, then falling into periods of shallow, fitful sleep at odd hours. She'd left her apartment at night to walk the beach alone, following the dark curve of the coast up to Santa Monica Pier, then turning back to retrace her steps several miles to the Marina. The beaches late at night were empty but for the people who lived on them, shadowy figures crouched outside of tents murmuring to each other, their faces illuminated briefly by a flared match or dimly lit phone. Bonnie moved soundlessly past them until she was at the water's edge, the cold water lapping at her bare feet. There, it was quiet. There, she could walk and think undisturbed. When the sky lightened and the first surfers began to dot the shore, she returned home. She had not seen or spoken to anyone since the attack.

Bonnie looked through the peephole and saw Peachy's freckled face pressed against the hole, attempting to peer in. Without a word, she cracked the door. He spread his arms to her.

"You don't call, you don't write. You playin' hard to get with me?"

Bonnie ducked her head.

"Come on in, Peachy."

He walked into the living room and looked at the bare floors, single beach chair, and bags of empty take-out containers.

"Wow, I like what you've done with the place. Minimalist."

"Really?"

"Fuck no! This looks like where a murderer takes his victims to dismember them. By the way, you don't do that, do you? Hired take-outs and the like?"

Bonnie gave him a look of such genuine anguish, he squeezed her shoulder reassuringly.

"I'm kidding. Kind of. I mean, after the way you went off on that guy . . . Talk about a killer instinct."

This was the moment Bonnie had been dreading. She felt her entire body go cold. It was time for her to face reality. She deserved whatever came.

"He's dead, isn't he?" she said flatly. "I killed him."

Peachy looked at her in surprise.

"Oh, hun, that's what you've been thinking? He's just fine."

Bonnie sank into the beach chair behind her and placed her head in her palms.

"Oh god," she exhaled. "Thank god. I thought . . . Oh, thank god."

Peachy let out a chuckle.

"You bruised his ego more than anything."

Bonnie lifted her head from her hands and raised an eyebrow.

"Yeah, okay, and you definitely broke his nose and gave him a concussion," conceded Peachy. "But still, that shit's mostly cosmetic."

Bonnie groaned again.

"What am I going to do, Peachy?"

"Look, we can handle it. And you've done the right thing already by staying away from the bar. He came 'round yesterday saying he had half a mind to press charges. Can I smoke in here, by the way?"

Bonnie looked around the barren room. She hated smoking, but there wasn't exactly much in here to protect. She nodded. Peachy lit a cigarette and inhaled with palpable relief.

"Do you think he will?" Bonnie asked.

"Honestly? I could see his heart wasn't in it. He's embarrassed, you know. Who'd want to advertise it? Getting beat up by a chick?" Peachy threw his hands in the air. "I mean, woman! Getting beat up by a very strong, independent, professionally trained woman."

Bonnie smiled.

"But, to him, still a chick," she said.

"Exactly." Peachy nodded. "So I'd just lie low for a while and let it all blow over. Take a vacation."

"For how long?"

"A few weeks, a month to be safe?"

"That's a long vacation, Peachy!"

Bonnie couldn't afford this place without that income. She looked around. Peachy was right, it had never been a home anyway. She would have to give the landlord notice, but since these were short-term rentals she would only have to pay through the end of the week.

"I know, I know." Peachy gave her a sympathetic look. "Look, I'll give you last week's paycheck early. You got any friends you want to visit?"

Bonnie shook her head.

"I don't really do that," she said.

"Do what?"

"Have friends."

"Jesus, that's sad, is what that is. Who do you talk to? If you're having, you know, issues?"

Bonnie thought about this for a moment.

"I used to talk to my trainer, Pavel. Now just my sisters, I guess."

"That's good, sisters are good. My sis is a raging narcissist, but I'm glad you like yours. Can you stay with one of them?"

Another shake of her head. That would involve telling them what had happened.

"They don't live in the country. But—" The apartment. There was always the apartment. She said the words quickly, before she had time to take them back. "My parents have an empty place in New York I can stay in for a bit. They're selling it, but they need help packing up anyway."

"You're *kidding* me. Why didn't you say? That's perfect. New York fuckin' City! Next club I'm opening, it's New York. I'm over the Hollywood crowd. I'd come with you, but it might not sit right with my new bird."

Bonnie chose not to mention the fact she hadn't invited him. For Peachy, life was a door in which he was always on the list. She nodded along as he continued airing his grievances with the Hollywood "swine and dine set," as he called them, her mind racing. Could she really go back to New York after everything that had happened there? But there was an air of inevitability about returning that she couldn't shake. She had no other options. Peachy had broken off his rant and was now rubbing his chin thoughtfully.

"You think it's romantic my new bird wants us to share our locations on our phones or weird?" he asked. "It's weird, right? Like a tracking device? She wants to track me."

"I don't know, Peach. Depends how much you like her, I guess."

Peachy shook his head and exhaled a cloud of smoke.

"Women," he mused seriously. "They're always too close or too far, eh?"

Bonnie tried to nod in an understanding manner. She had often felt the same about Pavel; but whether he was too close to see her clearly or too far away to notice her as anything other than a boxer, she wasn't sure. But there were moments, however fleeting, when there was no distance between them at all. She thought of them shadowboxing together, flitting around the ring like twin flames, moving in a secret rhythm only they shared. When they were like that, there was no leader and no follower, no trainer and no student, only their shared breath, the soft shuffle of their feet on the canvas, the whisper of air around their swinging limbs, the feeling, unspoken but known by both, that they were a single body split in two, dancing around itself. Bonnie missed that feeling more than anything on earth, except her sister.

After her last fight, Bonnie had not spoken to Pavel again. She had changed her phone number and left for L.A. directly after the funeral. He had no way of reaching her; she didn't even know if he'd tried. But as soon as she suggested returning to New York, it was Pavel she thought of, Pavel, she knew, she was really returning to. She looked up at Peachy, who was pacing around the room, clearly enjoying this slice of drama.

"A cheeky little hideout in New York and she forgets to mention it!" he mused to himself. "Are you secretly rich? You can tell me, babe, mum's the word."

Bonnie shook her head.

"It's just where I grew up. My parents bought it cheap in the seventies. My sister and I used to live there and then . . . I don't know, it's just been empty for a while."

"That settles it, then. You head to New York and if anyone comes 'round asking, I'll say you no longer work with us."

Peachy opened the front door and tossed his cigarette out over the landing. The shrieks of a passing flock of seagulls filled the air. He made to leave, then turned back.

"You want to get an ice cream before you go? I could murder a Twix ice cream bar right about now."

Bonnie smiled. She hadn't eaten ice cream in probably a decade or more.

"Sure," she said.

She followed him out onto the landing, wincing as a bright bar of sunshine striped her face.

"And by the way, you're wrong," Peachy said.

"About what?"

He punched her softly in the arm.

"I'm your friend, Bonnie Blue."

No New Yorker, no matter how cynical, is immune to the feeling of flying into JFK at night. Tired though she was, anxious though she'd been, some hidden hope alighted in Bonnie as soon as the plane touched down. She was back in New York. City of sirens, city of secrets, city of her sisters. She had dreaded returning, but it was surprisingly comforting to see the city lights wink in their bed of black below, each one a little life of its own. She was home, the only one she knew, not because she'd always lived in it, but because it always lived in her.

In the lobby of their building, Bonnie waved her keys at the new night doorman, who gave her a sleepy nod. Everything was exactly as before. The building had once been a hotel, and the foyer maintained a feeling of faded luxury with its scuffed marble floors and sun-bleached brocade seats. The gold dial above the elevator was still stuck, exactly as it had always been, at number eleven. Bonnie stood before it without pressing the button. She had told herself she would never enter that elevator again after what happened. But now that she was there, she felt strangely numb. Bonnie pressed the button and stepped through the sliding doors as if in a dream. It glided up to their floor. Bonnie exited and walked to the front door feeling mercifully blank. With her hand on the knob, she braced herself for whatever feeling would come.

The smell was what she noticed first. It didn't smell like home at all, that familiar yet unnameable scent that only becomes known to you once you leave. The odor was strangely medicinal, as though someone had sprayed the place with antiseptic. But the rest was the same. The long hallway with the threadbare Moroccan runner, the far wall that was covered in pegs of various heights for all their coats. In the winter that wall would be so laden with puffers, peacoats, and vintage furs it was impossible to pass by without knocking at least one off, a fact that irritated their mother endlessly. Bonnie felt all the life in this home rushing just beneath the surface of the present moment, like running water trapped beneath a layer of ice. If only she could break through and return to the living moments beneath, her sisters in the kitchen making a race of peeling boiled eggs for egg salad sandwiches, her sisters pulling each other down the hallways on a towel they'd turned into a magic carpet, her sisters flopped on the couch watching TV after school, the ordinary, everyday miracle of being all together.

Bonnie wandered into the living room without turning on the lights. It was past midnight, and the city below was quiet, a thin trickle of traffic lighting its veins. The furniture was a mismatched mingling of their mother's and father's tastes. From their mother: a leather Noguchi knockoff chair, a huge dining table made from the door of a church, various found object sculptures by friends from her gallery days. From their father: some dark paintings of ships and storms, a dusty navy velvet sofa that doubled as a pullout, the complete works of Charles Dickens stacked proudly on the mantelpiece. Bonnie sank into the sofa, which released a familiar sigh, and listened. She could hear the city all around her, the absence of silence that was New York.

She didn't want to remember, but everything was a reminder. Above the mantelpiece, the oil painting of the four of them stared back at her. Nicky was on Bonnie's lap and Lucky was on Avery's. In a strange twist of genetics, Avery and Nicky had dark chestnut hair and Bonnie's and Lucky's was blond, but they were all unmistakably sisters. The painting was by a friend of their mother's, an Israeli artist with a gentle, mournful air who had the habit of dipping her paintbrush into her tea and absent-mindedly drinking the murky concoction.

It wasn't a flattering portrait, or rather it wasn't intended to highlight the girls' childish beauty. The artist had given their faces a caprine quality; huge, fearful eyes set above narrow noses and pointed chins. Their pupils were eerily large, so black they were almost violet, and fixed in tense, watchful expressions. Each of their heads was tilted slightly toward the others, as though pulling away from whatever was beyond the painting. The four of them *were* like a little herd of goats back then, Bonnie thought. She pictured them picking their way across the craggy mountain range of their childhood, that rocky, inhospitable landscape; Avery and Bonnie the strong, agile does leading the way, Nicky and Lucky the fluffy kids capering behind.

*It is good you have each other,* the artist had said, regarding them seriously as she worked. *You never have to explain yourself to sisters.*

It was true. Being one of four sisters always felt like being part of something magic. Once Bonnie noticed it, she saw the world was made up of fours. The seasons. The elements. The points on a compass. Four suits in a pack of cards. Four chambers of a human heart. Bonnie loved being a part of this mystical number, this perfect symmetry of two sets of two. *Until you know my sisters,* she used to say to Pavel, *you don't know me.*

But it wasn't all harmonious. Around the time the painting was made, Nicky reached an age where all she wanted was her older sisters' attention. She and Lucky were still a pair, but she wanted admittance into the realm of the big girls too. Nicky followed Avery and Bonnie from room to room peppering them with questions, attempting to impress them with whatever skill she'd recently learned, a card trick, or flipping backward onto her palms. One evening, Bonnie and Avery had barricaded themselves in their bedroom and laughed, closer, then, for having someone to exclude, as Nicky pled for entry on the other side. They could feel the door shudder as Nicky grew frenzied with frustration, smashing herself against the barricade again and again wordlessly. Any pleasure was drained from their game as Bonnie and Avery listened to the stoic *thud, thud, thud* of their sister throwing her body against the door until, in a hasty anticlimax, they opened it and let her tumble in. *Stop it, you freak, you're hurting yourself.* Bonnie knew it was normal childhood stuff, the inevitable pairing of siblings against one another, but now that Nicky was gone, the memory was unbearable. What would Bonnie give to go back now and hurl that door open? To never have closed it in the first place?

She wandered through the apartment and let the memories come, the best and the worst ones. It was a Friday afternoon in summer. Their father had come home early from work full of bluster and joy, bringing the sunshine inside with him. He maintained a boyish, playful streak well into adulthood; eventually the alcoholism would decay this, too, but for years it remained. He could make anything a game. That day, it was catch with their mother's favorite teacup, the one painted with wildflowers and nettles from the countryside she grew up in. Beckoning for the girls to spread across the living room, he tossed the cup to each of them as they shrieked with delight and dread, the fragile china sailing toward their trembling hands. Bonnie could still feel the jubilance of the catch, the pleasurable fright of the throw. Lucky, not yet nine, fumbled her turn, but the cup plonked onto the carpet unharmed. They all yelped with relief, then kept playing. Their mother was there, too, standing in the kitchen doorway, feigning outrage but in on the game. It was the good kind of fear, a fun made more thrilling for its proximity to danger. The cup survived unscathed, and Bonnie had felt it then, a fact as simple as a sugar cube, and just as easily dissolved: She loved her parents.

A few months later, their father would smash that cup, along with her parents' entire collection of wedding china, in a blackout. Afterward, he had sobbed, inconsolable as a child, as he gathered the shards of porcelain to his chest. He did not remember breaking them. Avery had hidden the sisters in her and Bonnie's bedroom, her arms around them, murmuring nonsense poems and rhymes from their childhood, trying to drown out the sound of shattering china beyond the door. *Monday's child is fair of face, Tuesday's child is full of grace . . .*

The last year they all lived together, he had stormed through the house flinging open all the closet doors. They had too much stuff, he thundered, and they needed to make space. To his credit, he only destroyed his own clothes. That powerful anger that raged inside him—ceaseless, directionless, relentless—she saw how, even drunk, he tried with all his might to direct it inward. Bonnie had that anger within her, too, but unlike him she had found an outlet in boxing. With his bare hands, he tore apart his silk shirts, beautiful items chosen by their mother in her gallery days, dusty pinks, cornflower blues, and mint greens, the kind of shirts he could never wear to the bank. The next morning, he attempted to make a game of picking up the silk-covered buttons that lay scattered across the hallway floor. For the first time ever, Bonnie refused to play.

She sat back on the sofa, staring at the painting of the four of them until her eyelids became heavy. She could have gone to her old bedroom, but she wasn't ready. She closed her eyes and drifted off right there on the couch. She was home, but not any home she knew anymore.

THE NEXT MORNING, SHE WAS eating her usual deli order of egg and cheese on a roll on one of the benches lining Central Park West, when Avery called.

"I've been trying to reach you! Where have you been?"

Bonnie placed the last few bites in the scrunched silver foil and cleared her throat.

"I'm in New York."

She heard Avery inhale.

"You are? What on earth are you doing there?"

"I thought about it and . . . I wanted to say goodbye to the apartment."

"You *did*?"

"And go through Nicky's stuff. One of us has to, and I'm the closest."

"Wow, that's a huge weight off my shoulders," said Avery. "Thank you, Bon Bon. I've been trying to work out when I could go. But you sure you're okay being there alone after everything that happened?"

Bonnie tilted back her head to look up at the dappled light falling through the tree above her. All around her the city was making its usual complaint of car horns and sirens. On a playground out of sight, children shrieked and cheered.

"It didn't feel right to not say goodbye. And . . . I'm thinking of starting training again," she said. "It's time."

As soon as the words came out of her mouth, she knew they were true. She had no idea how Pavel would feel seeing her, nor how she would feel seeing him. She only knew that she had to find out.

"Oh, that's brilliant!" exclaimed Avery. "I can't believe it. What made you change your mind?"

There was no way Bonnie was going to tell Avery about the incident at the bar. At best it would only worry her, at worst she would take it as evidence of Bonnie's need for therapy or professional intervention.

"It was our conversation, actually. Yeah, you really made me see how being a bouncer wasn't, you know, serving me."

Anyone who thinks boxers aren't smart are fools. Fighters understand lying better than anyone. What else is a feint? A hook off the jab? A combination switch-up? Boxers are trained to telegraph one thing and do another.

"*This* is what I'm talking about!" declared Avery triumphantly. "I am a *helpful* person. I just want the best for you, for all my family. I wish I could get Lucky on the phone to hear *exactly* what you just said."

"Why? What are you two arguing about now?"

Like most families, their sibling alliances shifted constantly, but ultimately, they remained split by age. Bonnie and Avery had remained on one side of the door, Lucky and Nicky on the other. But there were other, subtler bonds too. Bonnie knew that Avery and Nicky could talk for hours about books, for instance. Meanwhile, Bonnie's natural reticence offered space for Lucky's shy nature to unfurl. And Bonnie had her own bond with Nicky. After all, Nicky was the first person to ever see her box, had accompanied her to all her early training sessions. It was Avery and Lucky, the eldest and youngest, who had struggled to connect.

"I'm really worried about her, Bonnie."

"What happened?"

Avery launched into a graphic description of finding Lucky crumpled on her top step.

"She was covered in glitter, with lipstick all over her cheek and neck, basically naked except for a pair of angel wings and this dirty feather boa she'd tied around herself."

Bonnie smiled in spite of herself. She knew it was wrong, but she admired Lucky's commitment to partying, which was nothing if not consistent. She thought it all sounded pretty glamorous.

"She's twenty-six. She's just a bit of a wild child. You really think it's that bad?"

Avery practically barked with frustration.

"She'd traveled *all the way home* by herself like that. Like some wounded animal just waiting to be picked off from the herd. It's a miracle she wasn't raped."

Bonnie shuddered at the word.

"Look, you have to remember Lucky's been by herself in foreign cities since she was fifteen. She's savvier than you give her credit for."

She was trying to convince herself as much as Avery. Bonnie would never forgive herself if something bad happened to either of her remaining sisters.

"You didn't *see* her," said Avery. "She kept slipping in and out of consciousness, going limp in my arms. It was terrifying. I didn't know what to do. I felt so useless."

"You're the opposite of useless," said Bonnie gently. "What happened?"

"Well, I stuck her in a cold shower and basically slapped her back to consciousness. Not totally unsatisfying, I must admit."

Bonnie exhaled a soft laugh. She couldn't think of anyone better prepared to violently deliver someone back to reality than Avery.

"Then I managed to get her to drink a can of Coke," Avery continued. "I read if she'd taken MDMA or anything like that the sugar would help her come down. Anyway, she's been sleeping all day."

"Probably for the best."

Avery's voice dropped to a low murmur.

"When I was holding her, I kept thinking about Nicky. I can't imagine what that must have been like for you, Bonnie."

Bonnie tried to respond, but she couldn't. That moment, the moment when Nicky died, was beyond language for her.

"Look, I've gotta get to the gym," she said. "But I'm glad you told me. You want me to call her?"

"No. Yes. Maybe. I don't know. Let me see how she is when she wakes up. I'm sure she'd rather hear from you. You've always had a softer touch, ironically."

Bonnie hung up and tried not to remember. But it was impossible. She sat on the bench as the city rushed around her and thought of Nicky. They had spoken on the phone in the morning; Bonnie was coming in from her training camp in New Jersey for the evening to see her. As soon as she let herself into the apartment, she could feel something was wrong. The air was too still. Then she saw her through the doorway of the bedroom, her dark hair partially covering her face. She looked like something that had just spilled, like a vase of violets tipped over.

It took her less than five seconds to cover the distance from the door to Nicky. When she crouched over her body, she noticed Nicky's fingernails and lips were a pale shade of blue. She must have called 911, though she had no recollection of doing so afterward. The next thing she knew the operator's voice was asking for the apartment number, but Bonnie couldn't remember it. She had to rush back outside and check the iron numbers nailed to the door. *My sister has had an accident,* is what she said. She did not think she was dead.

Bonnie didn't want the paramedics to waste a single second getting to them, so she picked up Nicky and staggered with her to the elevator. This would have been hard for most people, but Bonnie was strong. She was the strongest of anyone in the family. She held her sister tight to her chest as the elevator groaned down fourteen flights, then carried her into the lobby. The doorman shot up from behind the desk when he saw them. His mouth was a small, helpless "o." Then the paramedics rushed in and ripped Nicky out of her arms. Bonnie could hear them saying something about her being unresponsive, about not being able to find a pulse.

*What's her name?*

*Nicky. Nicole. Nicole Blue.*

*How old is Nicole?*

*Twenty-six. Wait! Twenty-seven. She just turned twenty-seven.*

*What's your relation?*

*Sister. I'm her big sister.*

*Has Nicole taken any drugs that you know of?*

*I don't think so. I don't know.*

*Was she responsive when you found her?*

*She was on the floor. Her lips were blue. I-I picked her up. Was that wrong? Was that bad? Did I hurt her?*

The human heart is an amazing thing. It can stop for up to twenty minutes before starting back up again, more if the body has been in cold water. In fact, most organs can survive death for considerable periods. Blood circulation, for instance, can be stopped in the entire body below the heart for at least thirty minutes. Detached limbs may be successfully reattached after six hours. Bone, tendon, and skin can survive as long as twelve. But the brain, as every boxer knows, is another story. It injures faster than any other organ. Without special treatment, full recovery after more than three minutes of death is rare. And by the time Bonnie found Nicky, she had already been dead for four.

BONNIE TOSSED THE REST OF her sandwich and headed toward the gym before she could change her mind. She had done this journey so many times, her feet guided her without thought. She passed the elementary school whose playground was converted into a flea market on weekends, the dusty Italian bakery Avery would order all their birthday cakes from. She walked until she was almost at Columbus Circle, where the traffic thickened and congealed into a slow crawl. There, on a quiet run-down block in the sixties was Golden Ring. It had a large front shop window, so the entire gym was visible from the street; Bonnie had often glanced up after sparring to find a gaggle of tourists or students from the nearby high school pressed against the glass watching. Now, she was in their place, peering inside as the July heat beat down on her. Pavel was there, as she knew he would be, leaning against the far wall watching the darting, flitting figure of a young man shadowbox.

———

THE DAY AFTER NICKY DIED, Bonnie sat with her family and described finding her over and over again. Lucky and Avery had flown overnight from London and Paris; they begged her, faces hollow and exhausted, to go over each second again, as if by mastering every part of what happened they could somehow change it. Bonnie told them every single detail except one: that Nicky had called her to ask her for the drugs. Whether this was to protect Nicky or herself, she did not know. It was the police who found the Ziploc bag of pills on the kitchen counter. There were ten of them, pale pink, Nicky's favorite color. Bonnie was so naive. She had never even heard of fentanyl before. That evening, when everyone went to bed early, Bonnie went back to the gym. She didn't know what else to do. Pavel found her working the heavy bag in the dark, the streetlamps outside casting long orange streaks across the floor. He touched her shoulder gently, but she did not stop. When he spoke, his voice was heavy with sadness.

*I cancel the fight.*

Bonnie kept hitting the bag. Jab, jab, cross. Jab, hook, cross. Jab, jab, uppercut.

*Bonnie, did you hear me?*

Bonnie shot another hook off the jab.

*I'm taking that fight,* she huffed between punches.

*Bonnie, stop. Go be with family now.*

Bonnie kept hitting.

*You said it,* she said, her voice flinty. *Boxing first, family second.*

Pavel looked at her with a pained expression.

*Not like this.*

*Isn't*—jab—*that*—jab—*what you told me?*

She shot her straight right so hard the chains holding the bag groaned. Pavel put his hand on her back to stop her, but she swung around and pushed him away from her. He stepped forward again, but she shoved him back. Her voice tore out of her.

*Isn't this what you wanted me to be?* She pounded her chest with her glove. *You made me this! You made me!*

He tried to stop her hands, but she turned her gloves on him, beating at his chest. She was not hitting hard; her punches were too ragged to be forceful. Pavel took the hits without flinching until, in one quick movement, he wrapped his arms around her and pulled her to his chest. She leaned against his heart, heaving.

*Is okay,* he murmured, though of course it was not, would never be again. *Is okay.*

He ran his palms over her head, from her crown to her neck, like a benediction, like a blessing. Then, clutching either side of her face, he pressed his forehead to hers, holding his face an inch from hers. It was the closest their lips had ever been. Bonnie was still between his hands.

*What do I do?* she whimpered.

*If you want to fight,* he whispered. *We fight.*


SIXTEEN YEARS AFTER SHE'D GAZED through the window for the first time beside Nicky, Bonnie stood outside Golden Ring gym again. Pavel looked at her through the glass. He was not a man who was easily surprised, but she saw him flinch. What did he see when he looked at her now? Bonnie with her pale blond hair and paler blue eyes, her compact body in which nothing was superfluous. She was like a still stone in the river of his gaze. Half her life had passed since the first time they met, but she was still young, still capable of surprising herself and him. If Nicky had been there, she would have grabbed Bonnie by the hand and led her inside. So, Bonnie imagined it, her sister's warm palm in hers, and opened the door.

## CHAPTER SIX

# Avery

IN HER PERFECT LIVING ROOM, DECORATED WITH A VINTAGE SOFA reupholstered in handmade fabric from a third-generation block printer in Jaipur, a coffee table consisting of a marble plinth shipped from Denmark, and £840-a-roll gold-embossed wallpaper from Soane Britain, interior designers to the Royals, Avery was preparing to excoriate her less-than-perfect youngest sister.

"It was a *party,* Avery," said Lucky, going on the defensive before Avery could even begin the blistering opening statement she'd practiced in the shower that morning. "Remember those? I drank too much, like everyone did, and had a bit of trouble getting my key in the lock. Please don't make a big deal out of this."

"I found you half naked and unconscious outside my front door and you're asking me not to make a big deal of it? Why are *you* not making more of this? Do you have so little concern for yourself?"

Lucky rolled her eyes with such force Avery was surprised she didn't cause ligament damage. They were standing on either side of the room, the coffee table laden with its glossy gallery exhibition books and *New Yorker*s Avery never actually got around to reading, forming a buffer between them. Lucky was silhouetted against the large sash windows overlooking the street. Outside, the sunshine from yesterday had vanished with such completeness it was as if it had never been at all. It was a typically English still, gray day.

"*Everyone* was drunk!" Lucky said. "You're just out of touch, not to mention a born catastrophizer."

Avery emitted a derisive snort.

"A catastrophizer? Where do you even get this stuff? I'm a realist. I live in *reality*. Maybe you should try it."

"Negativity isn't some higher version of reality. It's just being judgmental. By your standards every person in Britain would have a drinking problem."

"Um, hello, they *do*. Have you seen the men in this country? They *all* look fifty."

Now it was Lucky's turn to snort.

"As someone who is actually interested in men, I can promise you they do not."

Avery flicked her head in exasperation.

"You know I had boyfriends before Chiti. Remember Steve?"

Lucky barked a dry laugh.

"That guy who used to bring the Tupperware containers of deviled eggs over to the apartment? Steve does *not* count."

Avery turned away in frustration. Steve had undeniably been a dud. She should not have brought up Steve.

"Who's being judgmental now?" she rebounded. "Anyway, all that is beside the point. You want to normalize this shit? Fine. But I am not going to sit here and tell you it's okay. You are *not* okay."

"I think I should be the judge of whether or not I'm okay. And I am. I'm great. I'm fucking thriving."

Avery turned to Chiti, who had appeared in the doorway, clutching her hands in front of her chest.

"I can't talk to this person," Avery said, gesturing toward Lucky. "It's pointless."

"Sweetheart," said Chiti to Avery. "Sit down. Let's make some tea and discuss this like people who love each other."

Lucky and Avery looked at each other and almost smiled. It was just like their mother. Familial strife, emotional turmoil, cancer, the climate crisis . . . There was seemingly nothing she did not believe could be remedied, or at least relieved, by a cup of tea. But Lucky looked away and the moment passed. Avery's rage rushed back in.

"She's fucking killing herself, Chiti!" Avery turned back to Lucky. "Did Nicky not teach you anything? Do you still not get the part about the fucking fragility of life?"

"She doesn't mean that," said Chiti to Lucky.

"Oh, fuck you," spat Lucky back at Avery. "You act like you're so much better than us. You're not. You're not better than anybody. You've always been an uptight asshole. Now you're just a rich one."

"She didn't mean that," said Chiti to Avery.

"And by the way, you're not my mother," continued Lucky. "I already have one useless one, I don't need another."

"She's *my* useless mother too!" said Avery. "And I don't *want* to be your mother. You're twenty-six years old, Lucky. It's not *cute* anymore. Being a total mess isn't something to be proud of."

"You're not a mess," said Chiti to Lucky, then to her wife, "That's unfair, Avery."

Avery rounded on Chiti.

"Why are you defending her?"

"I'm not defending anyone. I am trying to get you both to see that attacking each other will not help the situation."

Avery gave each of them a long look. Suddenly, and with a surprising and searing clarity, she missed her mother, that woman who had so consistently let her down. At least with her mother, she was allowed to remember that she had once been a child. Around her sisters, she was always the eldest, which meant, in comparison to them, she was never young. But she was tired of being the grown-up. She was tired of being herself.

"You know what? I'm sick of this," she said. "I'm sick of having to play the bad guy all the time."

"That's because you *are,*" shot Lucky. "Ever since you bought this house, you're like some corporate cyborg with a blowout."

Avery turned to Chiti.

"I can't call her a mess—which she categorically is—but she can call me a corporate . . . whatever she called me. How is that fair?"

"No one's agreeing with her," Chiti tried to soothe.

"I am!" chimed Lucky. "I am agreeing with me!"

"You know what? You're right," said Avery, her voice dripping with scorn. "I'm sorry for making a success of myself. I'm sorry for not being like our parents and forcing my family to live in a fucking shoebox while I drink myself to oblivion. I'm sorry I wanted something better than the upbringing we got."

"And you think I don't?" Lucky gasped. "Why do you think I do what I do? You think I like getting my measurements taken every year like I'm fucking cattle? Do you know how degrading and dumb ninety percent of the shit I have to do is? You think I want to wear *pink tulle*? But I made more money by the time I graduated from high school than most people make in . . . I don't know! I made a shit ton of money!"

"I have no doubt you did," said Avery. "But where is it, Lucky? Do you have savings? Stocks? Where's that money today?"

Lucky looked away.

"I'll make more," she murmured.

"And it will go up your nose too," declared Avery.

"Enough!" said Chiti. "I can't listen to you two attack each other anymore. You both work hard. You both have been through a lot. There's no competition."

But Chiti didn't understand what it was like to have sisters. Against their parents, against the world at large, they were fiercely allied. But among themselves, everything was a competition. There was never enough attention, never enough money, never enough love to go around. So they fought for every scrap.

"I don't need this," Avery said. "I'm going out."

"That's right, leave," Lucky said. "Treat me like you treat everyone else when they don't meet your exacting standards."

"Ignore that," said Chiti to Avery. "Where are you going? Don't go."

"I don't know," said Avery, launching herself toward the door. "Back to the office."

"It's a Sunday," pleaded Chiti.

"So? I need to be anywhere but here."

"We're not done with this conversation," said Chiti.

"You might not be," said Avery. "But I am. I am so fucking done."

"This is why you have no friends!" Lucky called after her as she left the room.

Avery slammed the front door and walked down the road. She waited to check that no one was following her, then she called him. He answered on the second ring.

"So we're doing phone calls now?" he said.

"What are you doing? Want to smoke a cigarette?"

He laughed softly.

"I would, but I'm home."

"Where's that? I can drive."

"You want to come to where I live?"

"I want to see you."

A pause. Avery forgot to exhale.

"I'll text you my address," he said.

IF AVERY HAD NOT GONE back to AA the previous week, if she had not chosen a sparsely populated meeting that she had never been to before, if he had not happened to be sitting in the back row when she snuck in late, he may never have become the rocks upon which she would dash her marriage and life. But she did and he was, and the rest was inevitable.

She'd been relieved that the meeting was at the same time as her former home group, so it was unlikely anyone she knew would be there. She didn't want to be asked where she'd been for the past year or how she was, if she was maintaining her spiritual condition or living in her character defects. Because Avery, by her own estimations, was living in all of them: stealing, lying, judging, fearing, and resenting everything and everyone. To avoid the pre-meeting small talk or eager questions about whether she was a newcomer, she had waited on the corner until fifteen minutes after the meeting started, a hard act for someone like Avery, for whom punctuality was a kind of religion.

The speaker, a middle-aged woman with a heavy face of makeup, was already well into her story by the time Avery slipped in. She did a quick scan of the room; no one she recognized. She took a seat in the back next to the table of digestive biscuits and trays of lukewarm tea. The speaker was cataloging a seemingly never-ending list of abusive relationships with men, starting with her father (of course) and ending with an ex-husband who'd embezzled money from her, then left her for a friend's daughter. Now, in her third year of sobriety, in addition to alcohol, she was abstaining from all her "triggers": sugar, cigarettes, coffee, shopping, gossip magazines, and sex. Especially sex, she took care to reiterate.

"The other day I was dying to go out and pick up a man," she said. "But then I had to ask myself, would that bring me closer to or further from a drink? Is that what my Higher Power really wants for me? So I turned it over and went to a meeting. And guess what? I picked up a sponsee instead!"

Indulgent chuckles from around the room. Avery involuntarily rolled her eyes. Somewhere during this rotation, they landed on the man next to her. He was writing with earnest concentration in his notebook. Could he seriously be taking notes on this? Then she remembered that she had done that herself when she was younger. She used to love meetings, love the stories, the depth of identification that could bubble up from nowhere like a hot spring in a desert. She could be listening to someone ostensibly nothing like her who would describe, with almost uncanny precision, her exact feelings and thoughts. That was the magic of the fellowship, when it worked: the realization that the parts of yourself that were the most hidden, most shameful, were what connected you most deeply to others. In AA, you were never an outsider, never alone. For years it had felt like she always had a golden lattice of sober people beneath and around her, ready to catch her if she fell. But she had been falling for a year now, and no one had caught her yet.

The truth is, she knew she was the problem. Relating to others was a muscle; a little over a year ago she would have loved this share too. What was it she'd been told the *ism* in alcoholism stood for? *I separate myself.* That was her, all right. Separating herself, then wondering why she felt apart. Avery let her eyes scan her neighbor's page. He appeared to be writing poetry. She smiled to herself. A sober poet, just what the world needed. As she was thinking this, he glanced up. He could have been embarrassed, as she would have been, and closed the page, but he only smiled in collusion. They looked at each other. He was young, Black, and striking, though not exactly handsome. He had an unusual face: a straight, serious mouth and wide eyes the shape of two drawn bows. Avery was struck.

After the meeting, she found him outside smoking. He was alone, standing just a little away from the group that was discussing which Le Pain Quotidien to go to for fellowship. She sidled up alongside him.

"Could I bum one of those?" she asked.

*Thank god for smoking,* she thought, the universal conversation starter for shy, socially awkward, or self-destructive strangers the world over. He pulled one from his pack and leaned over to light hers with an old silver Zippo.

"I'm Charlie," he said, as the flame shot up between them.

"Avery," she said, inhaling. "So, you're a poet?"

He had an irrepressible smile, as though in a constant and amusing dialogue with himself.

"Guilty," he said. "And you're an American."

She smiled.

"Guilty too," she said.

A moment of silence drifted down between them like a balloon losing helium.

"I didn't know real poets still existed," she said.

"I don't know how real I am," he said. "But I exist. Are you a real American?"

"I'm from New York," she said.

"So no," he said, and she laughed.

"And you can make a living? As a poet?"

A flicker of self-consciousness shot through her. She sounded like she was giving a job interview. When had she become this conservative? She had written poetry herself when living on the commune. Charlie's face, however, remained open and sanguine.

"Some can. But I make my living as a lowly copywriter."

"That doesn't sound so lowly to me," said Avery.

The Le Pain Quotidien group, including the speaker who was swearing off men, was shuffling toward them, ostensibly to invite them to join. Charlie and Avery shared a look that communicated a mutual desire to avoid this. It was bad, she knew, to pair off and separate from the group, an old form of bonding that didn't serve her sobriety, but then Charlie touched her elbow and all she could think about was the quickest way out of there.

"Hey," he said, giving her a knowing look. "You walking to the tube?"

*Fuck it,* she thought.

"Let's go," she said.

Before the others reached them, they took off together in step, both taking regular drags of their cigarettes, a heady sensation of escape quickening their pace. It was a beautiful summer evening and the light, as they set off up the hill, was the rich yellow of good French butter. London was so lovely when it chose to be, Avery thought. Charlie turned to her and smiled.

"What about you?" he asked.

"What about me?"

"What do you do?"

"Don't you know that's a rude question?"

That smile again. His teeth were surprisingly small and cream, like tiny pearls.

"Forgive me," he said.

Avery looked at his funny face, so close to handsome yet slightly off the mark, and felt she could forgive him anything.

"I'm a lawyer," she said.

"Ah!" He nodded. "The least lowly of trades."

Now, Avery smiled. It was true.

"So what are you doing here?" he asked, nodding back toward the meeting. "Too much champagne and cocaine for you? Had to call it quits?"

This was so far from the truth of the last years of her using as an itinerant drug addict, Avery had to laugh.

"What makes you think those were my drugs of choice?" she asked.

"You just seem like kind of a fancy lady."

"Why?"

"I don't know. Your shoes, maybe."

Avery looked down at her Gucci loafers with the horse bit buckle. She had been wearing them last weekend when she stole a quilted wallet from Chanel. No one ever suspects the woman in loafers. She blushed.

"Nah, don't get me wrong. They look good," he added. "I'm just surprised to meet someone like you at a meeting, is all."

"How much time do you have?" she asked.

"I just picked up my ninety days."

He was barely able to conceal his pride. So, he was a newcomer, she thought. Probably still on a pink cloud, that euphoric period of early recovery when you're through the physical withdrawals but reality hasn't quite set in yet. A brief window of time when anything seemed possible. How she missed it.

"You'll see, there's all sorts here," she said. "In New York we say this disease gets everyone from Park Avenue to the park bench."

He grinned.

"I like that. What would the London equivalent be?"

"I don't know, from Mayfair to—"

"My bedroom," he said.

The blush would not leave her cheeks.

"That works," she said.

"How come I've not seen you here before?"

"I stopped coming for a little," she said.

"Why'd you stop?"

"Honestly?"

"Sure."

"I stopped being able to listen to people talk about God."

Charlie raised his eyebrows.

"Go on," he said.

"I just . . . I couldn't handle hearing about how someone's Higher Power never gives them anything they can't handle. If that was the case, we wouldn't have rape or child abuse or incest or domestic violence, and people wouldn't develop PTSD or complex trauma or crippling drug dependencies, all of which are the direct results of being given *exactly* what you can't handle."

Charlie was listening to her closely, with respect or reservation Avery couldn't tell.

"So you don't believe everything happens for a reason and all that?" he asked.

She took a deep breath. She could give some pat, newcomer-appropriate answer, but she was, indeed, a lawyer and the compulsion to be right, to hammer home her case, was as deeply entrenched in her as breathing.

"I believe that everything *happens*," she said. "Period. Or full stop, as you would say. That's it. Things happen and we have to learn to live with them, as long as suicide is off the table, that is. If we can find meaning in them, fine, but even if we can't, we *still* have to live with them. The meaning is an afterthought, an anesthesia. *Happens* is the only word in that statement that's empirical. The rest is whatever helps you sleep at night."

Charlie looked at her as if he were evaluating the cover of a book he'd picked up but wasn't sure he wanted to read.

"I guess I can't argue with that," he said.

They walked together in silence through the quiet residential streets. From over an ivy-covered brick wall two children on a trampoline in their garden careened in and out of view, their blond hair lifting and falling around their faces as they shrieked with joy.

"Also, my sister died," Avery said.

When Charlie looked at her again, his assessment seemed to shift and soften. There was a tenderness in his face that was entirely unforced.

"I'm sorry to hear that," he said. "Recently?"

Avery nodded.

"Last year."

"Do you mind if I ask you how?"

"No, it's fine." Avery cleared her throat. "She overdosed."

"Oh man." Charlie shook his head softly. "Your sister was an addict too?"

Avery shook her head. She had never thought of Nicky like that when she was alive, and it felt like a betrayal to do so now.

"No," she said firmly. "She had chronic pain. It's this condition called endometriosis. Men don't get it." She tried to keep the bitterness out of her voice as she continued. "She went to lots of doctors, she had surgeries, but they couldn't seem to help her. In fact, they were fucking useless."

She remembered sitting with Nicky in the emergency room when the pain had become too much to sleep. Her sister curled in on herself, as though she could make herself small enough for the hurt not to find her. The nurses in the hospital treated her like a criminal. They thought she was there for the drugs. All she was asking for was comfort, a little relief. In that sense, perhaps she was no different from an addict. Weren't all addicts looking for relief from some invisible pain? Weren't all people?

Avery tried to modulate her voice, so she sounded reasonable, like someone simply conveying a tragic series of events and not a woman half mad with rage and grief.

"Understandably, given the pain she was in," she began judiciously, "she took painkillers. That's what they're there for. They *kill pain*. But she developed a dependency and ended up buying a batch on the street that contained fentanyl and . . ."

Avery inhaled sharply. Would it ever be easier to tell this story? Would it ever not make her want to grab the world like a sheet of drawing paper on which a terrible mistake had been made and rip it up, rip it down, and start again?

But there had been a slither of relief, too, which Avery never admitted to anyone. Nicky had been suffering for years by the time she died. The problem with her pain was that it was invisible. Avery wished she could have given it crutches, some object that made it obvious to everyone around her, but she had learned now that most pain is private.

Language grasped at, but never caught, it. Each time Nicky tried to find the right words, it seemed to change shape. Sometimes she said it was a dull, low ache, foreboding and inevitable, like the darkening of the sky before a storm. Sometimes it was hot electric bursts that shot and pinged through her, leaving her doubled over and gasping for air. Sometimes she said it felt like crashing waves gathering momentum and receding, her insides the beaten and unyielding shore. And when it was gone, she waited for it, like a volatile husband who has left in a rage but will inevitably return. Sometimes, she said, the waiting felt like the worst part of all.

Where language failed, numbers were no better. How many times had Nicky been asked to rate her pain on a scale of one to ten? It was a riddle: Choose too low and she might not get the relief she needed, choose too high and she'd be dismissed as hysterical. What was the magic number? She tried six, seven, eight, nine . . . She never dared consider herself a ten. Avery had watched her writhe in hospital waiting rooms and doctors' offices trying to find the right combination of words and numbers that would unlock permanent relief.

She never found it, but Avery left for London anyway. She could still remember the howl of grief escaping through the phone when Nicky called to tell her what the doctors had said. It was late on a Friday night in London and Avery was at a bar in Soho, where she'd been meeting some of Chiti's other therapist friends. She had wanted to make a good impression, was unwilling to answer the call. But she did, she reminded herself now, she did answer. The rain had stopped just in time for the weekend and the streets were still slick when she stepped outside. *Hysterectomy.* She'd pressed a hand to her ear to drown out the noise of passing revelers, everyone drunk and high-spirited after the rain. *Could you repeat that?* The neon lights of the bar splashed and smeared along the wet pavement. *Hysterectomy.* That was the word she hadn't been able to hear. The removal of the uterus. The key to permanent relief.

The last time Avery saw Nicky, she knew her sister was different, though it was impossible to say exactly why. Afterward, it was her eyes she remembered. Her pupils were too small, two tiny dots that would not hold Avery's gaze. Nicky had a face like water, always moving, rippling, dancing. Their mother used to say she should have been an actress; she could convey any emotion—amusement, irritation, incredulity—with the slightest widening of her eyes or jump of her eyebrow. But the last time Avery saw her, she was strangely still, as if holding herself braced against something.

They were walking in Regents Park; Nicky had come to stay for spring break, and it was her final day before returning to New York. She had been herself for most of the trip, but during the last two days she became withdrawn. Avery realized afterward that she had likely been running out of pills, lengthening the space between each dose to make her supply last until she got home. It was an unseasonably warm spring day, so Avery bought them both Cornettos from the café by the pond. As they walked, Nicky struggled to unwrap the paper from the cone, her hands seemingly uncooperative.

*Are you okay, Nicks?* Avery asked, glancing at her trembling fingers. She took Nicky's ice cream and smoothly unpeeled the wrapper, then passed it back. *You sure you feel up for flying?*

*Why do people keep asking if I'm okay?* snapped Nicky.

Avery glanced at her in surprise; she didn't know that anyone else was asking.

*My period's due,* relented Nicky after a pause.

*Oh, I'm sorry.* Avery motioned toward a bench they could go sit on. *Is it . . . painful?*

She never knew quite how to talk about Nicky's condition, aware, as she was, of the unfair fact that her own periods had always been remarkably uneventful.

*Yeah, well, obviously,* said Nicky sharply, then seemed to try to mollify her peevishness. *And it's a busy semester, so I have a lot of grading to do on the plane. But it's not a big deal. I'm good, I promise.*

*I get it,* said Avery, wary of pushing her further. *They're lucky to have a teacher who cares as much as you do. Remember the nuns?*

Nicky gave a dry laugh. All four of them had gone to a Catholic middle and high school run by a group of nuns who were either oblivious or actively ill-suited to meeting the needs of children. They sat down now on a wooden bench under a shady ash tree and watched the ducks waddle around the pond imperiously. Twin toddlers, each dressed in bright overalls and mini Converse high-tops, ran toward a mallard, shrieking with delighted terror as it opened its wings and quacked irately at them.

*Look at that,* said Nicky, suddenly smiling.

*So cute,* said Avery dutifully, though, in truth, she thought they should leave that poor duck alone.

*You know I got bitten by a duck when we were little?* Nicky said.

*You did? When?*

*In Central Park by the Turtle Pond. I was probably, like, four, but I hid it from Mom so she wouldn't know.*

*Why'd you do that?*

*I thought I'd get in trouble. She was always so exasperated when we needed anything. I think I knew, even then, it was better to deal with it myself.*

Avery nodded. She could imagine the scene exactly; Lucky would have been only two; Nicky, four; Bonnie, seven; and Avery, nine. A day out at the park with them would have been treated as equivalent to navigating a military assault course by their mother. Amazing, thought Avery, that at only four, Nicky had already understood the reality of their family, but of course they all had.

*Well, if you ever get bitten again,* said Avery, taking her sister's hand, *I hope you will tell me.*

Nicky smiled sadly.

*My kid is always going to be able to tell me,* she said. *Always.* She looked at her and Avery saw the hope beneath her exhaustion, like the sun peeking through clouds. *Anyway,* Nicky added with a laugh. *Fuck ducks.*

Avery could have pushed her then, she could have asked more questions, but she didn't. She sat on the bench holding her sister's hand, watching the ducks glide across the glassy water with their ducklings in tow, and she stayed silent, happy just to be with her.

Of course, Nicky refused the hysterectomy. She wanted to be a mother more than she wanted to be free. Or, rather, motherhood was the form of freedom she chose; not a life without pain, but a life assembled around it, love coupled forever with fear, a paper dollhouse built around an open flame. That was why she had been taking the painkillers, to hold off one kind of pain to make way for a better one. And now here was Avery promising Chiti a child. But was it what she wanted? This dream Nicky had lived for? Died for? Could she love a child because her sister would have loved a child? Because Chiti would? Could that be enough for her? Should it be?

"Shit," Charlie murmured beside her. Avery had almost forgotten he was there. "I'm sorry that happened to her. And to you. I-I don't know what else to say."

He gave her a nervous look and she was suddenly aware of his age. He was young. Early twenties probably, mid at most. What could he know of loss?

"There's nothing to say," she replied, her voice returning to its quality of crisp control. "It happened and I have to live with it. End of story. No reason why, no hidden lesson, no *attitude of gratitude.*" She almost spat the words. "She died and I'm still alive. Life's random and unfair and sometimes it's random and more than fair. That's it."

The yellow light was cooling to a dusty blue. Avery still marveled at how long the summer evenings were in London. In New York, they seemed to be over as quickly as a pop song, relinquishing themselves to equally hot nights, but in England the light lingered like a note held on and on.

"I had a brother who died too," Charlie said.

Avery's eyes darted to him in surprise.

"You did?"

"Yeah, of leukemia. I was still pretty young, so I didn't really understand what had happened until I was older. I just remember my mum crying all the time."

"That's awful. Your poor mom. And you."

"The thing that doesn't change is that I still think of myself as one of three, even though it's just been me and my sister since I was seven. It's like this invisible limb no one knows I have, but it's always there. It's part of me."

Avery nodded vigorously.

"*Exactly.* I feel exactly the same. Except I'm one of four—or I was. All girls. I'm the eldest."

"Yeah, see, that's really hard. And you're older so you feel like you've got to be strong for the others, at least that's how it was with my sister. I'm really sorry you're going through that. I don't get it, but I get it. You get it?"

Avery nodded.

"I do."

Charlie glanced at her and smiled.

"Pretty weird, right? That we've both been through that? I knew there was something about you."

Avery allowed herself the slightest smile. It had been a long time since anyone had made her feel special. She dropped the cigarette and ground it out with the heel of her ridiculous loafers.

"So, what about you?" she asked. "Do you believe everything happens for a reason? That there's a benevolent God watching over us?"

Charlie ran his hand over the back of his neck and offered her something between a grin and a grimace.

"Recovery really robs us of the ability to make small talk, right?"

Avery gave a low laugh.

"You don't have to answer."

"No, it's a good question."

He looked up as a cluster of wood pigeons fled the tree above, leaving in unison, as birds somehow magically knew to do.

"I don't," he said quietly. "But I wish I did. I wish I had my mother's God, actually. Not all the Jehovah's Witness stuff she practices, that's a bit much for me. But she believes in something that believes in her—or at least she *believes* it believes in her. And it comforts her, I can tell. I envy her that."

Avery followed Charlie's eyes to the now empty tree. The leaves glowed electric green in the evening light.

"I wish I had your mother's God too."

Charlie nodded thoughtfully.

"If I did, I definitely would have spent a lot less money on cocaine," he said.

Avery barked with laughter.

"True. And I probably wouldn't have shot heroin into my groin," she said.

Charlie glanced at her in surprise.

"Really? I can't picture that. Or were you one of those heroin chic chicks?"

Avery colored ever so slightly. As far as she knew, no one had ever thought of her as chic at doing anything, heroin or otherwise.

"I lived in a commune for a while with a group of libertarian Marxists and anarchists and then in a parking lot in the Tenderloin. I guess it was meant to be some kind of twenty-four-hour protest against the system, but we mostly just shot up and gave each other head lice."

Charlie laughed and the sound was like a smooth banister she could slide down to another floor, another life.

"And did it work?" he asked. "Did you feel free of the chains of capitalism?"

"Mostly, I just felt itchy," she said.

"How long did that last?"

"The itching?"

"That life."

"Until I was twenty-three and got clean."

"So you have . . ."

He was fishing for her age, but she let him have it.

"Ten years next month," she said.

Twenty-three plus ten. She was thirty-three years old, had been sober now for longer than she ever drank or used drugs. But she didn't feel sober at all. She felt lost.

"Wow, that is . . . sensational," Charlie said, and the word in his mouth sounded like something smooth and delicious, like a fruit from a foreign country she had yet to try.

"I don't know what it is yet," said Avery. "But it's definitely something."

At the tube station they exchanged numbers and an awkward, lingering hug. When she got home, she went straight to her study to search his name. She was surprised to find there were dozens of articles about his work and videos of his readings; she had taken him for an amateur, but he was just that rarest of things: humble. Checking over her shoulder to make sure Chiti wasn't nearby, she pressed play on the first video that came up. It felt illicit, as though she was watching porn, not a poetry reading.

He was standing in front of a packed crowd at one of the East London bars Avery never went to, the audience's faces upturned to him. They were all slim and young and able to sit cross-legged on the floor without issue. She could see one woman wearing a vintage military beret. Charlie looked relaxed in a red hoodie and jeans standing above the others, everyone's eyes on him. Then he began to speak, without ceremony, without self-consciousness, reciting from memory with a half smile on his face that seemed to suggest that yes, he was there, earnestly taking part in this ancient social tradition of oral poetry, but he was also lightly laughing at himself for being there, laughing at all of them, at the whole enterprise. As he spoke he flitted seamlessly between gravity and levity, the cosmic and the comic, never landing in one place too long.

By the time the poem ended, Avery didn't feel that she wanted *him,* exactly; she wanted to *be* him. She wanted to make a bed in the chamber of his chest and live there. She wanted to speak and have his words come out of her mouth. She wanted to be a man onstage with a woman in a beret staring at her like she had just invented language. She wanted to see the world as he did and make it into an offering.

The next day, Charlie texted her that he was going to a meeting at six that evening, and Avery answered immediately that she would meet him there. It was the earliest she had left work in months; she often stayed in the office until after eight P.M., then took more work home with her to look at after dinner. Chiti had long ago accepted this and sometimes even scheduled clients that late herself, ostensibly ones who, like Avery, struggled with work boundaries.

But they spent enough time together, Avery told herself. They took weekend walking tours in the Lake District and went to dinner regularly at the Italian place at the top of the high street where the pasta came baked in tinfoil and the host always brought them a complimentary slab of tiramisu. But Avery had not left work early to spend time with Chiti in a long time, and it was this, more than anything else, that nagged her as she walked to the church. Then she entered the meeting and saw Charlie sitting coolly in the last row, one arm slung over the back of a chair he was saving for her, and she stopped thinking about anything at all.

"Hey, American," he said.

"Hey, poet."

He offered her the copy of the *Twelve and Twelve* the group was reading from that week. They shared the book, heads bowed close together, following along as one by one each person read a passage. AA had often left Avery feeling like she was in school again, the reading aloud, the Big Book studies, the step work with a sponsor that felt so similar to homework. She loved the way meetings always started and ended on time, each beginning with the familiar preamble and ending with the same prayer recited as a group. After years of chaos and turbulence, it felt safe, structured—which was, she supposed, the point.

But now, sitting next to Charlie, she really did feel like a schoolgirl again, the hot flush of a crush creeping into her cheeks as she inhaled the scent of smoke and a musk that was simply male wafting off his skin. At closing, when they formed a circle, and she slipped her hand into his cool, dry palm, Avery felt something she had not felt in a long time: a frisson of desire.

Later that week, she met Charlie at another meeting. Lucky was arriving from Paris that evening, and she knew she should go straight home after work to meet her, but it felt so good, for once, to not do what she was supposed to do. And, if she was honest, she wanted an excuse to be out of the house. Chiti had promptly started looking at sperm donor websites online after their conversation on Nicky's anniversary, happily peppering Avery with life-altering questions with the blithe breeziness of someone asking what she wanted for dinner— Did she have a preference on the donor's race? Height? Did she want to know where they went to college?—while Avery felt like the air was slowly being siphoned out of the room.

She met him in the basement of a church in Belsize Park at a meditation meeting where they discussed the eleventh step. Avery opened her eyes during the meditation to find him watching her with his calm, still gaze. At first, she'd attempted to make light of it and pulled a silly face to make him laugh, but he had continued regarding her with serene composure. Eventually, she stilled, too, and they sat like that, each looking into the other's eyes in a silence that seemed to reach for eternity. Only when the timer went off and the room sprang back to life with the usual sighs and shuffles did their eyes break away from each other. As the secretary read from the script, Avery glanced down into her lap, overcome suddenly by the desire to shake herself out like a wet dog or hoot with laughter or stretch her mouth into a scream, *something* to release the intensity of the past handful of minutes. Her entire body was buzzing with a new electricity. *Chemistry,* she thought with wonder. Impossible to force or fake. Inexplicable and undeniable. Who knew why she had it with Charlie? She only knew that she did.

He was walking her back toward Hampstead after the meeting when she turned to him.

"I watched some of your readings online," she said.

Charlie raised his eyebrows in surprise.

"You looked me up?"

"Just doing my due diligence. I am a lawyer, after all."

"What did you think?"

She smiled.

"To borrow a word from you . . . sensational."

Charlie beamed, making no effort to hide his delight.

"Were they what you expected? My poems?"

"I guess I thought maybe they'd be more political. They're sort of party poems."

He laughed.

"No, I mean that in a good way!" continued Avery. "Like, they could be read in the middle of a party and not interrupt the flow of festivities. Even when they're sad they still feel like a celebration."

Charlie plucked a leaf from a bush and began breaking it into green confetti.

"It's interesting that you say that. I think there's an expectation that someone like me has to stand for something political, but I'm philosophical. I'm really into this idea that my ethical code doesn't have to come from any doctrine. There is no intrinsic right or wrong, only what's right or wrong for me."

"So essentially moral nihilism crossed with psychological egoism?"

"Yeah, that's pretty much exactly what it is," Charlie said, giving her an impressed look.

"I studied philosophy at undergrad, a fact that usually renders me insufferable to ninety-nine percent of people."

"I think you are the opposite of insufferable," said Charlie. "I suffer you gladly."

Avery blushed, then blushed some more when she realized she was blushing. She cleared her throat.

"So you act in your own self-interest at all times?" she asked.

"Pretty much."

"Even at the expense of others?"

"Sometimes."

"But if everyone acted that way and my interests and yours were in opposition, how would there be order? If there was no agreed-upon value system or moral code?"

Charlie brushed the remains of the leaf from his hands.

"Look, man, all I know is that I was raised in a strictly religious household that told me most of what I wanted made me morally wrong. I felt so bad so much of my life, I thought that was just the way it had to be. Then I started pushing back *hard* in the other direction and I realized it wasn't. Total moral independence, that's what I believe in. Answering to myself and no one else."

Avery smiled. He sounded like her ten years ago.

"And how do you feel?"

"Free. I feel free."

Charlie ran ahead of her and leapt up to clasp a bar of scaffolding. He hoisted himself higher in a quick succession of pull-ups, his T-shirt riding up to reveal his narrow hips. He was lithe and muscular as a fish. Avery came to stand beneath him, unable to hide her admiration. She looked up at his face, which was creased with effort.

"Oh, you're so big and strong," she teased.

He dropped lightly onto his feet in front of her and stood with his face inches from hers.

"What did you say?" he asked.

His face was cracked open with a grin, but his eyes did not leave hers.

"You're so big," she said.

He pulled her into him.

"And?"

"And strong," she said.

Then he kissed her, and Avery finally understood the true meaning of the phrase *Blew my mind*. His lips met hers and it was like the hushed *pop* of a fuse blowing out. Everything inside her was cast into welcome darkness. Her mind was beautifully, blissfully blank. What a relief not to have to think anymore. Not to have to pretend to be whole anymore. They kissed for an hour, his hands grabbing and kneading her body with such force it felt like he could pull her into a new shape, a new person altogether. When she eventually broke away from him to meet Lucky, she already knew that she was too late.

———

AVERY STOOD NOW OUTSIDE THE address Charlie had given her and exhaled slowly. Was she really going to do this? A kiss was a transgression, but this, this would be a betrayal. Was it worse that he was a man? Chiti had only ever been with women, had always known that was right for her. Avery had been with men as a teenager but not since; *boys* was probably more accurate. She always said that she had only ever loved Chiti, but that wasn't entirely true. First, there had been Freja, though equating what she had with Chiti to that relationship was like comparing a fireplace to a forest fire. One was comfort, the other carnage.

Avery met Freja in a class called HOPE: Human Odyssey to Political Existentialism during her final year at Columbia, where Freja was also a philosophy major. She was originally from Sweden, and she looked it. Her eyes were like sea glass with bright white eyelashes and eyebrows, and her skin turned the color of wet sand in the sun. Fiercely intelligent and arrogantly determined to live according to her own principles, she believed that personal satisfaction was the noblest activity, and the pursuit of independence was the moral purpose of life. Naturally, she read a lot of Ayn Rand. She was, Avery thought now with a start, not unlike Charlie. It was Freja who had introduced Avery to heroin—*horse,* she called it with cool insouciance, insisting it wasn't truly addictive unless injected. Given her commitment to radical self-determination, it wasn't all that surprising that Freja left before graduating to join an anarchic, nonhierarchical, consensus-driven community in Northern California, though, with her ethos of independence above all, Avery imagined she might struggle with the consensus part. The group lived on the empty ranch outside of San Francisco owned by one of the founding members' grandparents, a trust fund kid not quite anarchic enough to believe in abolishing inheritance, who kept Freja hooked to a steady supply of downers. Drug dependency, it turned out, was an effective suppressor of independence.

Salt and pepper, everyone called them, for the way Freja's white-blond hair looked next to Avery's black bob, but also because they were inseparable. They belonged together. Freja was the first person

Avery truly loved outside of her family, the first woman she'd ever slept with, the first person to give her an orgasm. They were in the tiny furnished bedroom Freja rented near campus from an elderly couple she'd met through the Swedish Church's housing board. The room had been their daughter's—since either married or dead, Avery had never confirmed which—and was covered in crochet, china dolls, and Virgin Mary memorabilia.

The first time Freja had disappeared beneath the bedcovers to kiss Avery's sex, Avery had looked up to see a portrait of Mary smiling down at her. Time melted and slowed; little waves of pleasure lapped and pooled in her like warm rock pools. It felt so good, so right. Freja's mouth soft and insistent as the sea's waves, a sensation inside her like light on water. Not at all like with the boys before. Above her, the Virgin Mary smiled down, and, staring up into her benevolent gray eyes, Avery had orgasmed powerfully for the first time. She'd maintained a secret soft spot for the Mother of God ever since.

Avery liked the effects of heroin, but it was Freja she really got high on. After Freja left for California, Avery went through one of the worst withdrawals of her life. She missed everything about her: the silky blond hairs on her shins, her salty-sweet taste, her loud, coarse laugh, her way of adding a questioning *no* to statements, as if both inviting and daring Avery to contradict her. *Too much sunshine is bad for critical thinking, no? Let's make love in the library, then get ice cream, no?* Avery waited until after she graduated and her sisters had all left home, aching with longing all the while, then moved west to follow her. They'd been living on the ranch together for a few months, aimless and increasingly strung out, when one of the other commune members climbed through their bedroom window and raped Freja while Avery slept next to her in drug-stupefied unconsciousness. The next day when Freja told the group, the mostly male members informed her that rape was a *choice;* she had the agency to view the experience as consensual if only she would exercise it.

The two of them fled to San Francisco, slept on the streets or in motels when Freja's parents sent money, and stole everything else they needed. They were both too thin, afflicted by head lice, thrush, dry skin, and intermittent withdrawals, but they were still salt and pepper, Avery believed, still made for each other. Then, Freja overdosed. She survived, but her parents, tall and blond, arrived at the San Francisco General Hospital looking like Norse gods, picked her up, and took her back to Sweden without saying a word to Avery. It was Nicky she called from the hospital pay phone, Nicky who used up all her air miles to book her a flight home, though Avery wouldn't show up to thank her in person for another month. Her pride would not allow her to be seen in that state by any of her sisters, so she went to the free detox straight from the airport, back when it was still possible to show up unannounced and stay for twenty-eight days. She never heard from Freja again but, with time, she stopped trying to reach her and was relieved. That love had been a type of madness and, just like the second step in AA says, she needed to be restored to sanity.

But now, standing in front of Charlie's home, that old insanity was back. What was it in her that loved a wildfire? It was pointless to pretend to herself that she wasn't going in after coming all this way. The torturing herself before, that was part of the process. She couldn't even self-sabotage in a spontaneous way. Hedonism, she was discovering, didn't really work when you were sober, grieving, and thirty-three. The address he had given her was for a modest redbrick terraced house in the heart of Willesden Green. He probably had roommates, she thought grimly, the kind of bathroom with too many people's shampoos cluttering the edge of the bath. Avery walked up the short narrow path to the front door, which was painted a jaunty green, and raised the knocker. Her hand was shaking. She stared at it; she was, she realized, trembling all over. She could stop this right now, she reminded herself, she could turn around and go home. But she knew she wouldn't; she felt too alive.

Charlie opened the door in a pair of black track pants and no shirt. The muscles in his shoulders and arms rippled as he opened the door. Avery almost laughed. He was dressed the part, at least. She walked through the doorway and kissed him. His chest under her hands felt like something pulled taut and ready, not soft with the give of flesh she was used to. She kissed his chest and ran her tongue over his stomach, dropping to her knees right there in the hallway. It was like licking marble. Sensational.

"Not here," he said, laughing as he pulled her up.

Now she had decided to do this, she was feeling high on her own recklessness. It would almost be a relief to get caught. Only something outside of herself could stop her now. But the house was quiet. Avery followed him up the narrow staircase, glancing into the small living room as she went. She saw a faded floral sofa, a mantelpiece filled with pictures of smiling faces. Charlie as a little boy in glasses and a tie. A teenage girl in a graduation robe. A black-and-white photo of a beautiful woman, probably his mother, in a long white wedding dress next to a stiff-backed man in a three-piece suit. In his bedroom, books were everywhere, piled on the small dresser and stacked against the walls. The gray sheets on his low twin bed were meticulously folded and pulled stiff like in a hotel.

"You have a single bed," she said.

He smiled.

"It's my parents' place."

Avery dropped her bag to the floor, slipped off her shoes.

"Of course it is."

"Hey, London rents ain't cheap, man."

"I'm not going to have to meet your mother, am I?"

"She's out with her church group and Dad's at work," he said. "So you'll just have to make do with me."

"You never mentioned your dad before," said Avery.

"Not much to say. He's just a solid, nice man."

"Like you?"

It could have been a statement, but it was a question.

Charlie gave a slow, sly smile.

"I don't think you came here to talk about my family," he said.

He deftly unwound Avery from her wrap dress until she was standing in just her black cotton thong. His eyes widened as he took her in. She had a slim snake coiled around one arm, its daggered tongue licking her elbow. A small starling nestled under each collarbone.

"Nice ink," he said.

Avery shrugged.

"Past life."

"How many do you have?"

She gave him a mischievous look.

"You'll have to find them."

He pressed her onto the twin mattress and crept his fingers over her body in a tender excavation, checking the soles of her feet, her inner thighs, under each breast. He found the little boat riding the waves of her rib cage, the face drawn in one line like a Matisse sketch on her inner arm, the anarchy symbol on her shoulder blade she'd let Freja give her with a stick-and-poke needle while high. Across her heart she had three small letters: BNL. He traced them with his finger.

"My sisters," she said.

He nodded wordlessly.

"There's just one more," she said.

He sat back on his heels.

"I give up," he said.

She pulled down her bottom lip to reveal a four-leaf clover inked into the pink flesh of her inner mouth.

"You're full of surprises," he said.

"Like an Easter egg?"

He climbed onto the bed, laying the length of his body on top of her.

"Not any Easter egg I ever had."

Avery closed her eyes as Charlie slipped his hand into her underwear. Eight years with Chiti and they still had sex, but she had to *choose* to get turned on. It wasn't instinctive anymore, the way it had been at the beginning, a carnal impulse impossible to ignore or deny. These days, an internal alarm would go off in one of them that it had been too long, and they would decide to have sex. It was still enjoyable, but it felt like maintenance as opposed to lust. This was different. Her body acted without thought, without instruction.

"Wow," he said.

He pulled his hand from between her legs and his fingers were slick with her wetness.

"Sorry," she whispered, though she wasn't sure why. It felt excessive, somehow, evidence of something too much in her.

"No, I love it, I love it," he murmured.

And then he was on his knees, pulling down her underwear, and his mouth was on her, his hot breath, his tongue. She pulled him back up.

"Not that." She reached between his legs. "*This.*"

He freed himself from his sweatpants in one movement and she realized he was not wearing any underwear. He stroked himself with one hand and sank a finger back into her with the other.

"You sure?" he asked, his hands moving in tandem, one on him, one in her.

Avery nodded, closing her eyes. He braced himself over her, then pushed the length of himself inside of her in one long thrust. She gasped. How long had it been since she'd felt this? Ten years? More? She had never slept with a man sober. Charlie began to move in and out slowly and she heard herself making noises that weren't familiar at all, little animal moans and whines. He seemed to be touching the deepest part of her. As she whimpered, he cupped her head in his hands and looked at her. His face above her was utterly defenseless.

"I'm not hurting you?" he asked.

She shook her head.

"No."

"You don't want me to stop?"

"*No.*"

She squeezed her eyes shut again and pushed her mouth up onto his. She breathed his breath. He tasted vaguely sweet, like apple juice. Then he was moving inside of her again, deep rhythmic strokes through the center of her. She was sweating and so was he, their chests slipping against each other. He pushed her hair from her damp temples and kissed her there. She burrowed her face into the heat of his neck. She didn't think about anything except the feel of him. It was the not-thinking she loved most, the not-thinking that she never wanted to end.

"I'm close," he said eventually.

"Wait for me."

She grabbed handfuls of his buttocks and pulled him into her, thrusting him deeper and deeper in a succession of sharp, quick pumps. Then she squeezed a hand between her pelvis and his so she could touch herself as he moved inside of her. With a great throbbing wave, she came. She ached and ached with it. As the wave subsided, she felt the involuntary release and heard a soft sigh as he emptied himself inside of her. Avery's eyes rolled back in her head. There it was, that familiar sensation, unbidden yet unforgotten, of pleasure locked in consort with pain. Just like plunging down the piston of a syringe.

AFTERWARD, THEY LAY SIDE BY side, their backs against the wall, their legs hanging over the narrow bed. He leaned over to scoop up his crumpled sweatpants and draped them over his crotch with a self-conscious gesture that surprised her. She looked down to see his semen leaking out of her. It formed a wet, dark patch on the pale gray duvet between her legs.

"Shit," she said. "Sorry."

"Here."

He grabbed the leg of his sweatpants and held it to her as though stemming the flow of blood from a wound.

"Thanks," she said, wiping herself roughly with the fabric.

"Are you . . . on some kind of birth control?"

She glanced at him.

"Why is it that men only ever ask that *after* they've come inside you?"

Charlie ducked his head with embarrassment.

"Don't worry," she said. "I'll take care of it."

"I'm sorry I didn't ask," he said. "Let me know if I can pay for—"

"No, absolutely *not*," Avery said.

She stood up and pulled on her underwear, then began wrapping herself back up in her dress. She was struggling to find the little hole the sash went through to close the thing.

"I'm the one who should be apologizing," she said in a rush. "You're a newcomer and I'm—"

Charlie stood up and pulled on his sweatpants, clearly unperturbed that they had just been used to soak up his cum. He stepped toward her and took the sash from her hand, deftly weaving it through the slit in the fabric at her waist, then tying it in a bow with the other end.

"Look, I have three months but I'm not three months old. I'm twenty-seven, man."

Avery looked up at his face. Nicky's age. He was Nicky's age.

"Twenty-seven is young," she said softly.

"It doesn't feel it."

"It's just—it's your first year in the program. You'll see, it's a vulnerable time."

"I know, I know. But I've already changed a lot."

Charlie went over to a pair of jeans slung over his desk chair and pulled a pack of cigarettes and his silver Zippo from the back pocket. He opened his window and motioned for her to join him.

"When did you start smoking?" she asked, accepting the cigarette he offered her.

"When I was twelve. I smoked my first blunt and my first cigarette in the same day with my older cousin. I just wanted to be like him."

"Where's your cousin now?"

"He works in the City, got a wife who's a model and twins on the way. Turns out I was the bad influence. What about you?"

"Fourteen, I think. I was in Central Park walking home from school and bummed it off a Japanese businessman. I smoked it too quickly and promptly threw up in a bush. I promised myself never again."

"Yeah, I'm familiar with that tune. Never again, never again . . ."

Avery smiled sadly. She was telling herself that right now.

"You know a joke my sponsor told me?" Charlie asked. "An alcoholic will steal your wallet, but an addict will steal it *and* help you look for it. That's how I know I'm definitely an addict as well, because I swear to god, I've fucking done that. I've lied so much I didn't even know I was lying anymore."

Honesty? What did Avery know about honesty? She leaned her head against the window frame. A warm breeze paraded in.

"Now would probably not be a great time to tell you I'm married," she said.

"I know," he said.

She looked over at him in surprise.

"To a woman," she added.

"I know," he said.

"How?"

"I looked you up too. You had a wedding registry. Your wife has a really beautiful name. I can't remember it now."

"Chitrita," said Avery softly. "I could be divorced."

Charlie nodded.

"You could."

"But I'm not."

"Okay."

"And it doesn't matter to you either way?"

"Monogamy, fidelity, heterosexuality . . . These aren't words I put a lot of store in."

"Right," nodded Avery. "Because you're an amoral egoist."

"Exactly."

"Well, that's convenient for you, but, sadly, those words do mean something to me."

Charlie shifted so he was facing her in the window.

"The truth is, I'm not trying to get into anything heavy right now. You seem like a smart, cool person who's going through some shit. If you want to use me to feel better in the moment, I've got no complaints. I've been with men. I've been with women. Married, not married . . . I'm just not going to feel bad about something because someone else told me I should. I decide what feels good for me."

"Because you're free," she said.

"Exactly."

"Well, thank you for letting me use you."

Charlie grinned.

"Anytime. You're cool, you know? You're real."

"You're real too." She smiled self-consciously. "Whatever that means."

He glanced around his bedroom.

"Now all I need is my own flat and a bigger bed."

Avery laughed and looked out the window at the parched lawn of the garden below. A dilapidated football net stood at one end, a beautiful bush of frothy-headed hydrangea at the other. Somewhere through an open window she could hear an audience laughing on TV.

"You know what I think really makes me an addict?" she asked. "It's not how many drugs I took or how much I drank. It's not even the lying."

"What?"

She inhaled so deeply that her lungs burned.

"I find what gives me pleasure and I do it until it gives me pain," she said. "Every time."

Charlie looked at her with his funny half smile.

"Yeah, but how else would you know when to stop?"

## CHAPTER SEVEN

# Lucky

LUCKY HAD BEEN HUNGOVER FOR TWO DAYS, WHICH WAS A NEW REC-
ord for her. Saturday, she'd spent almost entirely in bed, waking up to
find first tea and toast, then plain pasta and paracetamol, and finally
soup and crackers placed on the nightstand by either Avery or Chiti.
Sunday had brought the inevitable blowup with Avery, whose uni-
verse of anal domesticity was not built to withstand the cannonball
intrusion of a freewheeling Lucky. Avery and Lucky had fought
plenty in their lives, but neither ever held a grudge. Quick to anger,
quick to forgive, that was their way. So Lucky had been surprised
when Avery had not returned until late that evening, heading straight
to her bedroom without a word while she and Chiti sat downstairs
watching a movie. Lucky had turned to catch Avery's retreating figure slipping silently up the stairs and felt, for the first time, that she
did not know her sister as well as she thought.

On Monday morning, a still reticent Avery left for work and Chiti
disappeared into her home office to see clients, so Lucky was left to

herself. Her body no longer felt like a pillowcase that had been filled with rocks and broken glass, then put in the tumble dryer, but she didn't feel great. It had been one of those contradictory comedowns that never let her settle in one place for long; she was lethargic and jumpy, chilled but sweaty, intermittently panicked by and numb to everything around her. She spent the morning watching cartoons on her laptop in bed and smoking the last of the weed she had managed to hide in her underwear on the Eurostar.

Around lunchtime, Lucky checked her phone for the first time in forty-eight hours. The screen, she saw, was cracked but still usable. She had been hoping for an apology text from Avery, but there was only a missed call and voicemail from Bonnie, a message in French from Sabina her brain could not bring itself to translate, and a flurry of texts from Troll Doll she didn't bother to read. Avery had probably gotten to Bonnie first, Lucky realized, with a sinking feeling. At least Bonnie could be relied upon not to yell at her, though her fumbling concern was often more distressing. In her inbox was an email from her agent from two days ago. She saw the subject line "We need to talk" and deleted it unopened, then went back to Bonnie's voicemail. She pressed the Play button and brought the phone to her ear.

*Hey, Lucky, just, um, checking in on you. Avery said you had a bit of a rough night. I'm here if you want to talk about it . . . or not talk. Whichever.* A pause, in which Lucky could feel her sister's discomfort. She was not talkative at the best of times, but a voicemail, essentially an enforced monologue, was, for Bonnie, the human equivalent of putting a bear in a tutu and making it dance. *Anyway . . . I'm in New York, which Avery probably told you. It's weird to be here without you. It would be great to have you here, actually, but no pressure . . . Oh, and I'm training at Golden Ring again. I figure I'll stay here 'til Mom and Dad sell the place, then decide what to do. I haven't looked at Nicky's stuff yet, but I'll keep anything for you that you want. Unless you want to come get it yourself? Please? But, yeah, like I said, no pressure . . . That's all, I guess. Call me back.*

Lucky sat down on the unmade bed, then pressed Play again. So Bonnie was boxing again, and here in London, Avery was having a baby. Everyone was moving forward with their lives except her. But Bonnie wanted her there, that much was obvious. Her sister almost never asked her for anything, but she had asked her to come (*no pressure!*) twice in one message. And it wasn't as if Avery wanted her here.

With the sudden surge of relief that always followed the possibility of escape, Lucky checked her airline app on her cracked phone. She had thousands of air miles saved up from her years of traveling, and there was a seat on a flight leaving tomorrow afternoon. She tapped quickly through the checkout process, then forwarded her flight details to Bonnie with simply a smiley face and "xx" in the body of the email. Better not to get into everything that had happened here until she was physically back with Bonnie, by far her more understanding sister. That gave her just over twenty-four hours left in London, a city that clearly did not have a great influence on her. It would be good to get out of here, she thought, and show Avery that she wasn't going to hang around waiting for forgiveness like a kicked dog. That would wake her eldest sister up. If there was one thing Lucky was a master at, it was leaving.

Lucky wandered downstairs into the kitchen, but she was not hungry. She wished she'd brought her guitar, but she'd left it in Paris. For the first time, she worried vaguely about what was to come next. Sure, she would go to New York to help Bonnie with the apartment, but then what? She knew she didn't want to model anymore, but at least it was something to *do*. That was the thing people didn't talk about, how much of life was just filling time. Her years had been broken into a particular set of seasons for so long, the twice-yearly loop around New York, London, Milan, Paris, then Haute Couture Week every January and July, photo shoots in lofts in New York, in parks in Berlin, at the top of skyscrapers in Hong Kong, on the beaches of Bali. For so many years she had been too busy, too jet-lagged, or too high to feel much of anything. Now, just when she wanted to feel the least, she had nothing to distract her.

She opened the fridge door, then shut it again with a wave of nausea. The worst part was the flashes of memory from Friday night. Fragments of scenes illuminated like matches struck then snuffed back out. She was dancing in the twin headlights of a taxi—or was she falling? Hands were grabbing at her feathered chest. She was like a bird being plucked. She was pushing the driver off her, ignoring his shouts, oozing away from him to slide up the steps like a backward slinky, and crumpling at Avery's door.

Lucky swung open the kitchen's double French doors and stepped into the garden. It was a beautiful, bright day. She lit a cigarette and exhaled. *Nicky's baby.* That was the part of the night that still lay just out of reach. Somebody had called her Nicky's baby. A person at that party had known Nicky, and Lucky wouldn't be able to stop thinking about it until she found out who. She picked up her phone and called Troll Doll, who answered on the second ring.

"Oh my *gawsh,* I thought you were dead," she said. "Look, sorry about those texts I sent you, yah? I was off my face."

"No worries," said Lucky.

"I was *cringing* the next day."

"Seriously, you're all good," said Lucky. "I've forgotten them."

This was sort of true since she had never bothered to read them. Troll Doll exhaled with relief.

"Legend. So, when do you leave? Can I see you again?"

"I'm gonna head to New York soon. Things are . . . weird with my sister."

"The lawyer one?"

"Yeah."

"Why don't you come stay with me? I'd love that!"

Lucky inhaled and rolled her eyes. She tried her best to sound polite.

"I wouldn't want to put you out."

"You wouldn't be putting me out! You'd be putting me *in,* like, heaven."

Lucky chose to ignore this.

"Look, I wanted to ask you, that place we went the other night? Do you have the address?"

"Why? You're not seriously thinking of going *back* there, are you? It's, like, an actual sex club, you know."

"I lost something and wanted to check if it's there."

"Your T-shirt? I have it! I actually slept in it last night, how sad is that?" She made a snorting sound of humiliation or, perhaps, hope. "Flopsy says you can keep her feather boa by the way."

"I don't care about the shirt. I'm looking for . . . something else."

"The drugs? I'm pretty sure you did them all, babe."

"Can you just tell me the address?"

Troll Doll hummed down the phone.

"If I give it to you, will you come see me after?"

Lucky stayed silent until she heard Troll Doll eject a little sigh of defeat.

"I'll text it to you now."

"Thanks, I appreciate it."

"I swear," Troll Doll said sadly. "You're worse than any boy, Lucky."


LUCKY SPENT THE AFTERNOON AT a dark, wood-paneled pub tucked on one of the winding streets near Avery's. Hampstead was so unrelentingly quaint it was hard not to be charmed by it. Especially when the sun was shining and would continue doing so until after nine P.M., especially when the ivy-trellised pub looked like something out of an eighteenth-century storybook, especially when there was a youngish and not-bad-looking bartender (he was in school for figurative painting, he assured her) giving her free pints in exchange, seemingly, for the pleasure of being able to cast his trained eye upon her. Lucky spent a cheerful handful of hours drinking and playing darts for cigarettes with a gaggle of sunburned older British men, all while being gazed at longingly by the starstruck bartender. She stepped outside for a smoke and checked her phone. Another message from her agent. Buoyed by the beers and feeling the liquid impenetrability that came from riding the first wave of a new drunk, she deleted it without reading it. For the first time since she was fifteen, she was out of a job. To celebrate, she went back inside for another round.

By the time she left the pub, she had won five cigarettes and was on a first-name basis with a throng of London's finest male retirees, all of whom agreed that having a job was a complete waste of time. She took the bus all the way to the club to kill time, a journey that took the better part of two hours. The novelty of riding on the top of a double-decker was not lost on her, especially as she had managed to nab the prized pair of seats at the very front, sprawling her long legs across both seats to ward off any potential neighbors. From this vantage, she could watch London through the huge plexiglass window unfolding beneath its leafy canopy of trees. Unlike in New York, in which heat was considered a right from May to September, every warm summer day in London felt special, fleeting. Women in the bright dresses they'd been waiting all year to wear flitted in and out of shops, barefoot men kicked soccer balls around huge green parks, old men in short sleeves relaxed outside of cafés, hookah pipes in hand. Lucky watched it all from her perch with a gentle remove only possible for her when several pints deep. She was perfectly drunk, not yet blacked out, but no longer fully in time and space. The best word she could think of for this state was *untethered;* she was a balloon slipping lightly out of the world's grasping hand.

As the bus meandered through the sun-dappled streets, she sat back and thought of Avery. Her sister was a fool for giving all this up to live full-time in reality. Avery had taken it too far by getting hooked on heroin, that was her mistake. She should have stuck with the classics: booze, weed, coke, pills, and the occasional psychedelic. Like Lucky, who knew what she was doing. She could handle her shit, she thought with drunken satisfaction, which meant, unlike Avery, she would never have to stop. A warm breeze curled from the fanning bus doors up to the top deck. The bustle of the city, of life in general, felt very far below. Like a bird safe in its nest, Lucky propped her sunglasses on her nose, tucked her chin to her chest, and slipped away.

SHE WAS NOT DREAMING SO much as remembering. The shoot was at a studio downtown by the Hudson River, which she liked because it had pinball machines in the hallway she could play on in her breaks between shots. She was better at pinball than modeling, she thought.

That day was particularly bad because she had to do lines. She was reading from a sheet of paper held behind the camera by the director's assistant, but she kept fucking up. She was bad at reading aloud and always avoided it at school, not because she couldn't read, but because she'd get too nervous and forget to breathe.

*All right, let's try it again,* said the photographer. *Take your time.*

But the more self-conscious she grew, the harder it was to catch her breath. The lights were too hot, and she could feel beads of sweat coalescing on her upper lip. That couldn't look good. She wanted to wipe her face on her sleeve but she was wearing silk and that probably wasn't allowed either. She wished she could get everyone to blink simultaneously, just give her one second to herself to at least dry her face off, but everyone's eyes stayed on her. It never occurred to her that she could ask for a break. She was trying to discreetly blot her face with the back of her hand when she heard snickers from two of the stylists by the racks. She glanced over to see them exchange a look that said, *Surprise, surprise, a model who can't read.* It wasn't the first time she'd caught sight of the contempt for her just beneath the surface of other women, nor would it be the last. She was five foot ten, one hundred and twelve pounds, and fifteen years old. She was the beauty standard these women were being held to and, whether consciously or not, they hated her for it. *Join the club,* she wanted to tell them. She hated herself too.

The photographer gave her an appraising look, then to her relief smiled kindly at her. He had long sandy hair and the insouciantly cheerful air of someone raised around an abundance of sunshine and money. He also, Lucky had been breathlessly informed by the makeup artist, had recently started dating a household-name supermodel. Lucky understood that he was very important and had been told multiple times by her agency how fortunate she was to be chosen by him in the very first year of her career. He stepped away from the camera and gave her another encouraging smile.

*You know what?* he said. *We'll just shoot some stills. In fact, why don't we clear the set for a second? Just me, you, and my assistant, Jared, here.*

Lucky nodded with relief and watched as hair, makeup, styling, and various crew began to trickle off set to wait in the craft services area, where they would all undoubtedly talk about her.

*Can I just?* said one of the makeup artists, quickly darting forward to blot her face and dust it with a fine powder. *Good luck,* she whispered without enthusiasm, then disappeared too.

The photographer picked up his camera and gave her a cheerful wink.

*All right, my love,* he said. *Let's have you standing.*

He circled around her, clicking away, and Lucky moved with him instinctively. The truth was, she was a natural. When Lucky saw photos of herself after the fact, she was always amazed by how different she appeared compared to how she had felt taking them. She looked mature and completely at home in herself. Like a woman.

*You're doing great, Lucy,* said the photographer.

*It's Lucky,* she whispered. Then added automatically, *Sorry.*

*Lucky, of course.* He made a show of slapping his forehead. *That's a perfect name for you. How old are you, Lucky?*

*Fifteen,* she said, then quickly returned her face to a look of blank inscrutability.

*Wow, I would have guessed older by the way you carry yourself. You must have an old soul, Lucky.*

Lucky was pretty sure her soul was also fifteen, but she nodded anyway. They kept shooting for a while, the photographer's face obscured behind his camera, Lucky focusing on looking sexy but a little scared, as she'd been taught, when he stopped suddenly. She was afraid he was going to tell her it wasn't working and send her home, but instead he ran a hand through his hair and grinned.

*Okay, I want to try something.* He handed the camera to his assistant without taking his eyes off her. *Let's try the Pentax with black and white.* He beckoned her closer. *Do you mind kneeling?*

She hesitated and the photographer motioned to his assistant.

*Sorry, Lucky, I should have thought. Could you grab her something, Jared? A cushion or something?*

The assistant grabbed a small towel from the makeup chair and folded it, placing it on the ground before her. It provided only the tiniest amount of padding between her shins and the concrete floor, but she knelt anyway.

*That looks great, Lucky.* He snapped a few shots. He was saying her name too much, she thought, probably to compensate for having gotten it wrong earlier. She sensed he wanted her to feel comfortable, so she tried her best to give off the impression that she was.

*Now, Lucky, can you open your mouth?*

His voice didn't change; he delivered this instruction with the same cheerful directness that he'd asked Jared to swap the cameras. She hesitated again, then parted her lips ever so slightly.

*That's perfect. A little wider.*

He stepped toward her and very gently slipped his thumb into her mouth. Above her, she heard the camera click. His thumb tasted like cigarettes, but there was an earthiness, too, like vegetable root, mixed with an unpleasant metallic tang. Without pulling her head away, she darted her eyes to the assistant, Jared, but his face remained impassive, bored even. She blinked, then opened them again to glance at the photographer's crotch, which was now eye level with her. She had never seen a penis before, but, somehow, she knew to check if he had an erection. Upon seeing that he didn't, she felt a dizzying surge of relief. This must be part of the job then.

*Eyes up here,* he murmured.

Only then did his voice drop and take on a husky quality, as if sharing a secret with her. He clicked away, pushing his thumb very slowly in and out of her mouth. She kept her jaw stiff and her mouth wide, tucking her tongue beneath her teeth, so as little of her as possible would touch his skin. In the years afterward she would dream of chomping down on that thumb, locking her jaw like a pit bull and biting through the skin until she hit bone, until he screamed for release. Instead, she lifted her eyes. He looked down at her and smiled.

*You're a natural, Lucky. Now can you close your lips and suck?*

LUCKY SNAPPED AWAKE WITH A jolt of panic. For a sickening moment, she had no sense of where she was. A bus? But where? She patted down her body. Wallet, phone, keys, cigarettes, it was all still there. She looked out of the window. Still light. She saw with relief that the bus was passing a tube station not far from the address she'd been given. Lucky exhaled. She'd let her guard down again, but she was safe. On the seat across from her, an older woman in a loose lilac blouse was smiling at her.

"You was having a little kip," said the woman. "Don't worry, I had my eye on you. Would have woken you up before I got off."

"Thank you," croaked Lucky.

She looked at the woman, whose softly creased eyes were watching her with benign interest. Lucky was embarrassed to find tears pricking her own. Her sunglasses had slipped into her lap during sleep; she pushed them back onto her face and swung herself to standing. It must be almost her stop and she needed to keep moving.

"Stay safe, dear," called the woman as Lucky disappeared down the stairs.

Lucky did have some memory of the club from Friday, but it was vague. The townhouse at the address given to her was a narrow, unassuming building on a quiet street. Wide black-and-white-tiled stairs led to its front door. Lucky checked for a name or business written beneath the brass doorbell, found none, then pressed it anyway. It emitted a shrill, high ring like a seagull's squawk. She waited. Nothing. She stepped back and tried to peer through the windows, but the heavy red curtains were all pulled shut. Lucky stood on the steps for several minutes, hoping someone would come.

When it became clear no one would, she wandered around to the other side of the building, where there was a small side alley. There, standing between large plastic-wrapped crates of drink deliveries, was a woman. She looked somewhat disheveled in a pair of battered Ugg boots and denim cutoff shorts, a pale pink T-shirt with a diamanté heart missing a few of its jewels at the center. Her face, however, was another story. It was skillfully made-up, her skin powdered an ivory white, red glittery lips like bejeweled ruby slippers, and huge sweeping eyelashes with two red feathers at the corner of each eye. On her head was a nude stocking the same color as her skin. She looked like a painted china doll whose hair had not yet been attached. Lucky advanced tentatively toward her. The woman watched her approach warily.

"Can I 'elp you?"

"Um . . . I don't know. I'm looking for someone."

The woman raised her penciled eyebrow.

"You looking to dance?"

Lucky shook her head. The woman exhaled a plume of smoke.

"Shame."

"A guy who does security here," Lucky clarified. "At least, I think he does."

The woman took a drag of her cigarette, which was scarred red with lipstick at the tip. She stared at Lucky wordlessly, then clearly decided she was worth answering.

"So what's he look like? The chap you're looking for."

Lucky closed her eyes and tried to conjure the image of the man she'd seen on Friday night. She saw a figure like a mountain, colossal, eclipsing the lights above them.

"Big," she said.

The woman laughed to herself.

"You'd be looking for BFG. You're lucky he comes in early. You want me to get him for you?"

"If you could, yeah."

But she made no suggestion of leaving, so Lucky simply waited. The woman carried on smoking, eyes flicking up and down Lucky appraisingly. Lucky looked at her feet awkwardly. What was she doing here? What did she think she was going to find? She was just killing time, she supposed. Killing time instead of killing herself. She shook the thought away immediately. What was wrong with her? Of course she wasn't going to kill herself. She was just hungover.

"You a model?" the woman asked eventually. "You look like one."

Lucky thought about this.

"Used to be."

"You're so thin," said the woman matter-of-factly.

Lucky nodded. There was nothing much to say to this. She was.

"You got anorexia? All you models do, right? *Nothing tastes as good as skinny feels.* Didn't Kate Moss say that?" She sniffed. "The cow."

"It's a genetics thing," said Lucky, giving the answer she always gave. "And Kate Moss did say that, but she was quoting someone else."

"Is that right?"

The woman looked at her, sniffed again, and spat between her feet.

"Also, I don't eat much, and I do a lot of drugs," said Lucky. "So there's that."

The woman threw her head back and cackled with delight. Lucky smiled shyly.

"I'd have died to be a model, growing up," said the woman.

Lucky smiled ruefully.

"You didn't miss much."

Another raise of the arched eyebrow.

"Missed out on looking like you; I wouldn't have minded that."

Lucky squirmed. All her life she'd hated compliments. Since other women often resented her on sight, she did her best to make herself nonthreatening. This was usually by not saying much or finding a way to make fun of herself. Amazingly, the only people she had never worried about being jealous of her looks were her sisters. They loved her too much to hold it against her.

"You have better boobs," Lucky offered.

The dancer cackled again.

"That's true. Bet you can't do this."

She raised her pink T-shirt to reveal two pert, creamy breasts. The nipples had been painted a scarlet red, like bull's-eyes, and her stomach was round and soft. She began whistling the tune to "We Will Rock You" through her teeth while lifting one breast at a time. Her left breast twitched, then right until—on *rock you*—both jumped up and down in unison. Lucky's mouth hung slightly open.

"Nope," she said, once the woman had completed several rounds of the chorus. "Can't do that."

The dancer preened, clearly pleased with herself.

"Didn't think so. All right, I'll go get BFG for you, hun."

She dropped her cigarette, ground it under her fleeced boot, and blew Lucky a kiss, disappearing through the back door. A few minutes later, it sprang open again. A colossal man was making his way out, dipping his huge bald head under the doorframe to avoid collision. He was wearing a loose black leather waistcoat that several cows must have been sacrificed to make. Around his thick neck hung a silver chain with a chunky skull pendant hanging off it. He looked at her and smiled.

"You forget something, love?"

Lucky cleared her throat.

"Do you remember me? I was here on Friday."

He barked a laugh.

"You mean the *Toffs Gone Wild* party? Sorry, sweetheart, there were too many to keep track of. What you looking for though? I can check the back to see if it's there."

Lucky felt like an idiot. What *was* she looking for? But she had come all this way and she had to at least try.

"You said something to me," she said. "You don't remember?"

BFG narrowed his eyes at her and took a wary step back.

"I've never made a pass at a patron," he said. "Whoever you're thinking of, it weren't me."

"No, no." Lucky waved her hands to dispel this line of thought. "You said something about my sister Nicky. About me . . ." She was cringing, but she had to say it. "Always being her baby," she said quietly.

BFG tilted his head to the side like a large bird and eyed her with curiosity.

"I don't know a Nicky," he said. "She was at the party too?"

Lucky shook her head. She was not being very clear, she could see.

"She's dead," she said simply.

BFG looked aghast.

"She died after the *party*?"

"No, she died last year of an overdose. I thought . . . I just thought you said you knew her."

He seemed to relax at this, nodding his head in understanding.

"Ah. Sorry to hear that. Terrible thing, drugs. Enough to put you right off 'em."

Lucky nodded her head in a vague gesture of assent, though, of course, Nicky's death seemed to have had the opposite effect on her. Lucky had always been a hard partyer, but for the past year she had to admit it had taken on a death-defying edge that was new, even for her.

"Stick with booze, I always say," he added.

"So you *don't* know Nicky?" Lucky clarified.

BFG shook his head.

"Sorry, love. I know a Becky if that helps?"

Lucky looked at her feet. She was sure she had heard him say it. She felt as if she was going mad. Of course, she hadn't exactly been in a lucid state of mind. But it felt so real, like a message just for her, a sunbeam piercing through the mist. *Nicky's baby.* Could her unconscious have known she wanted a message from her sister so badly she hallucinated it? She must have been even more fucked-up that night than she thought. When she glanced back up, BFG was looking over her head thoughtfully. He was a man who spent his life looking over others' heads.

"People have a hard time talking about death," he said. "You find that? After my dad died, no one knew what to say."

"Yup," said Lucky. "It sucks."

She was wasting her time. BFG didn't know Nicky; no one here did. She'd been a fool to come.

"It wasn't a good moment for him, my dad," BFG continued, oblivious. "Imagine it was the same with your sister."

"Did he . . . with drugs?" asked Lucky.

"Nah, 'anged 'imself. Same thing, though, innit?"

Lucky looked away down the alley. She didn't want to argue with this man, but it was not the same thing. Nicky had been taking the painkillers in order to *live,* not die. BFG lit a cigarette and Lucky joined him, shaking one out from the pack she'd won at the pub. That already felt like a different day entirely. He proffered a lighter and Lucky leaned over the flame, their eyes meeting in a moment of pleasurable collusion.

"You have fun at the party, at least?" he asked.

Lucky was about to give one of her usual vague responses, then stopped herself.

"I got too fucked-up and I barely remember a thing," she said. "Except that I really upset my sister. The eldest one," she added. "Not Nicky."

The man tutted.

"That's bad, that is. You should watch it. We had a regular whose nose caved in from coke. Got one big nostril instead of two now, I'm not pissing you."

Lucky laughed in spite of herself.

"I'll be careful."

"You know why I think people do drugs?" BFG asked her suddenly.

Lucky made the rock-and-roll sign with her hands, then rolled her eyes.

"Because it's cool?" she said.

BFG snorted softly through his nose.

"I think they're trying to fall in love with life again," he said. "That's what I see in the club every night. All the sex and booze and coke and shit, it's not really about that stuff. It's people who have fallen out of love with life trying to get back to how they used to feel, you know?"

She looked up at him. BFG was still nodding slowly, lost in his own thoughts now. Was that what was happening to Lucky? Had she fallen out of love with life? She certainly didn't see much point doing the things others did to make their lives meaningful: working, marrying, having children, building a home. But she couldn't remember a time when she had. Could you fall out of love with life if you were never in love with it?

Once, a few years after Lucky started modeling, she and Nicky had hiked around the cliffs surrounding Lake Minnewaska together. From the forest along the ridge, they'd looked down upon the flat black surface of the water, reflecting the white clouds and green trees above like glass. In the very center, a tiny splashing dot was traversing the lake. Mesmerized, they looked closer to find it was a solitary swimmer. Her red swim cap bobbed just above the water as her arms sliced tiny white tears into the lake's surface. They sat side by side on a slab of rock, looking on like two watchful eagles, until finally the tiny, thrashing figure made her way to shore and pulled herself out, disappearing into the dense woods below. Afterward, Nicky had turned to Lucky.

*That's you,* she said. *You're the swimmer.*

Lucky shook her head and laughed.

*But I'm right here.*

*But down there,* she said. *That's how I see you.*

Nicky knew. No matter how many people Lucky surrounded herself with, part of her was always swimming alone through a wide, dark lake. The only time she ever felt that there was someone in the water with her was when she was with her sisters.

But Nicky was different. Nicky was always the first person to ask a question in the Q&A section of a talk because she couldn't bear for the person onstage to experience awkward silence after having made themselves vulnerable. She didn't need to have a drink to dance or make a speech at a wedding or go on a date like most people did. She threw herself into the center of things. Nicky took those drugs in order *not* to fall out of love with life. All she ever wanted was to stay. And now here was Lucky, alive when her sister was not, destroying herself. It struck her with sudden clarity that the best way to honor her sister would be to live life the way Nicky had wanted to, wide-awake and not numbing any part of it. But she didn't know how, and feared she never would, so she pushed the thought away.

She cleared her throat and looked back at BFG.

"Sorry about your dad," she said eventually.

"Ah." He waved his hand and returned from wherever his memories had taken him. "He was an old drunk."

Lucky smiled ruefully.

"Mine too."

He glanced down at her.

"That right?"

Lucky nodded.

"Love is a stranger, eh?" he said. He retrieved a penknife from his pocket and sliced open one of the plastic crates of drinks. He handed her a bottle of hard cider. "You want a drink for the road? It's on the house."

LUCKY CAME TO WITH HER face between Troll Doll's legs. Troll Doll's hands were clutching the back of her head, kneading her deeper into her surprisingly engorged clit, her thigh muscles squeezing Lucky's cheeks. Her mouth was filled with the briny taste of pussy. She remembered something a lover of hers in Paris, a French Caribbean model whose body had been the mold for a famous fragrance bottle, would say to her after he came. *I take my death in that pussy.* Lucky had laughed at the time, thinking it some error of translation, but now she understood. There was such a thing as death by pussy, and she was coming dangerously close to experiencing it. She yanked her head back and threw off the duvet cover, gasping for breath.

"I'm close," whined Troll Doll.

Lucky sucked in a large gulp of air.

"I'm dying."

Troll Doll took Lucky's hand and shoved it between her legs, using her fingers to furiously work her clit until, with a piercing scream reminiscent of foxes mating, she came. Lucky wiped her fingers on the bedcover and lay down next to the flushed and panting Troll Doll.

"That was . . ." Troll Doll sighed. "Heaven." She rolled over to face Lucky's profile, searching her face eagerly.

"You have any weed?" Lucky asked.

Troll Doll rolled her eyes.

"You're like a teenage boy," she said. She turned to pull open the drawer of the bedside table, producing a vape pen. "You'll be asking me if you can play video games next."

Lucky tucked one hand behind her head, then used the other to purse the pen between her lips. Troll Doll rested her head in the nook of Lucky's arm as she inhaled, stroking Lucky's bare stomach thoughtfully.

"I knew you'd come see me," Troll Doll said quietly. "I knew we had a connection."

"Mmm," murmured Lucky, watching the flume of vapor rise above her head.

Troll Doll kept stroking down and down until her hand was burrowed in Lucky's underwear. Very gently, Lucky reached down to remove it.

"I'm good," she said. "But thanks."

Troll Doll looked up at her.

"I want to," she said.

Lucky shook her head and took another toke. A silence passed between them and in it Lucky heard the echo of two words. *Nicky's baby.* She should let it go, she knew, chalk it up to drug-induced delusion, but something inside of her kept reaching to believe the message was real.

"Do you think the dead ever try to communicate with us?" she asked suddenly. "From, you know, wherever they go next?"

Troll Doll cocked her head and laughed.

"Okay, this is some *really* weird pillow talk, yah."

"But do you?" Lucky insisted.

Troll Doll rolled onto her back and giggled.

"I was *totally* into Wicca at school. We would do Ouija boards and try to speak to Princess Diana and stuff."

"Did it ever work?"

Troll Doll scoffed.

"Of course not! We'd attempt levitation too. You know . . ." She affected an exaggerated stage whisper. "*Light as a feather, stiff as a board, cold as ice, quiet as a barn owl* . . . All that nonsense. Anyway, why are you asking? You're not secretly all witchy woo, are you?"

Lucky frowned slightly.

"So, you don't believe we go somewhere then? After we die?"

Troll Doll propped herself up on her elbow and looked at her.

"If we did, wouldn't we know about it by now?" she said. "I can't believe people can still justify believing in heaven and hell. It's so . . . provincial."

If Lucky believed in anything resembling heaven, it was this: a square of chlorine-blue water in a wide, green field, her sisters lying beside her, heat stunned as lizards beneath a ripe, hot sun. It was their first real family holiday; after much begging and wheedling on their part, they had convinced their parents to rent a place upstate for a week in August. The house itself was dark and damp, but they didn't care; they spent all day by that bright square of incandescent blue. There were no trees to shade them, no umbrellas, and the old plastic deck chairs were terrifyingly temperamental, so their parents retreated to the porch or left for day trips around the area, leaving the four of them to enjoy the pool alone.

Each morning they filled a cooler with cans of Coke, potato chips, and ice pops, subsisting on these all day until the sun smeared along the horizon in a final frenzy of pink and gold and they were forced inside. They read voraciously, trading heat-curled paperbacks, bickering lightly over who got what next, who had dampened the pages beyond repair. After a little while, the heat would get to be too much and one of them would throw down her book and slide into the water, the others following behind like a gaggle of seals slipping from a rock.

Avery had taught them all to swim, but Nicky was the best swimmer of them all; she could swim three lengths of the pool without coming up for breath. Sometimes she would be underwater so long Lucky would grow nervous, watching her from the water's edge, but she always reappeared again, flinging fat beads of water like diamonds from her hair, gasping for breath. They'd stay in the water doing handstands and having tea parties along the slippery floor of the shallow end until they'd cooled off, then emerge to flop back onto the hot limestone perimeter, returning to soporific silence. They spent whole days that way, the sun baking them brown, as all around them the grass buzzed with bees, dragonflies, and cicadas, a thousand unknown forms of life.

*It's hot as heaven,* said Nicky, lazily swiping a hand through the air.

*You mean hell,* said Avery. *Hot as hell.*

Nicky glided her finger through the air as if she could unpick the stitches of the day and let it spill open.

*No, heaven is hot,* she said. *Like this.*


LUCKY STARED UP AT THE ceiling above her and Troll Doll as a passing car's headlights striped it with light.

"Hot as heaven," she murmured.

"What?" asked Troll Doll.

Lucky blinked and sat up. She had not meant to speak. Troll Doll gave a shrill laugh.

"Are you already high?" she asked. "Is that why you're getting all existential on me?"

Lucky swallowed thickly.

"Yeah, that's it," she said. "Ignore me."

Troll Doll's eyes brightened suddenly.

"You sure you don't want me to go down on you?" she asked.

Lucky shook her head.

"Sleep," she said. "That's what I want."

Troll Doll rested her head back on her chest with a little sigh. Lucky lay there with the weight of it pinning her to the mattress and stared above her. She could feel tears pricking her eyes as she pulled hard from the pen. She kept her gaze fixed on the air above her head for a long time, listening to Troll Doll's shallow snores until, thankfully, sleep pulled her under too.


LUCKY WAS AWAKENED BY A flash of light in the darkness. She looked up to see Troll Doll standing over her with her phone.

"What are you doing?" Lucky croaked.

Her voice was hoarse, her mouth brutally dry from the weed.

"Whoops, I didn't realize the flash was on." Troll Doll giggled. "Sorry."

"You were taking my picture?"

"You just looked so angelic sleeping like that. This is basically art."

"Delete that," said Lucky.

"Why?"

"Just delete it."

"What will you give me for it?" teased Troll Doll, holding her phone above her head.

Lucky leapt up and hooked her arms around Troll Doll's waist, toppling her to the mattress. Troll Doll's peals of laughter quickly turned to shrieks of alarm as Lucky shoved her down, pinching her wrists together. As her sisters had learned when they were younger, Lucky was wiry but surprisingly strong when provoked. She pinned the writhing Troll Doll beneath her with her knees and clawed the phone from her hands.

"That's *mine*," Troll Doll yelled.

With the phone in hand, Lucky jumped off the bed so Troll Doll could not grasp it back. She found the photo of herself, her pale face and bare chest eerily exposed in the harsh light of the flash, then pressed the delete icon. She went to the folder of erased photos and permanently deleted it there too. Troll Doll raised a hand to her flushed cheek, watching her sulkily.

"You scratched me," she said.

Lucky threw the phone onto the duvet next to her and began pulling on her jeans. Troll Doll's face hardened as she grabbed for the device, clutching it to her chest.

"You *hurt* me," she said.

Lucky cast around for her T-shirt and pulled it on.

"You're a fucking psycho, you know that?" Troll Doll said.

Lucky began lacing up her boots.

"Did you hear me?" she shouted. "Answer me!"

Lucky patted down her pockets. She couldn't find her cigarettes. No matter.

"You're, like, *deranged,*" said Troll Doll. "It was just a photo. You have your picture taken for a living, for fuck's sake!"

"Not anymore," muttered Lucky.

She grabbed the remainder of her stuff and walked out of the flat, slamming the door behind her. Lucky marched to the tube station, which was shuttered for the night. She'd forgotten that in London, the sleepiest of all capitals, the trains stopped running at midnight. She hailed a black cab on the King's Road and opened the door, but a memory of the taxi driver from Friday night hit her with a nauseating wave and she immediately waved it off again, backing away down the street. She checked the maps on her phone and zoomed out. It would take an hour and forty minutes to walk home. She stared at the blue circle on her screen, adrift in that unfamiliar patchwork of green and gray, and began walking.

IT WAS PAST TWO A.M. when Lucky let herself into the dark house in Hampstead. Through the living room, she saw Avery sitting at the dining table in a pool of yellow light, surrounded by piles of papers and several coffee mugs. She looked up as Lucky came in. She was wearing her tortoiseshell glasses, looking intelligent and exhausted.

"You're up late," said Lucky.

"Look who's talking," said Avery. "Where've you been?"

Lucky shrugged.

"Friend's."

"You seem to have friends wherever you go," said Avery.

Lucky frowned.

"It's a good thing," added Avery.

"What are you working on?"

"Prelitigation." She pushed her chair back in a gesture of defeat. "Very boring."

Lucky walked toward her and dropped to her knees. Without a word, she wrapped her arms around her sister's waist and laid her head in her lap. Avery's hands landed gently on her crown. They stroked her short hair, the velvety lobes of her ears, the nape of her neck.

"What's up, Lucky Lou?" she murmured.

Lucky lifted her head and looked up at her eldest sister. There were so many things she wanted to ask. *Why am I like this? Why are you? What is wrong with our family?*

"Remember our vacation upstate?" she asked instead.

Avery smiled at the memory.

"I got the worst sunburn," she said.

"You did?"

"Yeah, and Dad drove all over looking for fresh aloe vera for me."

Lucky frowned.

"I don't remember that."

"Mm–hmm. He brought that big leaf home and we made ice cubes out of it I'd melt on my shoulders."

"That doesn't sound like him."

Avery gave her head a gentle pat.

"You tend to recall the bad times with more alacrity."

Lucky scrunched her face at this. She knew that Avery and Bonnie remembered a time when their father inhabited more states than either catatonic or explosive. Maybe they'd gotten a different version of their father, one less drunk and more present to be a parent, but that didn't change the fact that by the time Lucky came along, he had pretty much given up. She thought about saying this, but it was pointless. If Avery needed to believe in him, that was her loss.

"Are you still mad at me?" she asked instead.

Avery shook her head.

"I was worried," she said. "It came out wrong. I should have handled it better."

"I'm sorry I scared you."

Avery kept stroking her head.

"You did but . . . I get it. Or maybe I don't and that's the problem. God knows I'm in no place to judge."

Lucky looked up at her and frowned.

"But you're, like, perfect."

Avery made a strangled noise that was not quite a laugh.

"You have no idea how far from perfect I am."

Lucky looked up at her sister's tired face. Momentarily, it occurred to her that there could be something going on with Avery that was bigger than their fight. She thought of what Chiti had said. *Sometimes your sister is like a medieval fortress.* But what could be happening? Avery never made mistakes, or at least she hadn't for a long time. That was Lucky's job in the family.

"Are you okay, Aves?" she asked. "With Chiti? And everything? You'd tell me if you weren't good, right?"

Avery's eyes shot to hers.

"Of course! Why? Did Chiti say something to you?"

Lucky was surprised by this, since Avery and Chiti had always seemed so unassailably in sync, but she tried not to show it.

"No," she said carefully. "I was just checking. Being a good sister, you know."

Avery shot her a relieved smile.

"You never have to worry about me," she said. "That's not your job."

Lucky frowned.

"I will if you want me to."

Avery shook her head.

"Just make sure you're keeping yourself safe, please." She reached over her head and gave a stiff stretch. "And I'm sorry we haven't had the chance to spend much time together. It's just a busy time of year for me."

"When's your slow time of year? I can come back then."

Avery gave her a worn-out look.

"When I find out, I'll tell you."

Lucky rested her chin on Avery's knee like a puppy and looked up at her.

"I'm gonna go to New York tomorrow," she said.

Avery blinked.

"So soon?"

"I thought I'd say goodbye to the apartment. And I figure Bonnie could use some help there."

"That's nice of you," said Avery doubtfully. "But I still think I can convince them to keep it."

"Maybe," said Lucky. "But Bonnie's there now, and I think she needs me."

If Lucky was hoping Avery would try to convince her to stay, she did not show her disappointment when Avery only nodded.

"What time's your flight?"

"In the afternoon."

"I could leave work early and drive you to the airport. How's that sound?"

Lucky nodded. Hellos and goodbyes, that was what their family was good at.

"I'd like that," she said, meaning it.

Avery smiled and patted her head, but her eyes were already roving back to the page she'd abandoned.


THE NEXT DAY, LUCKY WAS sitting on the bed beside her packed duffel bags, ignoring a stream of texts from Troll Doll that were intermittently pleading and attacking, when she heard a light knock on the bedroom door.

"Coming, Aves!" she yelled.

She looked up to find Chiti standing in the doorway.

"Is she here?" Lucky asked.

"She just called," said Chiti. "She's stuck at the office. I think she texted you."

Lucky looked at her phone and saw that between the manic messages of Troll Doll there was indeed a perfunctorily apologetic text from Avery.

"Oh," said Lucky.

She worried if she said any more her voice would betray her.

"I know she's sorry not to say goodbye," said Chiti. "I'll get you a car instead."

Lucky cleared her throat.

"You don't need to do that. I can get one."

Chiti looked up from her phone, which she had been busily tapping away at.

"Six minutes." She stepped tentatively into the room. "Do you have a moment before you leave? There's something I wanted to talk to you about."

Lucky scooted over to make room for Chiti beside her on the little bed with its rose-quartz-colored sheets.

"Look, sorry I'm leaving so soon," Lucky began. "You know I love seeing you guys. I just need to get to New York."

Chiti raised her hand.

"That's fine," she said soothingly. "It's a good idea for you to go home for a little. I wanted to speak to you about something else."

She reached into the pocket of her skirt and placed a small packet on the bed between them.

"I know it's none of my business," she said. "But I found this in the trash of the guest bathroom. And I just wanted to say . . . Well, if you need someone to talk to, I'm always here. I wanted you to know that."

Lucky picked up the packet and inspected it. It had an empty plastic circle in the center where a pill had been. She turned it over and read the writing on the back. It was Plan B. She looked at Chiti's face, which was creased with concern.

"Chiti," she said slowly. "This isn't mine."

Chiti's eyes widened slightly.

"But it was in your trash can," she said.

Lucky shook her head.

"I don't know what it was doing there, since I haven't had sex with a man in—" Lucky paused to think about this. The taxi driver. But she hadn't, thank god. "A minute," she landed on.

"I see," said Chiti quietly.

"Maybe it was one of your clients'?" tried Lucky.

Chiti gave her a distracted look. "I'm sure there's an explanation."

"Obviously." Lucky nodded hard enough to hopefully convince them both. "Definitely."

Lucky thought of Avery's face last night. *You have no idea how far from perfect I am.* A tense silence descended between them. Chiti stood up and smoothed the creases in her long silk skirt.

"Right, let me give you a hug before the car gets here."

She embraced her and Lucky did her best not to radiate the sadness she suddenly felt about leaving.

"I'm really sorry," she said into Chiti's hair.

"You have nothing to apologize for."

"I wasn't a very good houseguest."

Chiti pulled herself back and put her hands on either side of Lucky's face.

"You must take care of yourself, darling girl. Please, Lucky."

"I'm okay," said Lucky. "*You* take care of yourself."

Chiti leveled her in her dark, knowing gaze.

"No," she said. "You're not."

LUCKY STARED OUT THE LITTLE round cabin window at the black night sky and saw her own face reflected hazily back. Could the Plan B have been Avery's? But who on earth would she have used it with? Lucky had been so sure that the one person she could rely on to be a stable force in her life was Avery—but, of course, she'd thought the same thing of Nicky. They were two of four, but they were also undeniably a pair, as close as twins despite their age difference.

Nicky was just two when Lucky was born accidentally at home, elbowing out of the birth canal in only fifteen minutes as their mother squatted on the bedroom floor. Nicky could have resented Lucky for ending her tenure as the baby of the family so swiftly, but it was the opposite. Instead, she declared Lucky *her baby* and carried her everywhere in the following months, dragging a stoic Lucky like a sack of flour around the apartment.

When they were two and four, Lucky followed Nicky everywhere like a duckling, like a dog. Right from the start, it was Nicky she chose above everyone else. As far as she was concerned, the world began and ended with her sister.

Four and six was the two of them in the bath together, slipping over each other like seal cubs, laughing. It was Nicky's favorite toy, a pink cat with four kittens inside its Velcro belly who were born and returned to their mother again and again. It was an afternoon in Central Park licking Mister Softees, long cream rivulets dripping down their arms. It was Nicky insisting they feed some to the kittens. *Oh, they eat so sweetly,* she said, sighing.

Six and eight, they had matching bowl haircuts their mother gave them over the kitchen sink. They played hide-and-seek, choreographed dance routines, and spoke a language only the other understood.

Eight and ten, their dad shattered the wedding china. That Christmas, he pulled the Christmas tree down on top of himself while drunk. They stayed in their shared bedroom and played music softly when he was home. Lucky was Baby Spice and Nicky was Posh. They needed no other identities than these.

Ten and twelve, their small age difference was suddenly big. Nicky hit puberty early and hard, while Lucky was still a child. Lucky learned to fear the hot-water bottle, knowing that if Nicky had it pressed to her stomach, she was in no mood to play. For the first time, Nicky traveled to a place Lucky could not follow. It was scary and required Clearasil.

Twelve and fourteen, Nicky grew her hair out, bought a padded bra from Bloomingdale's, and started painting French tips on her nails. Lucky grew twelve inches, discovered the Ramones, and declared black her favorite color. They never looked alike again.

Fourteen and sixteen, Nicky came home early from school again after fainting on her period. Their mother told her she was being dramatic and, secretly, Lucky agreed. Why did Nicky find it so hard? The rest of them all managed. By the end of that year, the sisters were like four blue irises outgrowing their shared pot. They wanted their own bedrooms, their own taste, their own space. They yearned to crack the pot and escape.

Sixteen and eighteen, they did. Lucky was modeling full-time; Nicky started college and joined a sorority. Lucky smoked a pack a day. Nicky dated a guy called Chad. Lucky fell behind in her GED.

Nicky had a 4.0 GPA. Lucky was defiant. Nicky was compliant. They spoke every day.

Eighteen and twenty, Lucky went to Japan and Nicky was diagnosed with endometriosis after collapsing during her psychology final. Lucky felt guilty for ever privately thinking her sister was exaggerating her menstrual pain. While Lucky was in Tokyo, Nicky called her from the hospital, but she didn't say much. The medications they put her on made her sleepy and short-tempered. Lucky understood that her sister had gone to another place she could not follow. She was sure, however, that she would come back.

Twenty and twenty-two, they had their worst fight ever after Lucky got drunk at Nicky's graduation party and accidentally set fire to the hair of one of the three girls in attendance named Britney. She loathed Nicky's sorority sisters with their straightened hair and Tory Burch sandals and secret language they all seemed to share. She was sure they judged her for not graduating from high school. Try spending five years warding off the advances of grabby photographers, jealous attacks from other models, and constant inquiries into your weight and diet from agents, she wanted to tell them. *That* was an education. In the bathroom, Nicky splashed Lucky's face with water. *When did you get so boring?* Lucky slurred over the sink. Nicky grabbed her shoulders and shook her until her skull rattled. *There is nothing wrong with wanting to be normal!* she shouted. The next night, their parents had plans to take them all out to dinner to celebrate, but Nicky told them she was never speaking to Lucky again. *Okay,* their mother said. *But the reservation is for seven P.M., so can you stop speaking to her after that?* They ended up splitting dessert.

Twenty-two and twenty-four, they kept losing each other. Nicky moved back to New York to get her teaching degree and Lucky flitted around Europe before settling in Paris. Nicky tried acupuncture, breathwork, ice baths, and infrared saunas to help manage her pain, all to no avail. Lucky drank every day and smoked a joint each night to fall asleep. Their daily phone calls became weekly, sometimes monthly. But, like their games of hide-and-seek as children, sooner or later one of them was always there on the other end of the phone or at the airport gate, waiting for the other, hoping to be found.

Twenty-four and twenty-six, Lucky came back to visit Nicky in New York. She was early to pick her up from the high school she was teaching at, so Lucky wandered the quiet halls until she found the right room, then peeked through the glass to see Nicky standing in front of her class, relaxed and smiling in a bright summer dress, making twenty teenagers laugh. Her sister, Lucky thought, was a magician. In the playground, some students had installed an art piece called a wishing tree, which asked passersby to write out a wish on one of the thin strips of paper and tie it to the tree, filling its branches with blossoms of hopes. Lucky kept trying to peek at Nicky's paper as they scribbled, but she laughed and clutched it to her chest. *If you look, it won't come true!* Afterward, when Nicky ran back inside to grab some papers, Lucky found the branch she'd tied hers to and unfolded it. She already knew what Nicky would wish for, a husband and a baby, the same things she'd wished for over her birthday candles every year since she graduated from college, but she felt a strange compulsion to check. She opened the paper and there, written in Nicky's feminine cursive were three words: *no more pills.* Afterward, when Lucky had asked her about it, she denied the wish was hers.

For Lucky's twenty-fifth birthday, Nicky sent her a pair of framed blue butterflies. For Nicky's twenty-seventh, Lucky forgot and called her hungover the next day. Shortly after, she offered to fly Nicky to Paris as a belated birthday present; it was the summer after all, Nicky's time off, and Lucky could book the flights for as soon as the next day on air miles. But Nicky made an excuse.

*I'm not feeling so good, Lucky Lou,* she said. *Maybe another time.*

Lucky sighed down the phone.

*Please don't be mad at me forever,* she said. *Please let me make it up to you.*

Nicky paused.

*You know what I really want for my birthday? Find out what makes you happy, then go fucking do it.*

Lucky looked down at her hands. Who would she be if she knew how to do that?

*I've got to go,* she said finally. *I love you.*

Nicky sounded like she was going to say something else, then paused and said what she always said.

*I love you too. Without the too.*

They hung up and Lucky went to get ready for some party or other and that was the last time she spoke to her sister.

As the plane flew steadily through the night to New York, Lucky drank vodka straight, ignoring the minicans of soda placed alongside her plastic glass. She did not sleep. In that suspended haze, she kept returning to the same thought. She was alive. It sounded obvious, but Lucky had spent the last year denying that simple fact, existing in a drug- or alcohol-induced state that was neither living nor dead. She was alive and Nicky was not. It wasn't right, it simply was. And since she was the one who was still alive, she was going to have to find a way to live.

When she stumbled off the plane, weaving unsteadily between passengers and baggage carts, she found Bonnie waiting for her in the JFK arrivals hall. Lucky saw Bonnie before her sister saw her, hopefully scanning the crowd under the harsh fluorescent lights. She was clutching a sign that said Lucky's name. She had drawn two dots over the "U" to make it a smiley face. Lucky crashed through it into her arms.

# CHAPTER EIGHT

# Bonnie

BONNIE HAD NOT YET BEEN BACK IN THE GYM FOR A WEEK, BUT IT WAS clear her old life was gone for good. Pavel had greeted her with cold formality after she showed up unannounced. If she was expecting an apology, she wasn't going to get one. If he was expecting one from her, he wasn't getting one either. Any plan she'd had to explain the details of why she left after the funeral and what had happened in the year since evaporated on her tongue as soon as she found herself standing before him. She could train at Golden Ring, he made that clear, but he would not train her. She was going to have to find some-one else. She realized now that she had never before cared about the gym's covert hierarchy and system of favoritism because she had al-ways been at the top of it, the gym's undisputed rising star and Pavel's primary fighter. Now, she was learning how cold it was outside the spotlight of his attention.

She positioned herself in his sight line while warming up, waiting to see if he would notice. He was sitting gingerly across from a young

Bulgarian fighter, Danya, who had recently won his first two professional fights, the last by knockout. Bonnie glanced over at them as Pavel turned the young fighter's hand between his own and felt the twin threads of jealousy and longing twist inside of her. It was one of a thousand tender gestures common between a boxer and a trainer. For years, Pavel had wiped her brow, removed her mouthguard, wrapped her hands, laced her gloves, buckled her headgear, poured water into her waiting mouth, smeared her brow with Vaseline, and performed a litany of other daily devotions. This brusque, unselfconscious intimacy was not that of any lover. It was parental, but not exactly paternal. The closest thing to it, Bonnie supposed, was a mother's touch. Bonnie watched Pavel murmur something to Danya and wondered what precious lesson he was learning that she was excluded from.

She remembered Pavel teaching her a step jab while Nicky watched from her perch on the wooden bench by the ring. Bonnie was learning how to close the gap between her and her opponent by throwing the jab as she moved forward with her front foot, then quickly sliding her back foot up as she recovered the hand. It was a simple and essential move that, once mastered, would allow her to start building her combinations.

*Plant feet, Bonnie,* implored Pavel.

But every time she moved forward with the jab, she did a little leap like a deer skipping forward on ice. Pavel shook his head. He turned to Nicky.

*Nicky? I want that you listen too.*

Nicky nodded seriously. He turned back to Bonnie, who was panting in frustration.

*Bonnie, from where does your power come?*

She gave him a confused look.

*My punch?* she lisped through her mouthpiece.

Pavel turned back from her to Nicky.

*Nicky, from where does Bonnie's power come?*

*Her rage against the patriarchy!* she cried.

Bonnie snorted through her nose.

*In fact, the opposite,* said Pavel. *It come from the mother.*

Bonnie and Nicky both cocked their heads.

*Mother Earth.*

He knelt and tapped Bonnie's feet, which were laced in the elegant red boxing shoes she had been given for her sixteenth birthday.

*Mother Earth is source of all power. It come from the ground through your feet, up your knees, which are bent, thank you*—Bonnie dutifully bent her knees—*into hips, through shoulder, then fist. Every time you take feet off ground, you lose source of power. Understood?*

*Mother Earth,* Bonnie lisped.

Pavel nodded.

*We go again.*

She shot forward, this time using a quick shuffle step movement instead of the leap she had been doing before. She looked at Pavel, whose face split into an irrepressible smile. He had a large gap between his two front teeth that gave his usually brutish countenance a surprisingly boyish quality. His pale eyes were lit up and looking at her with something like delight, or respect, or love. Then he set his face back into an expression of cool inscrutability and cleared his throat.

*Better,* he said. *Again.*

And though her feet never left the ground, she knew Nicky could see she was flying.

THESE DAYS, BONNIE FELT THE weight of gravity more acutely than ever. Her whole body ached as she finished her stretches. She glanced over at Pavel and Danya, still locked in their private consort, picked up her gloves, and headed toward them. She was tired of this shit. But this rush of confidence soon waned when she found herself standing before Pavel. She avoided the eyes of the Bulgarian fighter, who was sizing her up with ill-disguised contempt.

"Thought I could get back to sparring today," she said.

Pavel gave a short shake of his head without looking up from wrapping Danya's hand.

"Not ready."

Bonnie scuffed one foot against the other.

"Look, I didn't stop everything. Did roadwork. Still in shape."

Pavel ran his gaze up and down her.

"Not ready," he repeated.

Next to him, Danya exhaled a soft snort of amusement. Bonnie narrowed her eyes.

"I can spar with him. We're similar weights."

"No," said Pavel.

Danya raised his hands and smiled.

"I don't fight women."

At this, Bonnie saw a flicker of annoyance cross Pavel's face.

"Patience, Bonnie," he said. "Please."

If Bonnie had been a different kind of person, she would have stamped in frustration.

"Felix will take you on the pads," said Pavel and inclined his head away to signal the conversation was done.

Felix was a new trainer in the gym, a Mexican former middle-weight known for being even-tempered and soft-spoken, a rarity in a sport of big, combustible personalities. Pavel called his name and he appeared from the gym's back office, taking in the three of them with a swift, all-seeing look.

"Let's go, Bonnie," Felix said softly. "Get your gloves on."

He guided her to the other side of the gym, then took her gloves between his hands and began lacing them. It was the kind of brusque proximity Bonnie was used to; boxers spent their lives being touched and handled. Once both wrists were secure, he glanced up at her from beneath his eyelashes, long and straight as an elephant's, and gave her a look of such gentle compassion, she marveled that this was the same man who once punched an opponent so hard they found two of his teeth on the canvas at the bell.

Bonnie worked with him on the pads, and her mind soon cleared. They were practicing three-punch combinations, then stepping to the side. She could feel Felix's focus as he absorbed her patterns and instincts, murmuring instructions in a voice barely above a whisper.

There was nothing else for her to do now but breathe and move. Jab, right, hook, breathe. Jab-to-body, jab-to-head, hook, breathe.

An image of the man she'd punched in Venice crumpled on the sidewalk flashed in her mind's eye, the look of horror on his girlfriend's face. But Peachy had said he was fine, she reminded herself, and had texted to let her know he had not been to the bar again. With great effort, she pushed the image away. Jab, jab, right, breathe. She needed discipline now more than ever, not just physically but mentally. She could not let anything distract her from her training. She could not keep getting in her own way.

"That's nice, Bonnie," Felix murmured at intervals. "I like that straight right."

Bonnie gave a curt nod of acknowledgment and kept working, but she felt the compliment spark a familiar warmth within her. She had forgotten what it was like to be praised. That was the thing about training, as tough as it was, as grueling as it could be, there was a sweetness to it. Being observed, feeling nurtured and encouraged, Bonnie had loved that more than anything. She had never really concerned herself with whether she was a good boxer; she had only worried about pleasing Pavel. And whatever she did now, she was still aware of him. He might studiously ignore her, but she knew the effort it took for him not to watch her. Even at their closest, Pavel had not spoken much. But she could *feel* his awareness of her too. Barely perceptibly, unnoticed by anyone, they leaned toward each other, like plants for whom the other was the sun.

Aside from traveling for fights, they'd spent little time together outside the gym. But there had been moments. Once, ten years after they started training together, Bonnie had been walking to the gym when she stopped suddenly. Across the street, sitting alone in a booth in the window of the diner on Sixty-eighth Street, was Pavel. A server was walking toward him with a slice of cheesecake held aloft; his face lit up as she approached. Bonnie considered continuing to walk; there was something so innocent about the scene, so tender, that it felt almost violent to intrude upon it, but she found herself crossing the street and opening the diner door, drawn toward him like a bee to a bud. Pavel looked up as she approached, a large bit of cake hovering on his fork. He gave her a self-conscious grin.

*You catch me,* he declared.

He motioned for her to sit across from him, and she slid into the booth. Without taking his eyes off her, he scooped the cake into his mouth, clearly delighted by the experience.

*You discover my one weakness,* he said between bites.

*Cheesecake?*

*Cheesecake.* Pavel nodded. *This one is very good. We don't have like this in Russia. You want a piece?*

Bonnie was about to decline—she kept to a strict training diet that included very little sugar—when she surprised herself by nodding.

*Sure,* she said. *Why not.*

He ordered her a slice and watched with a fervent intensity as she took the first bite.

*What do you think?* he asked eagerly. *Is good, no?*

To be honest, it tasted like regular cheesecake to Bonnie, but his enthusiasm was irresistible.

*Delicious,* nodded Bonnie, her mouth full.

Pavel beamed.

*Next fight you win, I get you this,* he said.

They sat in peaceable silence eating their cake until both their plates were clean. Bonnie assumed Pavel would immediately hurry them along to the gym, but he sat back and smiled at her contentedly.

*You want coffee?*

Another indulgence she rarely allowed herself since Pavel discouraged reliance on any stimulants, including caffeine.

*Are you getting one?* she asked in surprise.

*Today, we live a little,* he announced and ordered them two cups.

The mugs of steaming dark liquid were placed before them and Bonnie took a tentative sip, watching over the rim of her cup as Pavel took a long, satisfying gulp.

*Aaaah,* he exhaled, placing his down in front of him and regarding her with his amused, knowing stare. *So how are you, Bonnie?*

How was she? As . . . a person? Bonnie didn't know how to answer that. In the past months Pavel had asked her how her combinations were flowing, if her right shoulder was still bothering her, whether she was out of gas between sparring rounds, if she was keeping her chin down and her guard up, but never how she was. She mumbled something about being fine, then took a large swig of coffee, burning her tongue.

*And your sisters?* he pressed. *How's Nicky?*

This was easier for her.

*She's good.* Bonnie nodded proudly. *Just started her teaching degree. She wants to be an English teacher.*

*Good for her.* Pavel tapped his head and smiled. *That Nicky, always taking notes.*

*That's right.*

Bonnie smiled back, pleased, as always, to be talking about her special younger sister. A silence descended between them again; she wrapped her hands around the mug and cleared her throat.

*And . . . how are you?* she tried cautiously. *How's Anahid?*

She didn't know why she'd asked that. Pavel rarely mentioned his wife and Bonnie never asked. The few times Anahid had visited the gym, Bonnie had found her very striking and serious, exactly the kind of impressively intimidating partner you would expect for Pavel until you knew him better and discovered his silly side, the goofy, childlike version of him that loved to dance and juggle. *And,* Bonnie thought, smiling to herself, *eat cheesecake alone in diners.*

*I think she is well,* he said.

Bonnie knit her brow together. Think?

*We call it quits,* he clarified. *A little while ago now.*

*Oh.*

Bonnie didn't know what to say. Talking about anything outside of boxing, let alone something as personal as a breakup, was like trying to walk with Pavel on ice; neither of them quite had their balance.

*In fact,* he continued, *I just signed the divorce papers today.*

He gave a self-effacing laugh, seemingly marveling at the strangeness of the statement he'd just uttered. Bonnie searched his face for signs of heartbreak, but he was the same Pavel he had always been. Same flat, square nose—a true boxer's nose, he'd joke, broken many times into submission—set beneath bright, surprisingly gentle eyes.

*I'm really sorry, Pavel,* she said quietly.

He shrugged.

*Is hard, this life we chose,* he said. *Is not for everyone.*

Bonnie nodded seriously, but a frisson of delight passed through her at that *we.*

*So . . . cheesecake,* she said.

Pavel's face split into his boyish smile.

*Sometimes we need cheesecake,* he agreed.

Pavel paid the bill, waving off Bonnie's attempt to reach for her wallet. They stood up together and he held the door for her, guiding her through it with the slightest touch at the small of her back. Bonnie felt it then, a flutter of hope, like the lightest breeze, that life could be this way with him, so sweet and so simple. Breakfasts before the gym together, his hand on her, not to correct her, but simply out of tenderness, the two of them talking not as a trainer and boxer but as two people, conversations full of affection and laughter. They had walked together to the gym side by side, and Bonnie had let that light breeze carry her all the way to its doors. Then they had entered Golden Ring and Pavel had stridden ahead of her, instructing her gruffly over his shoulder to warm up quickly since she was late, and Bonnie understood that sometimes cheesecake was just cheesecake, and let the breeze die.

BONNIE BROUGHT HER MIND BACK to the pads Felix was holding. She needed to focus. *Thwack, thwack, thwack,* pivot. But from her periphery, Bonnie saw Pavel glance at them. His gaze was like a cool current in the air. Immediately, she hit a little harder, slipped a little quicker. *Pow, pow, pow.* As if pulled by an invisible tide, he wandered over to her side of the ring. Bonnie snapped through the combination, emboldened by his gaze. *Hiss hiss hiss.* But Pavel betrayed nothing as he watched her. The next time she glanced over, he had already turned away.

BONNIE RETURNED HOME LATE TO find Lucky's long body curled on
the sofa, her chin tucked into herself. Out of instinct, she lurched
forward to check that she was still breathing, but Lucky's chest was
rising and falling softly. Bonnie exhaled. She perched on the side of
the sofa, watching her sister's supine form. Lucky reminded her of a
sleeping fawn or fox, some elegant and mysterious woodland creature
just out of reach of human companionship. This close, she could see
that Lucky's pale skin was covered in a damp film of sweat. Her face,
even in sleep, was tense. She wore a threadbare white T-shirt, her
spine protruding like a string of pearls. Bonnie frowned. Had she
always been this thin? How could she possibly protect herself like
that? The sister that had stumbled off the plane from London, un-
steady as a toddler, terrified her. She knew Lucky was a prodigious
partyer, had always secretly admired her for it, but there seemed to be
no joy in Lucky's drinking these days.

Bonnie's gym bag was still dangling from her shoulder; she shucked
it to the floor and stood to take a shower, but she found herself turning back to watch Lucky a little longer. Her youngest sister was not
okay, she could see that now. But still, just having her close, Bonnie
could feel herself relax. Some atavistic part of herself was never at
peace until she was with one of her sisters. After Nicky died, Bonnie
feared that she would never feel stillness, real calm, again. *That was
family,* she thought sadly, *the root of all comfort and chaos.* But sitting here
now, watching the slumbering Lucky, she felt it faintly, an old ease.
She would take care of her. As long as she was near her, she would
protect her. Forgetting the shower, Bonnie lay down on the rug
alongside the sofa like a dog beside its master and, eventually, found
asleep.

SHE WAS JUMPING ROPE THE next day when Pavel approached her. She
felt him coming, though her eyes were glued to Psalm 18, which had
hung framed on the wall for as long as she'd been at the gym. The
paper behind the glass was old and yellow, the words faded from sun

exposure. It didn't matter; Bonnie knew them by heart. The psalm was what she stared at while jumping rope, had been her point of focus year after year. The words were a part of her now as if she'd written them herself.

> *It is God who arms me with strength*
> *and keeps my way secure.*
> *He makes my feet like the feet of a deer;*
> *he causes me to stand on the heights.*
> *He trains my hands for battle;*
> *my arms can bend a bow of bronze.*
> *You make your saving help my shield,*
> *and your right hand sustains me;*
> *your help has made me great.*
> *You provide a broad path for my feet,*
> *so that my ankles do not give way.*

This was Bonnie's secret, the one she never told anyone in her family: She believed in God. Her father was a lapsed Catholic and her mother a staunch atheist; they didn't baptize Bonnie and her sisters, and there was no discussion of faith, spirituality, or the afterlife in the house. When Bonnie's pet hamster died, their mother had crisply informed her that a pet's *purpose* was to teach her about death. But they had been sent to Catholic middle and high school, and something had clearly sunk in. It wasn't that Bonnie believed in heaven exactly, or a God that looked like any human, but she believed in something.

It had started when she was in middle school. First, she'd started having panic attacks, shortness of breath and dark waves crashing in from the corners of her vision. It seemed to her that the only times her father wasn't angry was when he had just started drinking or was watching Bonnie play sports, loudly instructing her from the sidelines to drive harder, dig deeper, be stronger. If she told her mother about the panic attacks, it would get back to him, and she couldn't allow that. Eventually, she found a way to deal with them without involving anyone else; she would secret herself off to the only single-person bathroom in the school, situated on the top floor by the dusty art supply room, and pray. Bonnie would talk to God until her heart rate would slow, and her breath would become steady. Afterward, whenever she needed to find calm or courage, she would think of that quiet, listening presence and automatically feel an inner peace.

Over time, her God became something more amorphous and expansive than the punitive Catholic God they were taught in school. It was a feeling of stillness that lived inside her. And, eventually, if she listened carefully enough, it spoke back to her. It or She or whatever God was had a voice barely above the sound of wind through sand. Bonnie could only hear it when she was very, very still. *This is right for you,* it would say. *This is wrong.* And when it spoke to her, she felt so supremely looked after, so deeply and existentially okay, its source could only be divine. It was a soothing and a smoothing, a drastic internal reconfiguration from chaos to harmony. When she heard it, nothing had to change for everything to be different. But she had not heard it in over a year.

Bonnie bounced with a soft, balletic movement from foot to foot, expertly flicking the rope in a crisscross in front of her. Jumping rope, like everything else in boxing, was about skill, but it was also about style. When Bonnie swung the rope, deftly passing it from hand to hand while her feet barely skimmed the floor, she made sure she moved like a swan on water, all the effort beneath the surface. Pavel picked his way across the gym to stand before her, regarding her with his now usual expression of blank inscrutability verging on mild hostility.

"Danya's sparring partner injured," he said. "You want?"

Bonnie gave a quick nod without missing a beat on the rope. She would not give him the satisfaction of seeing her excited.

"This afternoon," said Pavel. "Six rounds. Eat light lunch."

It was only after he had turned his back that she allowed herself a brief, ecstatic smile.

BONNIE CAME HOME FROM THE gym for lunch, partly because it was
cheaper to cook for herself, but mostly so she could check on Lucky.
She called her name as the lock clicked behind her and heard a low,
animal moan from the bathroom. Bonnie ran down the hallway to
find Lucky curled around the porcelain base of the toilet. Instinctively, she dropped to her knees and began patting down Lucky's
body, feeling for injury.

"What's wrong? Where does it hurt?"

Lucky lifted her cheek from the tiled floor and gazed up at her
blearily.

"Do you . . . have any weed?"

Bonnie frowned.

"You know I don't."

Lucky placed her cheek back down against the floor. She spoke to
the ground in front of her.

"I can't do it, Bon. I need something."

Do what? Her eyes darted over Lucky's prostrate form. Then she
thought of Nicky's body in her arms, her pale blue lips, and understood.

"You don't need that stuff," she said.

Lucky curled into herself and moaned.

"My stomach's cramping."

"That's normal," murmured Bonnie. "It will pass."

She had no idea what was normal. She had never been drunk or
done a drug in her life, let alone had to go through whatever Lucky
was experiencing right now.

"Where's your phone?" Bonnie asked.

"Why?"

"I want to look something up."

"Use yours."

"Mine's a flip, it doesn't do that."

"God, you're weird," groaned Lucky.

Bonnie smiled, just slightly. She still had an attitude; that was a
good sign.

"What's your passcode?"

"Nicky's birthday."

Bonnie gave Lucky a little pat of recognition without saying anything. It was typical Lucky, showing love in the most covert of ways.
She went and got the phone from the living room, then glanced at the
time on the home screen. She just needed to get Lucky into bed, then
she could get back to the gym in time to spar and come right back for
her. At her touch, the phone screen lit up with a series of messages
from someone called Troll Doll.

*where are you*

*seriously. answer your phone*

*okay im sorry i took your photo lol*

*bitch*

*did you leave for ny already???*

*i'm really raelly sorry pls talk to me*

Bonnie came back into the bathroom to find Lucky scrunched
into an even tighter ball.

"What's a Troll Doll?"

Lucky groaned again.

"Whoever they are," said Bonnie, "they're intense."

Lucky lifted her head and used seemingly the last of her effort to
give a pale, wolfish smile.

"You have no idea."

Bonnie dismissed the messages and opened the search engine on
Lucky's phone, hovering with her thumbs over the keyboard. She
didn't even know what to ask. She looked at Lucky's white face, the
dark half-moons under her eyes. She typed in *stopping drinking and
other stuff*. Tips from a rehab facility automatically popped up. Did
Lucky need to go to rehab? How much would that cost? Bonnie
wished Avery was there; she was decisive as an axe.

"Should we call Avery?" she asked.

"No!" cried Lucky with surprising force.

"But she's better at this," said Bonnie, a child's whine of fear
creeping into her voice. She cleared her throat. "She can help."

"She already thinks I'm a fuckup."

Bonnie knit her brows.

"I think you just remind her of her," she said.

And, more concerningly, of Nicky. Though she didn't want to say that part, didn't even want to think it. Bonnie glanced back at the phone.

"This says to drink plenty of fluids and eat fruits and vegetables."

Lucky sat up just in time to retch over the toilet. She produced long, guttural croaks that seemed to come from the deepest part of her belly. Her body shook violently as she dry-heaved some more. Bonnie winced; it hurt just listening to her. Lucky crawled away from the bowl and sat back against the low tub, wiping a tendril of saliva from her mouth. Her hands were trembling.

"Nothing left in me," she said between shallow gasps.

Bonnie swallowed, trying to keep her voice even and unemotional.

"That should stop soon. How many times have you thrown up this morning?"

Lucky rested the back of her neck against the curved lip of the tub and closed her eyes.

"A million." She rubbed a hand roughly over her face. "And I haven't shit in three days. Can you type that in too?"

"Sure." Bonnie did another search, but it just took her to more tips from rehabs. "Could you eat something?"

Lucky shook her head without opening her eyes.

"What else does it say?"

Bonnie scanned the list.

"Take a cold shower."

Lucky winced as though the icy droplets were already hitting her skin.

"Just let me rest here," she said. "Can I do that?"

Was it right to push her? Bonnie didn't know. She hated making Lucky do anything she didn't want to do, but was that only "enabling" her, as Avery would say? She kept reading down the list on the rehab's website until she got to the final point. *If there is one thing to remember when going through withdrawal it is this: Lean in. When pain presents itself, don't allow yourself to numb the pain and make it go away. Lean in and take a stand against your addiction.*

Bonnie nodded slowly as she read. Leaning into pain, that she knew how to do. Surely, if anyone was going to help Lucky through this, it should be her, who had made a life out of pushing past physical limits. She took a deep breath and knelt in front of Lucky, scooping her up under each of her arms, like she used to when Lucky was a baby. She lifted her tall, bony sister with ease.

"What are you doing?" wailed Lucky.

Bonnie pinned Lucky's body to her chest so she wouldn't slump back down. She felt sharp and breakable as glass.

"You're taking a shower," she said. "And you're going to eat something."

Lucky pulled back to look at her, so her face was inches from Bonnie's. Her breath was sour and her lower lip trembled, just as it used to when she was a little girl on the verge of tears.

"I can't," she whispered.

"You can," said Bonnie. "I'm going to help you."

Bonnie undressed her youngest sister with the greatest care. She thought of a painting she had once seen being installed at the Met, how the handlers had worn white cotton gloves to unwrap the padded casing, their fingers skimming the surface of the gilt frame with a tenderness that felt reverential. That was how cautiously she tried to handle Lucky, like she was the most precious piece at the Met. She gently peeled her T-shirt over her head, ignoring the tang of sweat that wafted from it.

"Sorry if I stink."

Lucky offered her a self-conscious smile. Bonnie dismissed this with a wave.

"You should smell the guys at the gym."

She knelt to shimmy Lucky out of her jeans. It felt like something devotional, like a prayer. Lucky rested her hands on her shoulder to step out of the fabric scrunched at her feet. Her legs were milk-white and bruised. Once she was in her underwear, Lucky tapped Bonnie softly.

"I can take it from here."

Bonnie stepped outside to give her some privacy, waiting on the other side of the door until she heard the burst of shower water. She headed to the kitchen to see what they had to eat that Lucky could keep down. Fortunately, she had stocked up on electrolyte drinks, eggs, fruit, protein bars, and big plastic buckets of spinach before Lucky arrived, food well suited for bulking up and, it turned out, drying out. She glanced up at the clock on the wall. If she could just get Lucky settled, she'd still have time to eat something quickly, then head back to the gym. She picked up a Gatorade—the blue flavor, Lucky's favorite—and snapped a banana from the bunch.

In the bathroom, Lucky was standing in a towel, her teeth chattering. Bonnie still wasn't used to her sister's new bleached pixie cut. Her own dirty-blond hair turned dark when damp, but Lucky's remained unchanged by the water, hanging from her head in wet peroxide-white spikes. She glared when Bonnie came in.

"I'm freezing," she said between chatters.

"Here, get started on this."

She handed Lucky the Gatorade and banana, grabbed the hair-dryer from under the sink, and led Lucky to the main bedroom. There were only two bedrooms in the apartment; the larger one, which had originally been Bonnie and Avery's but later became Nicky's, and the smaller, which had previously belonged to the younger two. This room had a queen bed and vanity; its bobbly cream carpet was stained from years of use. The other still housed the bunk beds all four of them had slept in at some point during their childhood, along with a dusty workout bike and Bonnie's first punching bag. Bonnie plugged in the hairdryer and sat down on the bed, motioning for Lucky to sit between her feet. The dryer roared to life in her hand as she ran it over Lucky's head, rubbing her scalp with her fingertips to loosen the wet clumps.

"Keep sipping that Gatorade," she called over the wail of hot air.

Lucky dutifully cracked the lid and tilted her head back to swallow a mouthful of synthetic blue liquid, then took a small bite of banana. Bonnie fumbled around her head like a bear pawing at a beehive. As it dried, Lucky's hair turned soft as dandelion seeds in her palms. Once she felt satisfied that Lucky would no longer catch a chill, Bonnie turned off the dryer and restored the room to silence. She cupped her sister's skull in her hands and awkwardly kissed the top of her head.

"All done. Shall we get you into bed?"

She helped Lucky into a large T-shirt and pair of sweatpants from her messy duffel bag, then pulled the covers up to her chin. Only her pale narrow face was visible, tiny amid the mounds of pillows and bedsheets. Bonnie tucked her in and watched as Lucky's eyes fluttered shut.

"Sorry for being a pussy-ass bitch about all this," Lucky said, her eyes still closed.

Bonnie snorted softly.

"I didn't expect to feel so bad," Lucky added.

"Yeah, you must have been . . ." Bonnie tried to think of the right words. "Hitting it pretty hard?" she landed on, immediately feeling like a loser.

Lucky opened her eyes and gave a dry laugh.

"I guess you could say that."

Bonnie didn't want to risk Lucky clamming up by asking for specifics. She was afraid to think of what her sister had been doing; she hoped what she imagined was worse than the reality.

"It's okay." Bonnie patted her down over the covers. "You're a Blue. You're made of tough stuff."

Lucky stared at her from between the mounds of pillows.

"Tough stuff," she repeated. "What does that make Nicky?"

From the corner of Lucky's eye, a fat teardrop escaped and made a run into her ear.

"She was tough stuff too." Bonnie wiped the wet trail the tear had left across Lucky's temple with the corner of the duvet. "She was just unlucky."

Bonnie closed the bedroom blinds against the midday sunlight and went to the kitchen to fetch a bucket in case Lucky was sick again. As she placed it on the floor beside the bed, Lucky's hand crept from under the covers and pulled at her sleeve.

"Are you leaving?" she asked in a small voice.

Bonnie didn't need to think before answering. She shook her head.

"I'm staying right here."

She perched on the edge of the bed, watching over Lucky like a sentry until, eventually, she appeared to doze. Once she was sure she was sleeping, she went back online and carried on reading. She could feel her heartbeat in her throat as she scrolled through page after page, trying to gather what tips she could. Most articles stressed the significant risks of detoxing at home. But Bonnie knew her chances of getting Lucky into a treatment facility were small to nonexistent. She wouldn't go willingly and, anyway, Bonnie didn't even know how to find a good one, let alone pay for it. She knew she should call Avery, but Lucky would never trust her again if she did.

Also, she couldn't shake the feeling that *she* was the one who was meant to help Lucky through this. Who else was as capable of helping Lucky lean into pain? Years of fighting had taught Bonnie that you must take an opening when you see it. She needed to take advantage of this small window of willingness that had opened inside of her sister and hoist her through it with all her strength. She had failed with Nicky, arriving minutes too late. She would not fail Lucky.

She returned to the kitchen to begin preparing a broth, following a recipe she'd found online by a holistic nutritionist who claimed to be able to cure everything from stomach cramps to cancer through diet. As she chopped the carrots, careful not to make too much noise, she glanced up at the black Kit-Kat clock swaying its tail on the kitchen wall. Danya would be warming up now. Bonnie used everything in her to push that thought away, returning her attention to thinly slicing the orange discs in front of her. She wanted to get them just right.

FOR THE NEXT FEW DAYS Bonnie stayed by Lucky's side, making sure she ate, bathed, and rested. Together, they watched terrible daytime TV and took slow, meandering walks around Central Park, Lucky wincing at the sunshine as she leaned on Bonnie, her hand tucked into the crook of her elder sister's arm. They sat by the Alice in Wonderland statue and watched children in bright summer clothes crawl over the toadstools into Alice's lap, its bronze patina rubbed smooth by the thousands of tiny hands and feet that had clambered on it.

"Remember when that was us?" asked Bonnie.

Lucky smiled wanly.

"Were we ever so young?"

Bonnie ignored all thoughts of the gym and instead read endless articles online delineating the best remedies for withdrawal. She blended juices and smoothies to slake Lucky's thirst, rubbed peppermint oil into her temples to ward off nausea, and led her in the healing pranayama breathing exercises she'd taught herself from YouTube for this purpose. It all seemed to be going to plan until the third night, when Lucky demanded to go out alone, where or why she wouldn't say, and Bonnie would not let her. She stood before their front door, blocking her sister's exit.

"You're seriously not going to let me out?" said Lucky.

As she had many times as a bouncer at Peachy's, Bonnie crossed her arms and shored herself up, keeping her face blank and inscrutable.

"I can't let you do that yet," she said calmly, her voice betraying none of the turmoil she felt.

"Seriously?" asked Lucky again, her voice rising with frustration.

Bonnie nodded.

"You've got to be fucking kidding me," shouted Lucky, turning as if to walk away.

Then she pivoted, barreled back down the hallway, and launched herself at Bonnie, trying to shove her to the side.

"You can't control me!" she cried.

"I'm not trying to control you," said Bonnie, easily pinning Lucky's arms to her chest and holding her still. "I'm trying to keep you safe."

"Safe? I can keep myself safe!" yelled Lucky. "What do you think I've been fucking doing all these years?"

Lucky thrashed like a caught fish in her arms. Her knees buckled beneath her and the two of them toppled over onto the hallway floor. All Bonnie's boxing training went out the window. They could have been children again, tussling over some game gone awry. Lucky untangled herself first and scrambled back up to lunge for the door, but Bonnie caught her ankles, attempting to drag her back down. She succeeded in yanking Lucky's sweatpants to her knees instead, revealing her pale butt cheeks bordered by a surprisingly girlish pink thong. With one hand tugging at her waistband, Lucky grasped desperately for the doorknob with the other before collapsing onto her knees, her ass still hanging over her waistband. She bowed her head, her shoulders shaking, and Bonnie realized with agony that she had made her sister cry. She had been too rough, just like when they were kids.

"Shit, I'm sorry, Lucky." She crawled toward her on the carpet and placed a hand on her shoulder as lightly as she could. "I'm really sorry."

But when Lucky turned to her, her face was cracked open with amusement. She let out another gulping laugh and yanked up her pants.

"All right, fuck it," she said, wiping her eyes. "You win. Let's watch a movie."

BY THE END OF THE week Lucky looked, for the first time, like she wasn't on the verge of either vomiting, nodding off, or killing herself, so Bonnie suggested they go for an early morning run.

"It's nice having you here with me," she said, nudging Lucky as they trotted along side by side. They'd done one mile, and Bonnie could feel the endorphins begin to kick in. She grinned. "Running buddy."

Lucky tried the best approximation of a shrug she could manage while heaving herself forward in time with Bonnie.

"Still . . . fucking . . . jet-lagged," she panted. "Also . . . I can't sleep . . . through the . . . night without . . . weed or Ambien."

Bonnie flipped herself through the air to run backward so they

were facing each other. She did the toe-tap run she used in the ring
to stay light on her feet and get points for footwork, bouncing ele-
gantly like a show pony as she talked.

"You will. Just need time to adjust."

"You're not . . . even sweating," heaved Lucky. "I . . . hate you."

Bonnie turned sideways, side tapping her heels to slow herself
down to Lucky's pace. Lucky pulled what sounded like a gigantic
wad of phlegm from her throat and spat mightily into the grass.

"Let's break," said Bonnie.

"Oh, thank god." Lucky collapsed onto the lawn and sprawled her
long limbs into a star. "I've got to stop smoking," she groaned.

Bonnie had read online that it was not advisable for smokers to try
to stop in their first year of sobriety since trying to kick too many
dependencies at once could lead to overwhelm and relapse.

"I wouldn't worry about that," said Bonnie quickly.

Lucky glanced at her.

"I thought you hated my smoking?" she said.

*Quit your addictions in the order they could kill you,* one website blithely
advised. Given that harrowing logic, Bonnie figured they should
focus on the drinking and drugs for now; everything else could wait.

"I'll stretch you." Bonnie lifted Lucky's leg from the ankle. "Hold
this straight."

Lucky let out a little yelp, of pleasure or pain Bonnie couldn't tell,
as she extended her leg. Her sister made a cushion for her head with
her hands and exhaled happily. Pleasure. She was finally doing better,
Bonnie noted with satisfaction. Now, she needed to make sure Lucky
didn't forget what she had just been through.

"Do you think you should go to a, um, meeting or something?"
she began, keeping her eyes on the task of stretching Lucky's Achilles.
"Like Avery does?"

Lucky made a *pffft* sound beneath her.

"She's not as together as you think, you know."

"Avery? What do you mean?"

Lucky opened her mouth to say something, then appeared to think
better of it.

"Don't you think it's a bit sad?" she said eventually. "Avery still needing meetings after all these years?"

Bonnie looked down at her and cocked her head.

"They help her. Why stop?"

Lucky sat up on her forearms.

"But isn't it a bit of a crutch? Like, now she's just addicted to meetings instead of drugs."

"Everyone's addicted to something. Might as well be something good for you."

Lucky tilted her head and peered up at her.

"You're not. You're, like, Miss Clean Dream Supreme."

Bonnie snorted softly and swapped legs.

"You know that was my second choice for ring name?"

"No, seriously," said Lucky. "Have you ever been addicted to *any-thing* in your whole life?"

"Sure, I have."

"What then?"

Bonnie bared her teeth.

"Pain, baby."

Lucky rested her head back in her hands and stared up at the blue swath of sky, unscarred by clouds. She sighed.

"The thing is, I think that's probably good for you too."

Bonnie dropped Lucky's leg and crouched next to her on the grass. There was something she'd been wanting to ask Lucky for the past few days and now finally seemed like the time.

"I have to ask . . ." She glanced at her sister. "Why now? What made you want to stop?"

Lucky sat up and folded her long arms around her knees.

"I don't know that I can put it into words," she said. "I only know I had to try. Also, I had you." She looked at her solemnly. "I wouldn't have been able to get through this week without you, Bon. I mean it."

Bonnie swallowed and placed her hand gruffly on Lucky's back.

"I'll always be here to help you," she said. "No matter what. You know that?"

Lucky looked down between her feet and nodded.

"Hey." She turned to poke Bonnie in the shoulder. "Don't you need to get to the gym?"

Bonnie dismissed this with a wave.

"I need to be with you."

"You can't watch over me forever, you know."

"Not forever." Bonnie grinned. "Just today and tomorrow and the day after that . . ."

Lucky shook her head.

"I don't want you to fuck with your life just because I fucked up mine."

Bonnie glanced over at her.

"You didn't fuck up. What you're doing is really brave."

Lucky made a small noise of disgust.

"Please don't call me brave. That is the opposite of what I am."

"You can't see yourself yet," said Bonnie. "You will."

Lucky plucked a blade of grass and twirled it between her fingers.

"My agency dropped me," she said quietly. "Or I dropped them. I don't know."

"What happened?"

Lucky looked down at her hands.

"I just . . . I don't want to do it anymore, Bon. This can't be it, you know? My career, my whole life, reduced to—" She lifted one thin arm and shook it. Bonnie nodded in understanding.

"A body," Bonnie said. "I get it."

Lucky rolled the blade of grass into a tiny green ball and flicked it away.

"Is that why you stopped boxing? Did you feel like that?"

Bonnie shook her head. Truthfully, she loved the physicality of what she did. Asking her body to do something nearly impossible and feeling it rise to the task made her feel invincible. She couldn't imagine spending her life doing anything that *wasn't* physical. It was the mental side of the sport that had got to her.

"After Nicky," she began slowly. "After having my title taken, I just couldn't see a way forward anymore. And without Pavel . . . I don't know how to box without him."

"Why *did* you leave Pavel? None of us understood that. He's, like, the best."

Bonnie took a deep breath. If she was going to be honest with anyone, it should be Lucky, who had been brave enough to let Bonnie help her this week.

"I started to feel——"

But she couldn't find the word. A *crush* felt ridiculous. *Feelings* was too wishy-washy. *Love* felt impossible to say. Instead, she fluttered a hand over her chest where her heart was and looked imploringly at Lucky, who gasped.

"For *Pavel*?"

Bonnie dropped her face in her hands. She was flushed all over. Her cheeks felt like asphalt baking in the sun.

"Wow, I did *not* see that coming," said Lucky.

Bonnie glanced up.

"Because he would never . . . like that? For me?"

Lucky's expression softened instantly.

"Are you kidding me? He should be so lucky! It's just . . . You know what, never mind. I see it, I do. He's pretty cute. In an I-survived-the-Russian-winter-by-wrestling-bears-and-using-my-own-stores-of-fat-as-sustenance kind of way."

Bonnie tried to smile, but she was still burning with embarrassment.

"So did you tell him?" asked Lucky. "How you felt?"

Bonnie shook her head. Lucky clicked her teeth and gave her the finger gun.

"A classic cut and run. Nice."

Bonnie grimaced.

"But now you're back at the gym together," continued Lucky. "So that's a good thing, right?"

"He has me working with this guy Felix, who's good, you know, but . . ."

"Not him. Right."

The two sat in silence contemplating Bonnie's conundrum. On

the path, a mother carrying a large Chanel purse and various shopping bags tried to grab her teenage son's hand.

"What are you *doing*?" he growled, shaking her off.

Bonnie and Lucky both smiled. Despite her embarrassment, it felt good to sit there with her sister, chatting about her life. Somehow, the Pavel situation seemed more manageable now that she'd spoken it aloud. For the first time in a long time, she felt something a little like joy, but lighter and more familiar. It was cheerfulness, she supposed. That ordinary, everyday sunniness that had buoyed so many of her days before Nicky died. She did not know how much she'd missed that feeling until it returned to her now. *Cheerfulness.* Uncomplicated as a sunbeam.

"So." Lucky turned to her. "Are you going to talk to him about your—you know?"

Lucky made a circular motion over her heart. But Bonnie didn't want to ruin this newfound lightness by trying to decipher how Pavel may or may not feel about her. *Not* feel, she reminded herself. He obviously did not feel anything for her, as proven by his attitude in the gym.

"Let's talk about you again." She jumped up and reached down to help Lucky to her feet. "What do you want to do if you're not being a pretty girl?"

Lucky laughed and took her hands.

"You're seriously going to change the subject?"

"I mean it. Do you have any ideas?"

Bonnie set off on a light jog and motioned for Lucky to keep up.

"I'm just a model," said Lucky. "I don't know how to be anything else."

Bonnie stopped. She took Lucky's shoulders between her hands and shook her gently.

"You are *not* just a model, Lucky." She gave her a meaningful look. "You are also, it turns out, a pretty hard-core drug addict."

Lucky gave a weak laugh.

"How could I forget!" She cast her eyes down. "I didn't even graduate from high school."

"High school? Pssh." Bonnie dismissed this with a wave. "Who needs it? You're Lucky–Fucking–Blue. You can do anything."

Lucky raised an eyebrow.

"Are you getting all last–act–of–a–sports–movie on me?"

"I mean it." Bonnie laughed. "You're the best person I know. You don't take shit from anyone. You've traveled all over the world. You speak *Japanese*."

"*Nihongo sukoshi dekimasu*," said Lucky softly.

"See!"

"That means I only speak a little."

"*Still* more than anyone else I know. Whatever you want to do, Lucky, you can do it. That's not true for everyone, but it's true for you. Nothing can stop you. Not even you."

Lucky attempted a smile.

"Okay." Lucky put her hands on Bonnie's shoulders, so they were like two sides of a bridge. "And what about you?"

"What about me?"

"I can do the locker room pep talk, too, you know."

Bonnie let her hands drop back to her sides. The difference between her and Lucky was that Lucky actually *was* exceptional. So was Avery, whose fast and terrifyingly efficient mind could be applied to anything. And Nicky had possessed the most social grace of anyone Bonnie knew; her students gathered around her as if warming themselves at the fire of her attention. But Bonnie just knew how to work hard. If her sisters were wild horses, she was simply a mule.

She turned toward home and started running again. The skyline of the Upper West Side rose above them, the pointed baroque towers of the San Remo building more familiar to her than any mountains. Lucky ran to catch up with her.

"Seriously, what about you?" she said. "If I can do anything, you can too."

"Sure," said Bonnie.

Lucky managed to pinch her arm while running alongside her.

"Say it!"

"Stop that!"

Another pinch.

"*Say* it!"

Bonnie batted her away, but she was laughing.

"Fine, you freak. I can do anything too."

Lucky, miraculously, picked up the pace, so she was ahead of Bonnie, turning back to her with a grin.

"That's the fighting spirit," she said.

Bonnie felt a surge of happiness that carried her all the way home, through the lobby, up the elevator, and to their floor. They were chatting merrily about what kind of smoothie to make for breakfast when Bonnie stopped, inhaling sharply.

"What is it?" asked Lucky, coming up behind her.

There, sitting in front of the door, was Avery. Avery had not yet looked up to see them, and for just a fraction of a second, Bonnie witnessed her sister as she really was. No polish. No facade. No deflection. She didn't know what had happened, but Avery was hurting. She could feel her sister's pain in her own chest. Avery was slumped in the doorway, her head bowed, limbs slack, crumpled in on herself. Then she glanced up and saw them. Watching Avery compose herself under their gaze was like watching a great marquee be erected, a slack pile of cloth swiftly transformed by a sharp pull of ropes into a towering structure. As Bonnie raced down the hallway toward her, she thought fleetingly that her sister was always pulling the ropes of herself taut. Before Bonnie could reach her, Avery had hoisted herself up to embrace her and Bonnie wished that just once, she would ask for a hand.

# CHAPTER NINE

# Avery

THE EVENING THAT LUCKY LEFT LONDON, AVERY CAME HOME FROM work late to find Chiti asleep on the sofa, a burgundy throw threaded with gold tangled around her legs. Avery perched beside her and placed a hand softly on Chiti's thigh, who stirred and peered up at her sleepily.

"It's late," said Avery.

"I was waiting for you," said Chiti.

"Let's get you to bed."

Avery made to free Chiti from the knot of blanket, but Chiti sat up brusquely, pulling something from her pocket and placing it between them. Avery knew what it was before the question came, but she prayed, futilely, that she might be wrong.

"Who is he?" asked Chiti. Her voice was cold and quiet.

Avery bowed her head.

"It's not about him."

Chiti raised her hand to stop her.

"You could have gotten rid of the evidence anywhere, but you kept it in our house. Consciously or not, you wanted me to know. So let's talk about it. Who is this man you fucked?"

Avery reached for the handle of her briefcase, as if preparing to run. But, of course, there was nowhere to go. She lifted her head.

"He's no one. You have to know that, Chiti."

Chiti clapped her hands in mock surprise.

"Oh, is this the script we're using? I've read this one before." She affected an American accent that was a cruel caricature of Avery's. "He is no one. It meant nothing. Please forgive me."

"He *is* no one," insisted Avery. "It *did* mean nothing."

"He is *not* no one," snapped Chiti. "He is a person. Is it this Charlie poet you've been watching on the internet?"

Avery's eyes sprang to her face. Chiti threw the blanket off her and stood up. She began to pace the living room, avoiding Avery's eyes.

"Yes, I checked your search history," she said. "And I have *never* done something like that before. But of course, I have never felt the need to. Until now."

"I'm so sorry," said Avery quietly, uselessly.

"So, it was this Charlie man?" asked Chiti, standing over her.

Avery hung her head again. Chiti put her hands to her waist, her silver bangles jangling.

"You fucked a man," declared Chiti.

"I swear he was just *there,* Chiti. It's not about him, it's about me."

Chiti circled around the sofa and Avery stood up. They turned to face each other.

"Do you not want to be with a woman, is that it?" asked Chiti. "You had your lesbian fling and now you're back to cock?"

Chiti uttered the word *cock* with such force Avery almost laughed, but when she looked into Chiti's face, she knew there was nothing funny about this moment.

"You're my *wife,* Chiti. You're not a fling."

"I know I'm your fucking wife!" screamed Chiti. "Do *you*?"

"Yes! That's why I've been torturing myself with this! I feel terrible. I hate myself for doing this."

Chiti was shaking her head in disbelief.

"Do you expect pity?"

"No! I—"

"So, you hate yourself? So what! You're not a teenager! You don't get to act on every self-destructive urge you have."

"I'm not saying it's an excuse, but—"

"I live in the house you wanted," Chiti cut her off again. "I eat the food you like. I treat your family as my own blood. And you *humiliate* me."

"I didn't ask you for this house," muttered Avery.

Chiti's attention snapped to her.

"What?"

"*You* wanted to buy the house I wanted. *You* insist on making the food I like. You make yourself the martyr so that I become the monster. You need me to be bad so you can be good."

Chiti shook her head violently.

"Are you seriously trying to argue that you didn't want my love? That you didn't benefit from it? Then why did you keep taking it all these years? *Why?*"

"Of course I wanted it! But you wanted to give it! You benefited from me needing you too."

Avery fell silent again. Chiti threw her hands onto the back of the sofa and leaned forward as if winded. She spoke to the cushions below her without looking at Avery.

"You've always wanted to escape who you are," she said. "Ever since I first met you. But I never thought you would want to escape—" Her voice broke and Avery winced at the sound of it, the raw, animal pain it contained. "*Me,*" she managed to choke out.

"That is not what this is," said Avery softly.

Chiti's eyes shot up to hers. They were a burning black.

"Then what is it?" shouted Chiti. "Talk to me! Why don't you *talk*? Why do you have to destroy our life to say you are unhappy? I know you are unhappy! I am unhappy too! So be an adult and fucking *talk* to me about it!"

"I . . . I don't know where to start," said Avery.

She was being a coward and she knew it. She was making Chiti voice Avery's feelings as well as her own, a cruel ventriloquy. Chiti looked at her and snorted with disgust.

"You know how they say the drink is the end of the relapse?" she said. "It always starts months before with the pulling away, the accruing resentments, the setting up of excuses."

Avery frowned in confusion.

"I didn't relapse," said Avery. "I swear."

"I believe you. But fucking a stranger is the *end* of the betrayal. You have been slipping away from me for a year. I have been waiting for this *for a year*."

"It only happened once," said Avery, as if that mattered.

Chiti's hands flew to her temples. She cast around as if frantically looking for something. Her entire body was shaking. Suddenly, she picked up a vase from the side table and launched it at the floor. It was one they had bought on their honeymoon in India, a beautiful glass cylinder blown in swirls of turquoise and pink. It hit the space between the wooden floorboards and the wall, exploding with such force it was as if it had been waiting all its life to shatter. Shards covered the carpet, winking and glistening in the light.

"That is one-tenth of how I feel," she said shakily.

As if feelings could be divided and delivered like that, thought Avery. If only.

"Stay there," said Avery. "Don't move. I'll get the broom."

"No," said Chiti, somewhere between a shriek and a plead. "For once in your life, I want you to stay in the wreckage you have created. Don't hide it, don't fix it. *Look* at what you have done." She was panting. "Please. For once in your goddamn life, Avery."

They stared at the shattered glass, glittering like rain. Chiti took a step onto it with her bare feet. Avery let out a yelp of pain as if it were her, not Chiti, whose soles were crunching the glass. She thought she saw blood, but it was only Chiti's crimson-painted toenails.

"Stop!" Avery cried.

Chiti stood in the center of the broken glass and looked back at Avery, her eyes ablaze.

"Do you think you are the only person in this house who is griev-ing?" she demanded.

"Chiti, please!"

"Do you?" she insisted.

"No, I don't," said Avery.

Chiti took another step, wincing slightly as the glass pierced skin.

"You are not the only person in this house who is having a hard fucking time, Avery."

Avery made an anguished sound.

"I know you miss her," said Avery. "But she was *my* sister."

From the center of her exploded life, Chiti gave her a look of pure contempt.

"Not only Nicky," Chiti said. "You. I lost *you*. For over a year now, I have been waiting for you to come back to me. I could feel it at the funeral when you wouldn't let me put my arm around you."

Avery frowned. She didn't remember that. The prayer book, she realized suddenly. She had stolen the prayer book and didn't want Chiti to feel it in her waistband.

"You have been slipping away from me for months," continued Chiti. "And now this! You think this is a surprise? You have been sabotaging our relationship in slow motion *for a year*."

"Please get out of the glass," said Avery. "Please, Chiti."

"Oh, now you care if I am hurt?" said Chiti. "*Now?*"

"Of course I care!" she shouted. "Your hurt hurts me! That's mar-riage!"

Chiti stood still and stared at her. Her hair had freed itself from its topknot and now hung loose around her shoulders. Avery observed its swirls and coils, more familiar to her than her own at this point. She had the urge to reach out and touch it, to bury herself in that dark curtain like a child hiding in her mother's skirt, but she knew there was nowhere to hide now.

"What do you want me to do?" Chiti asked, her voice shaking. "Do you want me to prove to you that you are unlovable? Undeserv-ing of happiness because you were too wrapped up in your own life to save your sister's? Because I won't. I *do* love you. Your grief, your anger, your silence, your secret cigarettes, even your lies. All of you. It turns out it is unconditional this love I have for you." She gave a shuddering inhale so sharp her nostrils blanched. "Though right now I dearly wish it wasn't."

With one light step, Chiti moved out of the shattered pile. They looked at each other in silent wonder, as though she had just vaulted a great distance to find herself standing before her.

"I'll fetch the tweezers," said Avery.

She returned from the bathroom with the first aid kit to find Chiti perched on the sofa. She took a seat beside her and motioned for Chiti to put her feet in her lap, then began inspecting her soles, plucking out slim splinters of pink and green glass as Chiti flinched. Chiti's feet were a constant source of wonder and frustration for Avery. They were completely flat, with arches so collapsed that they made suction sounds on the wet bathroom floor as she padded across it, a fact that Avery had never ceased to find hilarious. When they walked side by side on sand they had often marveled at the difference in their footprints; Avery's high arch gave her print the expected curve, while Chiti's resembled more of a splat. Her toes, too, were long and dexterous; practically fingers, Chiti often remarked cheerfully. Since they frequently ached and Chiti refused to wear proper shoes, they were also the reason the two of them were constantly taking cabs instead of walking, which Avery considered a waste of both money and the opportunity to get their step count up. Despite this, Avery had always thought Chiti's feet one of the loveliest parts of her. They were slim and long as silverside fish; holding them now, Avery felt as though she had plucked them from the water herself, these dancing, alive things caught in her hapless clasp. Angling the tweezers, she tugged the last sliver of glass free, stopping the ribbon of blood with a cotton ball. She held it fast to Chiti's foot and glanced at her face.

"Hurts?"

Chiti gave a grim smile.

"I'll survive. It was a silly thing to do."

Avery met her gaze.

"I've done worse."

Chiti narrowed her eyes.

"I know."

Now, Avery flinched. Suddenly, Chiti laughed.

"This is our worst fight ever, no?" she asked, incredulous.

Avery nodded, smiling timidly.

"Even worse than that New Year's we both got food poisoning because I made us order the seafood tower," she said.

Chiti released a short laugh again and stood up, hobbling on her sliced feet. She rubbed her eyes and sighed.

"I hate this, darling. I'm not cut out for histrionics. I just want to call it a night and go to bed. I know we can't, but . . . can we?"

Avery looked up into Chiti's open face. She took her hand and, somehow, they stumbled to their bedroom together. They lay on top of the bed without getting under the covers, clinging to each other, sleeping the whole night like that, knotted together, and Avery had dared to hope that, perhaps, the worst was over. Then the next morning, Chiti moved her things to the guest bedroom and a silence descended on the house that did not lift until, a week later, Avery fled to New York.

"WHAT ARE YOU DOING HERE?" asked Lucky.

Her tone registered more suspicion than surprise. Avery winced, just slightly. The three of them were standing in the kitchen, Bonnie and Lucky both looking flushed and streaming sweat under their workout clothes. Avery frowned. In what world did Lucky exercise?

"Wow, it's good to finally see you too," she said.

"You, like, just saw me," said Lucky, an edge of hostility creeping into her voice.

"I meant all together."

Lucky was clearly still mad at her for not taking her to the airport. Avery had told herself it was because she had too much work, which was partially true, but she knew it was really because she couldn't stand a long car ride alone with her sister after what she had just done with Charlie. She had been on such a high horse about Lucky's behavior, now look at her. Chiti had asked for no contact while Avery was away, ostensibly so she could think about what she wanted to do next and if that involved Avery. Now, Avery watched Bonnie shoot Lucky a look that communicated something like *be nice,* and the intimacy it contained bothered her immediately. Bonnie had always been her ally in the family. Now, without even Chiti, she had no one.

"Obviously it's good to see you, Aves," Bonnie said. "Why didn't you tell us you were coming?"

"I wanted to surprise you! I did, didn't I?"

Her voice sounded unnaturally high and grating, even to herself. Avery cleared her throat.

"It's amazing," said Bonnie. "The gang's back together! Well—" She looked at each of them with a sudden sadness. "You know what I mean."

"So, what's the plan?" Lucky asked, turning to the sink to fill a glass of water without looking at Avery. "How long are you here for?"

"However long it takes to go through Nicky's stuff," said Avery.

Bonnie knit her brow with concern.

"But I thought you said you weren't coming?" she asked.

"And we don't need your help," added Lucky.

"Guys!" Avery slapped her palm on the counter. "Is it that weird that I would want to come home and see my sisters together for the first time in forever?"

Lucky downed the water, then narrowed her pale eyes at Avery.

"How come Chiti didn't come with you?"

"What do you mean?"

"How come your wife is not here?" Lucky intoned slowly.

Avery blew a strand of hair out of her face. The apartment was stifling. Why hadn't anyone turned on the air conditioner?

"It was all so last-minute. She has her patients, you know. She can't just pick up and leave."

"That makes sense," said Bonnie. "Tell her we miss her?"

Lucky was staring at her with a weirdly intense expression. *Could she know? But how?* Avery thought. She needed to turn the conversation to anything but Chiti.

"And I'm going to look into what's actually happening with the apartment sale."

"Maybe they *should* sell this place," Lucky said suddenly. "Move on, you know."

"You don't mean that," said Avery.

"Why hold on to the past? Who cares."

"Nihilism is a luxury of youth," said Avery. "Trust me, you'll care once it's gone."

"Look, we don't *need* your help," said Lucky. "We've been getting on fine here without you."

"Oh yeah?" Avery put her hands on her hips. "How's going through Nicky's stuff going?"

Bonnie and Lucky exchanged a guilty look.

"You haven't started yet," said Avery flatly.

"We've had . . . other things to take care of," murmured Bonnie.

"What things?" asked Avery. "Is your training schedule already that intense?"

"I'm actually taking a little break from training," said Bonnie.

Avery frowned.

"Already?"

"We've just been doing other things," said Lucky.

"Staying out all night getting drunk with your friends does not count as things, Lucky."

Avery regretted saying it the moment the words left her mouth. What had she just been telling herself about her high horse? She was a scold, and no one welcomed a scold to the party.

"I'm not doing that," snapped Lucky.

"She's not doing that," confirmed Bonnie.

Avery looked from sister to sister.

"Why not? What's going on?"

Bonnie looked at Lucky for permission to speak.

"Seriously, guys," said Avery, feeling increasingly disconcerted by this new dynamic. Lucky opened her mouth to speak, then seemed to change her mind. She gave Bonnie a warning look.

"It's nothing," she said eventually. "I've just been jet-lagged. Let me take a shower and then we'll look at Nicky's shit."

"Nice," said Avery. "Very respectful."

Lucky was already heading out of the room.

"She was our sister, not a saint," she said over her shoulder. "Her shit is still her shit, Avery."


BEFORE GETTING STARTED, AVERY SUGGESTED the three of them head out and grab breakfast; she knew she was procrastinating, but she couldn't face Nicky's belongings on an empty stomach, and she wanted to do something to get on a better footing with Lucky before they opened the Pandora's box of their sister's life. They were walking back from the bodega, juggling their egg-and-cheese-on-a-rolls and coffees in the familiar Greek paper cups when Lucky stopped and gasped. She grabbed Bonnie's arm and pointed across the street.

"Holy *shit*," she cried. "Are you seeing what I'm seeing?"

They looked across Eighty-ninth Street, to where a pink Smeg fridge was standing placidly on the sidewalk, as though waiting for a friend. The streak of cotton candy pink against the gray pavement reminded Avery of a dove someone had dyed pink and set loose amid the sooty pigeons of Trafalgar Square during her first weeks in London. It was a surprisingly beautiful sight.

"Wow," said Bonnie. "That's nice."

"I'm sure it belongs to someone," said Avery, but Lucky was already darting across the street, frantically beckoning for them to follow her.

"Come *on,* before someone else gets it," she called over her shoulder.

Bonnie looked at Avery with an indulgent smile, shrugged, then crossed the street too.

"Guys, this is a waste of time," called Avery from her abandoned side of the street.

When it was clear they were going to ignore her, she gave up and trotted after them, dodging a slow-moving taxi. The three of them stood before the fridge, which was about Avery's height, in respectful awe. The fridge stared back. Lucky swung open its door and peered inside.

"It's in, like, mint condition," she said. "No gunk or mold or anything."

"I'll admit it's cool," said Avery. "But we don't need a fridge. In fact, the last thing on earth any of us need right now is a big pink fridge."

Lucky removed her head from inside.

"Aves, can't you see that this, like, *is* Nicky in an object? We have to take it."

"It's very Nicky," conceded Bonnie.

Avery gave her a look to show she expected better from her.

"Not to mention the fact these things cost thousands of dollars," continued Lucky. "It's essentially the holy grail of New York street finds."

"But we're here to get *rid* of Nicky's stuff," said Avery. "Not add some random kitchen appliance none of us need just because it happens to be her favorite color. Where would we even keep it?"

"In the apartment," said Lucky, as if this was obvious.

"Right, yes, of course, the apartment they're planning on selling in a month. Great idea."

Lucky's face fell.

"Okay, we'll store it at Mom and Dad's place upstate. Or I'll ship it back to Paris. Or Bonnie will take it." Lucky puffed through her nostrils with frustration, just like she used to when she was a little girl and couldn't keep up with her older sisters. "I don't know! All I know is we *have* to take this. It's Nicky, I can feel it. Nicky is giving us this fridge."

Bonnie went behind it and tipped it toward her, testing its weight.

"It's not as heavy as I thought," she said. "But it will take all three of us to carry it back."

Lucky looked at Avery imploringly, who shook her head.

"Absolutely not," she said.

"Pleeeeeeeease?" Lucky wheedled, shooting Avery her lycan-thropic grin.

"It's a ridiculous idea," said Avery.

Lucky's magic wolf smile disappeared and it was like the sun leaving the sky. Avery swallowed. Why, she asked herself, did she always have to be the naysayer? The adult? Wouldn't it be fun to be Lucky's carefree sister for once instead of her scolding mother? She placed a hand on the glossy pink surface.

"I'll take the middle," she said.

By the time the three of them got the fridge back to their building, they were winded less from the effort of carrying it than from laughing so hard. Several times, they'd had to set the Smeg back down on the sidewalk so they could give in to the fit of giggles that was overtaking them. It wasn't exactly clear why crab-walking down the sidewalk like the Three Stooges while carrying a ginormous pink fridge was so hilarious, but it was.

"Hey there!" said the doorman in surprise as they shuffled inelegantly through the entrance. "You ladies need help?"

"We're good," called Avery. "I think we need to take it up ourselves as a matter of pride at this point."

"It's our pink cross to bear," said Lucky, hitting the elevator button with her elbow, and the three of them dissolved into laughter again.

The doorman gave them a perplexed smile.

"If you're sure," he said. "Oh! Before you head up. Your mother stopped by and left this paperwork for the broker. Do you want to take it, or should I keep it at the desk for them to pick up?"

The three of them stopped laughing. They put the fridge down.

"Our mom was here?" asked Bonnie.

"Yeah, she came by while you were out."

"Did you tell her we were all here?" asked Lucky.

"Sure, I told her the three of yous had just stepped out."

"And did she say anything? Is she coming back?" asked Lucky, her voice rising.

"I–I don't think so," stammered the doorman, clearly thrown by their instant change in demeanor. "She just gave me the paperwork and left without going up."

Lucky checked her phone.

"She hasn't called or anything," she said.

"Of course she hasn't," muttered Avery. "She knows we're here."

"But why wouldn't she wait to see us?" asked Bonnie in a small voice.

Avery looked at her sisters' crestfallen faces. They were like flowers with all their petals picked off. She couldn't believe their mother would do this; first that ice-cold email about the apartment and now this. Except, of course, she could.

"Because she's a cunt," she said. The doorman gave her a shocked look. "Sorry," she added. "But she is." The elevator doors opened, and the three of them picked the fridge back up, without laughing this time, and only then did Avery have the thought that it was the exact shape and size of a coffin.

THE THREE OF THEM STOOD side by side in front of Nicky's closet and, as they stared at it, Avery felt as if it grew to an insurmountable height, one hundred feet at least. She had the overwhelming urge to simply lie down. They'd left the Smeg by the front door; the magic that had seemed to encircle it, and by proxy them, evaporating like heat. Suddenly, it was just somebody's old fridge.

"Right," Avery said, forcing herself to sound brisk. "We need three piles: keep, donate, and discard."

Thankfully, the ever-organized Nicky kept her closet tidy. She did, however, love to shop. Since her teacher's salary was not large, she favored high street brands like Forever 21, Strawberry, or Zara, places she could go for a pick-me-up, as she called it, and get herself something to wear that night like a going-out top or the kind of plated jewelry that left green marks on her skin. As a result, most items went in the donate and discard piles: stacks of pilled T-shirts, a tote bag filled with salt-crusted bikinis, a feather-trimmed cowboy hat, likely for some bachelorette party they all would have made fun of her for attending. Avery had often advised Nicky to save her money and spend it on one special thing instead of ten throwaway items, but Nicky liked the act of stopping in to a store after work the same way others liked a happy hour drink: It took the edge off.

In many ways, Nicky's taste hadn't changed all that much since she was a kid; she still loved feathers, florals, and flounce. Looking through her things now, Avery could feel every age Nicky had been present in that room: the gap-toothed child doing dance recitals in the living room, the preening teenager getting ready for a date, the sorority girl laughing with her friends. She touched the feathers of the cowboy hat gently. So what if Nicky had liked things that were a bit tacky? Looking through the piles of off-the-shoulder tops and maxi skirts, fake leather boots and tangled necklace chains, Avery regretted ever giving her sister a hard time. It was sweet that Nicky loved this stuff; if shopping had remained the worst of her addictions, she would have been lucky indeed.

"Motherfucker!" exclaimed Lucky from the other side of the room. "I knew she took this from me."

She was holding up a vintage Spice Girls tour tee. At the sight of it, Bonnie and Avery involuntarily smiled. Between Avery and Lucky's seven-year age gap and the vastly differently musical tastes of all the sisters, there was only one band that had ever managed to appeal to all four of them simultaneously and that was the Spice Girls. When Lucky was eight, Nicky was ten, Bonnie was thirteen, and Avery was fifteen, they'd convinced their mother to buy them tickets to the reunion tour. It was too expensive to go in Manhattan, but they had managed to find seats in the back of the Long Island venue. They'd begged to rent a limousine, as some of the other girls from their school had done to take them to the concert in the city, but their mother considered that a ridiculous expense in addition to the tickets, so they took the Long Island Railway instead. Since she didn't want to pay for five tickets, their mother had trusted Avery to chaperone them, handing her a credit card for emergencies only and strict instructions to come straight home after. The concert was three hours of heaven, all of them scream-singing the words to every song along with thousands of other girls, lifted together on a tide of riotous, unapologetic joy, the feeling that to be a girl with other girls was not some weakness, as they had been told, but a power, the best and luckiest power on earth. Afterward, still riding an estrogen-induced high, Avery had used the credit card to buy Bonnie, Nicky, and Lucky each a tour T-shirt. She claimed that she was too old to wear one, but really, she had just been worried about their mother seeing the credit card bill.

Bonnie picked up the tee, which was emblazoned with five grinning faces and the familiar invocation to SPICE UP YOUR LIFE.

"No, this one was mine," she said. "See? It's a large. I always bought everything size large."

"And you, extra small," said Avery, pointing at Lucky, who, true to form, was wearing a tiny cropped T-shirt and low-rise jeans, now topped with the feather-trimmed cowboy hat she'd fished out of the discard pile. "Which hasn't changed."

"I let her have it after she gave hers away to Carter Beaumont," said Bonnie.

"Carter-Fucking-Beaumont!" exclaimed Lucky, like it was all one word. "I'd forgotten about that asshole."

She glanced quickly at Avery to see if she was going to scold her, but Avery laughed. Carter *was* an asshole. The middle and high school all four of them had attended was a parish-funded Catholic school in the East Eighties. Because of this, it had substantially lower school fees than any of the surrounding private schools, including tuition breaks for enrolling multiple children, which was how their parents were able to send all four of them to it after their public elementary school. Despite its lack of extracurriculars, especially in the arts and humanities, it had a good reputation for offering a thorough, fluff-free education, which was why a number of wealthy Upper East Siders—especially the ones who worked in finance and lived in fear of spawning arts-oriented offspring who might aspire to fields as unlucrative as writing or, even worse, acting—enrolled their children in it. Also, no one loves a deal more than the rich.

This was why, though Avery and her sisters never lived in fear of not having food, shelter, new schoolbooks, clean uniforms, and even trivial niceties like sparkly stationery and matching pajamas, they often felt poor at that school. It had never seemed weird to them that their six-person family was squeezed into a two-bedroom apartment—after all, at their elementary school they'd known kids with all sorts of living situations, including grandparents, aunts, uncles, and cousins all in one home—until they met the likes of Carter-Fucking-Beaumont. Carter lived in a townhouse between Madison and Park, a home where the doorbell played the opening phrase of "Nessun Dorma" and each of Carter's six siblings had their own floor.

None of the sisters were great at fitting into this social milieu except Nicky, who by the end of her first week was already best friends with Carter and a blonde named Mary (there was a minimum of at least three Marys in any Catholic school) and calling themselves "the muskies," a take on the Three Musketeers. Spoiled and mean-spirited, Carter took great pleasure in pitting Mary and Nicky against each other and testing each of their loyalties to her. Shortly after the Spice Girls concert, Nicky had been invited to Carter's for a birthday sleepover during which they'd watched *Titanic,* made ice cream sundaes using the entire Dylan's Candy Bar assortment, and concocted a face mask following a recipe from one of Carter's mom's fashion magazines.

Two terrible things happened that night, according to Nicky. The first was that during a game of Truth or Dare, she had been dared to eat some of the face mask, formulated from a mix of avocado, coconut oil, and moisturizer, just one taste of which prompted her to throw up liquid ice cream all over Carter's en suite bathroom. This was bad enough, but the lasting effect was worse. Since this had been her very first taste of avocado, Nicky would never as an adult be able to enjoy the delight of a good guacamole, since even the slightest morsel of an avocado's creamy flesh immediately recalled for her the acrid savor of drugstore moisturizer, a fact that, to her dying day, remained one of her greatest grievances.

But worse even than the face mask fiasco was that their ever-abstemious mother, who, unlike every other mom on the planet, according to Nicky, did not have a goodie drawer filled with viable gifts for the endless tween birthdays she was destined to be invited to that year, had sent her to this sleepover armed with only a disposable camera she'd picked up on sale from the post office as a gift. When Carter had opened this present, the look on her face had not been disgust so much as confusion, a confusion so profoundly humiliating to Nicky that she had immediately leapt up, opened her overnight bag, and fished out the brand-new Spice Girls tee she had been planning on proudly wearing the next morning. She offered it to Carter, explaining that her mother hadn't had time to gift wrap it, who accepted it with a satisfied shrug.

"You gave her yours after that?" asked Avery.

Bonnie nodded, still gently holding the shirt.

"She was so upset afterward," she said. "Remember her crying when she got home?"

She had sobbed until a blood vessel beneath her eye burst, but Avery knew Nicky wouldn't have done it differently if given the chance. She wanted to fit in with those girls at any cost, and she had succeeded. Avery wished she had Bonnie's compassion, but what she remembered feeling was frustration. Why had Nicky given away something she loved, not to mention something Avery had gotten royally reprimanded by their mother for buying, to suck up to the likes of Carter? Why was she so quick to abandon herself to be popular? Even once she reached her twenties and, to Avery's relief, developed deeper friendships with more substantive people like her fellow teachers, she maintained the relationships from her youth. *Your sister has a knack for friendship,* their mother used to say, and it was true, but she also had a knack for becoming whoever anyone wanted her to be. Carter-Fucking-Beaumont had even attended the funeral, sobbing between her millionaire father and her finance fiancé, her hand weighed down by a hefty diamond engagement ring. *Don't dim to fit in,* Avery had implored her sister, but Nicky had only grown defensive. *Why does everyone in this family think it's bad to be normal?* she'd retaliate. *To be liked?*

But their family wasn't normal. Addiction whirred through all of them like electricity through a circuit. Even Nicky had it in her. Why else would she have secretly started buying more pills? She was addicted to the fantasy of normalcy she'd created for herself, the fantasy of an ordinary, pain-free life. And Avery had bought into the fantasy, too, turning a blind eye to Nicky's contracted pupils, her irritability, her growing secrecy. Staring at the piles of Nicky's things, each an attempt to fill her life with color and sparkle and joy, Avery felt her chest ache with the unfairness of it. Who could ever blame Nicky for wanting to be normal? It was Avery's fault for missing the signs, not Nicky's for creating them.

"Well, it's mine now," said Lucky, plucking the T-shirt from Bonnie's hands.

Bonnie laughed this off, but Avery flared immediately. Beneath the self-recrimination, there was another nagging thought too. Yes, she should have seen what was happening to Nicky, but *why* didn't anyone else? Where the fuck had her sisters been? Her mother? Her father? Anyone?

"Why should you get to keep it?" she snapped. "It was Bonnie's first. And, anyway, *I* bought it."

"It's fine, Aves," said Bonnie. "It's not like I'm going to wear it."

"And I'm the baby," whined Lucky, evincing that unique mix of self-indulgence and self-awareness that drove Avery crazy about her sister. She tried to snatch the shirt from her hands, but Lucky was too fast. She whipped off her T-shirt, exposing her bare chest, and pulled the new one on with an unselfconsciousness drilled into her early from modeling. Lucky never really acted like her body was her own, Avery thought fleetingly; it had been made public property too young. "Fits perfectly," Lucky declared, smoothing down the front.

"You don't *respect* anything," said Avery.

"Respect?" mimicked Lucky in a stuck-up voice that sounded

nothing like Avery's. "It's a Spice Girls tee! What the fuck am I meant to be respecting?"

Lucky had leapt onto the bed to escape her. She picked up the feather-trimmed cowboy hat from where she'd dropped it and plopped it onto her head to complete the look.

"It's not just this, it's everything!" Avery began counting on her fingers. "You didn't call us on the one-year anniversary. In fact, you never call me. You're barely helping with packing up her stuff. Just because you're the youngest doesn't mean you don't have to *deal* with anything."

Why was she picking this fight? Why couldn't she stop herself? Too many reasons to count. Because she was tired from the flight. Because she didn't want to be sorting through closets right now—she had simply wanted to make a point to Bonnie and Lucky that all you had to do to get something done was to *do* it. Because once again Avery's ruthless efficiency was backfiring on her, leaving her resentfully doing a task no one had asked her to do. Because Bonnie and Lucky were friends now and she should have been happy about it, but instead she was pissed. Because she was in the middle of destroying her marriage and she couldn't tell anyone because she was the eldest, and therefore exemplary. Because their mother had rejected them all over again and Avery had to make it okay. Because without Nicky the balance between them was off; they were meant to be an even number, and now they were odd. But mostly because her sister was dead, her beautiful, vivacious, silly, charismatic sister was gone, and nothing on earth would ever make that right.

"You seriously think I didn't remember what day July Fourth is?" asked Lucky. "Do you honestly think I'm that much of a fuckup?"

"Well, you forgot her last birthday," shot Avery.

Lucky winced as if struck.

"That is so unfair," she said quietly.

"Avery, stop," said Bonnie.

Avery turned to her.

"And you're no better! You just ran away to L.A. and buried your head in the sand. Did it ever occur to either of you to check in on how *I'm* doing? Heaven forbid you should worry about anyone but yourselves."

"You're right," began Bonnie, but Lucky interrupted.

"Oh, you're such a martyr," she said. "It must be *so* hard being you, in your perfect house with your perfect job and your perfect wife. I'm so sorry we aren't all more concerned about *you*."

Avery scoffed.

"Do you think you are the only one who wanted to throw your life away this year? To run away from all your problems? Do you think you're the only one grieving?"

She realized, as she said it, that it was exactly what Chiti had asked her.

"That's not what Lucky's doing," interrupted Bonnie. "She's actually been—"

"Shut up!" interrupted Lucky. "I don't want to talk to her about it!"

"Hey," said Bonnie, involuntarily taking a step back. "I'm trying to help."

"Talk to me about what*?*" asked Avery.

"None of your goddamn business!" said Lucky.

"What is going *on* with you two?" asked Avery. "Bonnie, why aren't you training? Lucky, why aren't you working?"

"I'm taking a break," declared Lucky, jumping off the bed. "I'm allowed to take a break!"

"Your whole life is a break!" shouted Avery, stepping forward and knocking the stupid feather-trimmed cowboy hat off her head.

"Don't touch me!" yelled Lucky, pushing her away.

"Don't touch *me*," said Avery, shoving her back.

The two began jostling and shunting each other until Bonnie got between them, swiftly separating them with professional efficiency.

"Enough!" Bonnie barked once she was sure she'd gotten them apart. "We're too old for this shit."

"She is," Lucky sulked.

"I said *stop*, Lucky," said Bonnie. "She's obviously having a hard time being back here. We all are."

"I'm not having a hard time," said Avery petulantly. "*You're* having a hard time."

Bonnie caught Avery's eye and gave her a gentle look.

"Come on, Aves," she murmured. "This isn't like you."

Avery let out a long exhale. Of course, Bonnie was right; being back here *was* hard. She hadn't anticipated quite how hard it would be.

"You're right." She softened. "Sorry, Bon Bon."

Lucky stepped back and looked at them both.

"I knew this would happen." She wiped her nose roughly on the back of her arm and pointed at Bonnie. "I knew you would take her side. Like always."

"That's not what's happening," said Bonnie.

Lucky shook her head.

"You are such a coward," she muttered. "You've always done whatever Avery says."

"Lucky, apologize to your sister," said Avery.

She knew it was the wrong move as soon as she said it. Knee-jerk mothering, an impulse guaranteed to infuriate Lucky.

"You think you know everything, don't you?" crowed Lucky. "You don't know Bonnie."

"What are you talking about?" asked Avery.

"Stop it," growled Bonnie.

"You want to know why she's not training? Because she's in love with Pavel and she's too chickenshit to tell him, that's why!"

"*What?*"

Avery turned to Bonnie in surprise, who, in turn, gave Lucky an outraged look.

"I'm not training because I've been helping *you,* you ungrateful little shit!" Bonnie said, as Lucky spun away from her.

"Bonnie and Pavel?" Avery thought about it for a moment. "Bonnie and Pavel!" she said again and smiled to herself.

Avery had never understood why Bonnie stopped working with Pavel after her last fight. Sure, it was a bad defeat, but Pavel had thrown in the towel to protect her, anyone could see that. She had always suspected Pavel was a little in love with her sister. She knew trainers and their fighters shared a unique bond, but it was hard not to notice the rapturous way Pavel watched Bonnie during her fights, flinching each time she was hit as though he, too, was absorbing the blow. For all his Russian stoicism, he'd always lit up like a jack-o'-lantern whenever she was around. And now, it turned out Bonnie was harboring a candle of her own. It made sense. She and Pavel were so similar, Avery thought, which was part of why they'd never gotten together. Both strong but shy, gentle but lethal, like two great orcas circling each other in the wild, never quite swimming abreast.

"Stop saying our names like that!" yelled Bonnie. She glared at Lucky again. "I cannot *believe* you. After everything I did for you this week?"

"Okay!" interjected Avery. "Someone explain to me what the fuck you two have been doing this past week."

"Don't," said Lucky, looking hard at Bonnie.

But Bonnie only shrugged. Whatever allegiance they'd brokered, Lucky had betrayed it.

"I was helping her get clean," she said quietly. "She's been sober since she got here."

Lucky rounded on her.

"Fuck you!"

Bonnie gave her a bewildered look.

"Fuck me? Fuck you!"

"Wait a minute!" called Avery, holding up a hand to each of them. She could feel hope squeeze into the room like a parade blimp, unwieldy and out of place. But there it was: good news.

"You're *clean,* Lucky?" she asked, trying not to let the excitement creep into her voice too obviously.

Lucky rolled her eyes and tossed herself away from them onto the bed. She grabbed a pillow to her chest, as if shielding herself.

"No! Well, yes. But it's not like that. I'm just taking a break. And I'm not going to go to one of your fucking meetings, so don't ask."

"What do you mean taking a break?" asked Bonnie quickly. "I thought . . . I thought you were trying to stop for good?"

"Isn't the whole thing meant to be a day at a time?" Lucky countered.

"But you said . . . Y-you said you'd *stopped* stopped," stammered Bonnie. "Now you just want a break?"

"I'm not like her," said Lucky, pointing at Avery. "She couldn't handle it. *I* can."

Avery released a snort of disdain. What was she talking about, handle it? She *handled* it by staying sober the past ten years and building a successful adult life. A life, she had to admit, she was currently doing a good job of burning to the ground, but Lucky didn't know that. She should be so lucky to *handle* things like Avery!

"And Nicky?" Bonnie asked. "What about her?"

"That's completely different," said Lucky.

Bonnie gave Avery a desperate look.

"She said she was ready," she said.

"I was!" cried Lucky. "I am! I don't know. I just don't need all this *pressure* from you two."

"It's not pressure," said Avery. "It's concern. We're concerned about you."

"Well, I don't need your fucking concern! Stop projecting onto me. I'm not you, I'm not Dad, I'm not Nicky. I'm just *me*."

Avery turned away, trying to keep her cool. Lucky was already making excuses for herself. It was typical of her youngest sister to wheedle out of any responsibility. Avery had once heard that mice didn't have collarbones, which was how they could fit through holes a fraction of their size. That was how an addict functioned. No collarbones—or, for that matter, spine. She turned back to Lucky.

"You're being spineless," she shot. So much for keeping her cool. "At least take responsibility for who and what you are."

"Don't you realize that I miss her every second of every fucking day?" screamed Lucky. "But she's not here, so I'm doing the best I can without her. Why is nothing I ever do good enough for you?"

"Please! Spare me the self-pity." Avery threw her hands in the air in exasperation. "You are not the only one who lost her. We knew her longer than you did anyway!"

This was a ridiculous claim and Avery knew it, but she was too infuriated to form a rational argument, which only made her more furious. Lucky let out a laugh of disbelief.

"Do you hear yourself? Just because you're older doesn't mean you knew her better. Neither of you knew her like I did."

"We all knew her differently," said Bonnie to the ceiling above her, seemingly resigned to the fact no one would listen. Ever since Lucky had suggested she wasn't planning on staying sober, the fight seemed to have gone out of her.

"Jesus, Lucky!" exclaimed Avery. "I'm so sick of you acting like it's worse for you than for anyone else. You didn't know her best. She was just more willing to put up with your bullshit than the rest of us."

Lucky stepped away from her as if pulling back the arrow on a bow, looking for her target.

"I do know that she thought you were a judgmental bitch."

It found its mark. Avery felt herself exhale involuntarily as the sharp point of this insult punctured her. The only recourse was to pull it out and hurl it back. She looked Lucky in the eyes.

"Better a judgmental bitch than a fucked-up addict," she said. "Destined to follow in her footsteps."

Bonnie's attention snapped back from the ceiling.

"Don't say that," she cried. "Don't even think that, Avery!"

But Lucky was narrowing her eyes at Avery with serpentine focus.

"I might be an addict," she said softly. "But you're a liar. I *see* you, Avery. Hypocrite."

Avery could feel herself go cold. Was it the stealing? The cheating? Both? But she'd been so careful. How could Lucky know? And even if by some bizarre twist of fate she did, who the fuck was she to judge her?

"How dare you," she said in a low voice.

Lucky smiled her lupine smile, exposing sharp canines.

"She's going to leave you, you know," she said.

Avery shook her head. As if she hadn't been telling herself this exact thing every moment of the past week.

"You don't know what the hell you're talking about," she said.

"What *are* we talking about?" interjected Bonnie. "Avery? Has something happened with Chiti?"

The question was asked without accusation, but Avery found herself leaning away as if from a flame. She and Bonnie were two years apart, but they had always felt a little like twins. They were connected on an unconscious level, able to feel the other's moods as instinctively as one feels shifts in the temperature, something Avery had historically found deeply comforting. But not now.

"I have no idea what she's talking about," she said. "She's just being a bitch."

Could Bonnie feel it, Avery's temperature change? She had gone cold, but now the shame of her affair was radiating off her like an ice burn.

"You don't deserve her," said Lucky.

Avery looked down. *You think I don't know that?* she wanted to shout. But she wasn't going to let Lucky win that easily.

"You're too young and stupid to know how fortunate you are," she said slowly. "That we don't all get what we deserve."

"What does that mean?" asked Lucky.

*Don't say it,* thought Avery. *Don't say it.* But she did.

"Because if we did, it would have been you in that casket, not her."

The regret was everywhere, instantly. Lucky looked at her in shocked silence, the same suspended quiet that comes after a toddler has fallen down and not yet decided to cry. But Lucky did not cry. She blinked back the tears that instantly filled her eyes and rubbed her face roughly with her palm.

"Well, I'm sorry to have disappointed you," she said and walked out the door.

Bonnie ran after her, but Avery knew Lucky was not coming back after that. Then the front door slammed, and Bonnie returned. She looked at Avery with a mixture of horror, contempt, and pity.

"How could you say that to her?"

Avery sat down on a pile of clothes and dropped her head in her hands.

"Don't, Bonnie, please."

"Do you have any idea how fragile she is right now? What if she drinks?"

Avery exhaled a weary sigh.

"I can't get her drunk and you can't keep her sober. The sooner you accept that, the better off you'll be."

"But I *did* get her sober. I . . . I gave everything to get her through this week."

"*Keep,* not get, Bonnie."

"So, what, you're just going to give up on her?"

Avery shook her head. She was so tired.

"I have carried this family on my back for too many years." She sighed, then added, apropos of nothing, "I wanted to go to Berkeley for college!"

Bonnie barked a laugh of disbelief.

"You went to Columbia! It was hardly community college. And then you *did* leave. You disappeared to California for a year before you moved to London. You've always done what you wanted."

That made Avery sit up.

"You think I *wanted* to pay for this apartment for the past year?" she countered. "I didn't want you two to lose your home *and* her. I wanted you and Lucky to have a place to come back to if you needed it. Everything I do is to protect you. I taught you *all* to swim. You know who taught me? No one! I had to pick it up myself, or I'd drown. I'm speaking both literally *and* metaphorically here."

Bonnie rolled her eyes.

"Yeah, I got that, Avery. You don't need to talk down to me. I'm not one of your clients."

"And who the hell are you to accuse me of giving up?" continued Avery. "You dedicated your entire life to boxing and quit after one loss. One!"

Bonnie looked down at her feet.

"You don't know what you're talking about."

"I know that you're letting your feelings for Pavel get in the way of a career you were born to have. So you love him? Big whoop! Grow some balls and tell him!"

"I have balls!" yelled Bonnie.

Avery would have laughed if it wasn't all so terrible.

"You are thirty-one years old," she said. "Your peak is *now*."

"Don't lecture me, Avery."

But she was not going to stop. She didn't care anymore. If Bonnie hated her as well as Lucky, so be it. All that mattered was that she did what she needed to do to get Bonnie out of this dynamic with Lucky, out of the quicksand of their family dysfunction, out of this moment of defeat for good.

"You want to throw that away to help Lucky?" she said. "Fine. But don't be surprised if all you end up with is another dead body on your hands."

Bonnie's face contorted with pain. She opened her mouth, then shut it again. How could she respond to that? Avery had now said the cruelest thing she could think of to both her sisters. But there was relief in it too. She could be free. The thought arrived like an electric jolt. Avery could be free of the responsibility of their love. They stood like that, each resolute in their silence, as below them the city offered its litany of noises. A garbage truck groaned down the street. In the place of birdsong, cars communicated with a flurry of horns. On a floor below, a dog released a long howl. Eventually, Bonnie dropped her sister's gaze. She walked to the door.

"Sometimes I think you forget that I'm the one who found her. Right there." She pointed to a spot on the bedroom floor. Her voice was quiet but there was a hardness to it Avery didn't often hear. "You're right that Nicky's death didn't only happen to Lucky. But it also didn't only happen to you."

## Chapter Ten

# Lucky

Lucky stormed out of the apartment and made it to the corner of the park before letting herself stop to think. She was breathing hard. Other than her phone in her pocket, she had nothing on her, not even her cigarettes. She gritted her teeth and dug her nails into her palms. She was not going to let Avery make her cry. She paced up and down near the park's entrance, watching for someone she could bum a smoke off, until she eventually clocked a businessman strolling past puffing on what looked like an American Spirit. He offered her one as soon as she asked, smiling at her as she leaned over the flame of his silver lighter.

"You look really familiar," he said.

"I'm not," she said, taking a deep inhale.

"Any chance I could get your—"

"Nope," Lucky said and turned on her heel, speed-walking away down the avenue.

Once she was a safe distance away, she stood under the awning of a quiet doorman building and took a deep drag, inhaling until her lungs crackled. She hated Avery. She exhaled. She hated Avery *so much*. She inhaled again, too quickly this time, and ended up sputtering up smoke and spit. She hated Avery so much she was *choking on it*. After a few more minutes of furious puffing, the doorman came out and stood beside her, wordlessly shepherding her along. She was done anyway. Lucky threw the butt into the gutter, instantly wishing for another, and headed south.

At the corner of Eighty-first Street, she stopped, lingering at the top of the subway entrance stairs. She felt a vague pull to be downtown, back in the neighborhoods where she felt most like herself, where there were fewer reminders of her sisters. She ducked into the entrance, made sure there were no transit employees around, then hopped the turnstile with a practiced swing, catching the C train just in time. She wished she had headphones so she could listen to music; instead, she stared at the various passengers and tried to pick one item of clothing from each of them to make an outfit of her own. An older Asian woman holding a potted plant on her lap, whose woven sandals Lucky had mentally decided to pair with the Dickies of the man next to her, looked up and smiled as she caught her eye. Shyly, Lucky smiled back. After spending the entirety of last week by Bonnie's side, it was strange to be in the city alone again, untethered by work, plans, or people to see. She had not lived in New York full-time for years, but when she did come back, she had always had Nicky to hang out with.

She emerged out of the Eighth Street exit by the one-dollar pizza slice place and, for no particular reason, turned west along Christopher Street. She stopped outside a boutique pet shop and stared at a cockapoo puppy galivanting in the window like a small cloud trapped in glass. At the sight of her, it hopped onto its back legs and fumbled eagerly at the partition dividing them, its fluffy paws slipping like feather dusters across the window. Lucky smiled and raised her hand to the glass. Should she get a dog? It would certainly be more loyal to her than either of her sisters. Maybe the dog she chose would, by some cosmic twist, have the soul of Nicky reborn inside it, a puppy with her exact temperament and spirit. Lucky kneeled, so she and the dog were eye level. She tried to stare into its bright black eyes, but it was now busy chasing its own tail, performing acrobatic tumbles on the shredded paper floor of its enclosure. Its fur was the color of warm ginger biscuits. She was still trying to catch its gaze—*Are you my sister?*—when a couple in matching college tees stopped beside her to coo at the puppy through the glass.

Lucky turned away and kept walking. Of course the cockapoo wasn't Nicky. That puppy had a crowd-pleasing, teddy-bear quality that might appear to be like Nicky to an outsider, but the people who truly knew her understood that wasn't the real her at all. If Nicky was a dog, she would be a breed both noble and fiercely loyal, like a saluki, those mythic creatures beloved by Egyptian royalty, not the kind of affable fluffball fawned over by any white couple in the West Village. But it would be a kind of magic, she thought longingly, to have Nicky by her side again, draping her silky form across her lap, streaking out ahead of her to chase off unwanted visitors (or sisters), a mute but knowing witness to her days and nights. She wished she believed in heaven like the Catholics or life after death like the Muslims or reincarnation like the Buddhists. She wished she believed in anything at all.

Nicky's funeral was held at the Church of Saint Ignatius Loyola on the Upper East Side, a decision their parents made without the input of the sisters. Lucky would have voted to put her ashes into a firework and shoot them into the night sky, Hunter S. Thompson style, but their parents insisted on a funeral mass and, if Lucky was honest, she thought Nicky would have liked the pomp and pageantry of the Park Avenue address. Lucky, Bonnie, and Avery had hidden out in the sacristy at the back of the church, sitting side by side in glum silence next to the rack of cassocks as, outside, the guests filed in. It was probably for the best that Bonnie stayed out of sight for as long as possible; she'd lost her fight the weekend before and her bruises were in the ugly stage of healing, sickly yellows, greens, and browns streaking across her cheekbone and under her eyes. Their mother poked her head through the door and gave them a daggered look.

*There you girls are! What are you doing back here? You're being rude.*

*It's our sister's funeral, Mom,* said Avery. *No one's expecting us to put on a show.*

*Who even are these people?* asked Lucky.

*They're people who knew Nicky,* said their mother. *Obviously.*

They peered past her through the door at the black–clad mourners jostling down the aisle to their seats. Their father, looking vacant and ready for a drink, stood making conversation with the priest. Two women, likely Nicky's sorority sisters, had obviously used the occasion to get dressed up, arriving in teetering high heels and plunging mini-dresses. One was wearing an elaborate feather–trimmed fascinator.

*I always said she had too many friends,* said Avery.

*Seriously,* said Lucky. *Like, who the hell is that?*

She pointed to an older man with oiled–back hair wearing an expensive-looking linen suit.

*That's Nicky's friend Carter Beaumont's father, I think,* said their mother. *Yes, see, there's Carter.*

*Carter-Fucking-Beaumont!* Lucky shook her head. *What are they doing here?*

*The Beaumonts always liked Nicky,* said their mother wistfully. She turned back to them sharply. *And you girls need to adjust your attitudes. It was nice of him to come. He's a very important man.*

Avery gave a snort of disgust.

*Why? Because he's rich?*

Their mother gave a distracted wave.

*He's helped a lot of people. He invented baby harmonicas or something.*

The sisters gave each other a bewildered look.

*Why the fuck would babies need those?* asked Lucky.

*I imagine they need them just as much as adults,* said their mother primly.

*Can they even control their mouth like that?* asked Avery.

*What?* asked their mother.

*Not to mention their tiny lungs,* said Lucky.

*It's not for their lungs,* said their mother. *Obviously, it's for their hearts.*

Lucky glanced at her sisters, who looked equally perturbed. Even Bonnie, who had remained practically mute since her fight, cracked the slightest smile.

*I guess music is always for the heart?* she offered softly, and Lucky and Avery tittered.

Now, their mother frowned.

*Music? What do baby heart monitors have to do with music?*

The mass was long and, as to be expected, heavy on the Jesus-died-for-our-sins narrative. *Whether in life or death, we belong to Christ,* intoned the priest as he placed the pall and cross on the coffin. Lucky thought Nicky would have preferred to belong to a good co-op board or a country club, but sure, yes, she conceded bitterly, Christ was good too. She sat blankly through the homily, the Eucharist, and the Old and New Testament readings feeling nothing, she assured herself, absolutely nothing. Only when the priest reached the final commendation did she start to crack.

He waved the silver thurible of incense over the casket, casting smoke over the length of where Nicky's body lay hidden, and Lucky watched as it curled over his hands and disappeared into the air above the nave. *Grant our sister may sleep here in peace until you awaken her to glory.* Lucky bowed her head forward. *She will see you face-to-face and in your light will see light.* She could feel her insides tearing apart, a physical sensation of ripping in her chest. *Until we all meet in Christ and are with you and with our sister forever and ever.* Lucky let out a gasp of pain. She was breaking under her grief. Beside her, she could feel Bonnie shuddering. Then Avery reached over to grab both of their hands, pulling them to her.

*Baby harmonicas,* she whispered and the three of them dissolved into a fit of giggles so inopportune and inappropriate, Lucky choked trying to keep them in. Their mother gave them a murderous look as they snorted into their hands, but they didn't care. Nicky would have laughed too.

————

LUCKY WAS WANDERING WITHOUT DIRECTION. She turned left, then left again until she found herself south of where she'd started, near the basketball courts by the West Fourth entrance of the subway. Shirtless, sweat-slick players raced up and down the courts, their sneakers squeaking on the asphalt as they pivoted and pushed past one another. Should she learn some kind of team sport? Would that give her life purpose? She had endured a brief and humiliating stint on the volleyball team in middle school, after the coach had persuaded her to try out, convinced that her unusual height would make her a natural fit for striker.

Her first practice, the team had initiated her by huddling in a circle with Lucky at the center and chanting *say what, what?* to which Lucky was instructed to respond *hot to trot!* She had looked around at the ruddy, cheering faces of her fellow female athletes, all screaming with the kind of glee that translated visually to anguish and terror, and walked right out of the circle, pushing between their unyielding bodies with mute determination. She still remembered the relief of breaking out of that hellish sphere, out of the gym, out of the locker room, out of the school altogether, until, finally, she was thrust back onto the streets of Manhattan, where she was anonymous and free. Now, she looked at the streaking figures on the courts, their faces twisted in an ecstasy of concentration and communion she would never know. No, she would not take up a sport. Lucky was not, nor ever would be, *hot to trot.*

She needed to keep moving or the memories would overwhelm her; she was turning away to continue her wandering when she heard her name being called in a breathless male voice with great excitement. It was Riley, the southern model she'd met in Paris. Today, his floppy blond hair was held back by an elastic headband that left his innocent, handsome face on full display. He was streaming sweat, looking at her with delight.

"I thought that was you!" he called.

He had a slow, gliding way of talking, with drawn-out vowels that sounded like they were dipped in honey. In his mouth, *I* sounded like a sigh of satisfaction more than a possessive. *Aaah.*

Lucky glanced behind her, but it was too late to pretend she hadn't heard him as Riley bounded over with puppyish excitement. He grabbed at the chain-link fence between them and grinned.

"Hot damn, I'm happy to see you again!" he said. "What are you doing here?"

"You know," she said. "Just wandering."

"Great shirt." He smiled. "I love the Spice Girls. You've got Posh written all over you."

"Actually, I'm Baby," said Lucky. *Nicky's Posh,* she thought but did not say.

Riley turned to gesture to his fellow players.

"Hey, guys! Look who it is! This is my friend Lucky."

*Friend* felt like a generous term for the two beer-soaked hours they had spent together, but Lucky smiled graciously. The other players, many of whom she recognized as fellow models, waved at her, then returned to shoving and jostling one another, laughing with boyish high energy. Lucky waved back at them self-consciously. That was another thing she remembered from middle school: the watching. The boys had the big sports games, the boys were in bands, the boys played tricks in class, and the girls looked on. It was initially what had made modeling so thrilling, as well as terrifying: For the first time in her life, she was the one being watched.

"I tried to message you after Paris, but I couldn't find your profile," said Riley. "And Sabina said she hadn't heard from you. You are one hard lady to track down."

"You know me," she said. "International woman of mystery."

Riley laughed and shook out his hair.

"I believe it." There it was again. *Aaah.* "So what you been up to?"

Detoxing about a decade's worth of drugs and alcohol out of her system.

"Not much. Hanging out with family and stuff."

"Right on." If Riley was waiting to be asked in return, he quickly clocked that was not going to happen. "Hey, what are you doing right now?" he asked, eagerness all over his face.

"I . . ." She couldn't think of an excuse. "Nothing. Absolutely nothing."

"Can you wait here a few minutes? We're just finishing up, then we're gonna head around the corner for a drink. You gotta come."

A drink. Lucky would kill for a drink right now. A drink would kill Lucky right now. She glanced up at the sky. Was this some kind of test? Did she even believe in those?

"Stay right here," said Riley, sensing her hesitation. "Don't move." He trotted backward toward the other players without taking his eyes off her. He was beaming. "Oh man!" he yelled. "Lucky-Fuckin'-Blue!"

Fifteen minutes later, Lucky found herself wedged around a small circular table in the shady courtyard of a Belgian brewery nestled off MacDougal Street, surrounded by half a dozen sweating models in basketball shorts.

"Now, Lucky, you're drinkin' on me," said Riley. "And I know you like your beer. What can I get you? They have a great blond here called Delirium Tremens."

Lucky made a slight choking sound but managed to maintain her composure.

"Just a soda water for me," she said.

Riley raised his eyebrows.

"You sure?"

"Yup," she managed to croak.

Lucky endured the first round of drinks by chain-smoking the other models' cigarettes and chugging seltzer, all while monosyllabically answering questions from the intensely curious Riley, who seemed intent on learning all he could about her. She kept imagining the taste of cool beer slipping down her throat. It was torture. When Riley finally left the table to go to the bathroom, she saw her opportunity to make an escape. She shot up from her seat.

"I'm just—" she mumbled. "I'll . . . be back."

She turned toward the exit and made it halfway there before she changed her mind and headed inside instead. The bar was dark and warm, untouched by the dappled sunlight outside. The scent hit her immediately. She could smell the beer in a way she'd never been able to when drinking it. It was so sweet and familiar. It was bread crusts and pine needles and caramel. It was earth and yeast and stone fruit. It was relief. The bartender sidled over to her, waiting for her order. She could do it. No one would have to know. She opened her mouth to order.

"Which way is the bathroom?" she asked.

The bartender gestured toward the back, and Lucky forced herself past the bar to where he pointed. There were two individual rest-rooms, each with a smoked-glass window in the door. Lucky waited outside them, vibrating with pent-up longing. A tall, attractive woman exited from one of them and did a double take at Lucky before leaving. Lucky was used to this. Women often checked her out more blatantly than men did, not out of sexual curiosity, or not al-ways, but as a kind of competitive research. It used to bother her, but since making the decision to quit modeling, she felt a novel remove from her physical self. Let her look. She wasn't profiting off her body anymore. Lucky waited without entering the vacated bathroom until Riley emerged from the other one. His face lit up at the sight of her.

"Hey, you," he said.

He held the door open to let her pass, but she grabbed the front of his jersey and pushed him back into the bathroom. When he opened his mouth in surprise, she pushed her own to his. Then she was kiss-ing him, hot, bruising kisses, fierce and ravenous, snaking her tongue into his mouth, bumping her teeth against his. She grabbed handfuls of his basketball jersey and wrung it between her fists. She wrapped her arms around him, crushing him to her. She felt the crunch of her ribs against his chest. They crashed back against the sink, and he lifted her up, pressing her tight to him as she coiled her legs around his waist. Her face was above his now and if she could, she would have unhinged her jaw and swallowed him whole like a snake with a smooth, round egg. She threaded her fingers through his hair, pulling off the stupid headband and flicking it to the floor. He stared up at her in wonder as she smoothed floppy golden strands of his hair away from his face with her palms. She pressed her lips to his breathlessly, messily, until his legs buckled beneath him, and she tumbled to her feet out of his arms. He reeled away from her and put a hand on the window ledge, catching his breath.

"Wow." He exhaled. "I wasn't expecting . . . Wow."

"Don't talk," said Lucky.

She launched toward him again, pushing her hand into the waistband of his basketball shorts. She closed her eyes and felt for him.

"Hey," he said softly, attempting to tug her hand away. "Hey, wait."

She opened her eyes.

"What is it?" she asked.

It could have been playful, but the question was tense with impatience.

"I just . . ." He swallowed and pulled her hand free of him. "My friends are outside—"

"We'll be quick," Lucky said and tried to return her hand.

"And I haven't showered—"

He attempted to take a step back and almost toppled into the toilet bowl. Lucky pressed forward.

"I don't care."

"And . . . *God,* Lucky." He grabbed her by the shoulders and held her still in front of him. "I like you. I think you're cool, you know? I'd like to take you out sometime."

Lucky stared blankly at him.

"You *like* me?"

He let go of her and ran a hand through his hair.

"Well . . . yeah."

Lucky blinked.

"But you don't know anything about me."

He threw his hands up.

"Well, I've been *trying,* Lucky, but you're kind of a hard book to crack. Maybe if you go on a date with me, I could find out more."

Lucky narrowed her eyes at him.

"A date? What kind of date?"

"I don't know, I hadn't planned it yet. We can do anything. What do you like to do?"

"I like to take drugs," said Lucky. "And drink until I black out."

Riley gave a nervous laugh tinged with something else, fear or fascination, Lucky couldn't tell.

"But . . . I'm open to other suggestions," she added.

At this, his entire being perked up like a dog who has just heard the front door open.

"So that's a yes?" He grinned. "That's great! Wow, okay. We could . . . I don't know, we could go bowling?"

Lucky shook her head.

"No sports. No organized fun of any kind. Next."

Riley frowned.

"Right. No fun. Okay."

"*Organized* fun," corrected Lucky. "I'm not a monster. I don't hate fun. I just hate it being forced upon me."

Riley gulped seriously.

"Totally," he said. "Me too."

Lucky swallowed her smile. This seemed patently untrue since Riley's personality so far was like every activity from a child's birthday party rolled into one. But she appreciated his effort.

"I know!" he exclaimed. "We could go dancing. I'm a great dancer."

Now, Lucky could not contain her smile.

"You're not meant to say that about yourself," she said.

"But I am. Seriously. I've had a lot of practice. I was part of the Kentucky Fried Hotties dance troupe back home."

Before she could stop herself, Lucky snorted through her nose.

"The *what*?"

"Kentucky Fried Hotties. We'd dance at, like, ladies' bachelorette parties. Sometimes birthdays too."

Lucky put a hand to his chest to steady herself.

"Wait a minute, you were a *stripper*?"

Riley grinned.

"I prefer adult entertainer, but yeah."

"Okay, I'm going to need to hear more."

Riley grinned, clearly delighted to have caught her attention so fully.

"I did gymnastics until college, but then I got injured and lost my scholarship, so I joined the dance troupe for a few years. It was great money, honestly. One of the bachelorettes ended up being a model scout, so that's how I came out here."

Lucky took a small step back and regarded him more thoughtfully. One thing she should never underestimate, she thought, was a person's capacity to surprise her.

"Before I say yes," she said seriously, "I'm going to need to see these famous Kentucky Fried moves."

Without hesitation, Riley lifted up his shirt and did a body roll that rippled from his head down to his chest and stomach, the muscles of his abs contracting rhythmically. He finished it with a liquid rotation of his hips. Lucky couldn't help herself, she squealed with delight like any bachelorette. Riley beamed.

"You should see me on a pole," he said.

Lucky shrieked again.

"You cannot do that on a pole!"

"Oh man, after gymnastics, I can do anything upside down. Only problem is, the nerve endings in your legs die." He patted the back of his knees. "Like here? I can't feel a thing."

Lucky stepped toward him and reached down so her face was at the height of his chest. She pinched the tender skin behind his right knee, and in doing so pressed her cheek to his torso.

"Can you feel that?" she asked, pulling the taut skin hidden behind his kneecap.

Riley looked over her head and tried to stifle his laugh.

"No, ma'am."

Lucky dropped to all fours. The bathroom floor was not exactly clean, but she didn't care. She was partially under the sink, its old iron pipes clanging softly. She twisted her head around so she could see the back of his leg and gently bit the skin behind his knee.

"What about this?" she asked, her teeth still holding his flesh.

He laughed lightly.

"That," he said, "I can feel."

Riley stayed very still, a willing prey in Lucky's wide wolf jaw.

Lucky left the bathroom with Riley feeling high on adrenaline. This was more like it. As they returned to the table, the fight with her sisters felt very far away. She took a seat, casting around for a cigarette, as one of the models slid a frosted pint of beer toward her.

"Hey, we ordered this for Petey, but he had to bounce. You want it?"

Suddenly, she couldn't remember why she had made such a big deal about stopping. Who was she trying to prove herself to, anyway? Bonnie? Avery? They didn't care about her. Avery had quite literally told her she would have preferred Lucky to die instead of Nicky. And Bonnie would always choose Avery over her. Why was she torturing herself trying to be something she wasn't to earn the love of people who didn't want her? *Fuck it,* she thought, and grabbed the glass. It tasted just as good as she remembered.

Beers turned into shots at a karaoke bar in Chinatown, which turned into bottle service at a club in SoHo they entered through the kitchen of a Mexican restaurant, which turned into warm tequila on the roof of one of the models' lofts, which turned into a four A.M. deli run for more booze, which turned into dancing and doing lines while one of the models played the latest single from his kind of cringe but quite fun band, which turned into Riley trying to get Lucky to put the Spice Girls T-shirt back on that she'd torn off her body while screaming *Fuck the Spice Girls!* and glugging half a bottle of cheap deli wine, which turned into Lucky telling Riley he was a fucking square who was trying to control her, which turned into Lucky making out with the owner of the loft right in front of Riley to show him just how little she cared, which turned into Riley threatening to leave, which turned into Lucky making a fake weepy face while giving him the middle finger and demanding the loft guy cut her another line, which turned into Riley actually leaving, which turned into Lucky drinking even more deli wine then projectile vomiting all over the loft guy's fancy cream Berber rug, which turned into him kicking her out, which turned into her standing on the corner of Greene and Grand at that totally dead hour between five and six A.M. when only the garbage trucks were out, which turned into Lucky realizing her phone was also dead and slumping down over a sidewalk grate determined to just sleep there, which turned into her looking up to find Riley walking toward her looking tired and sad, explaining that he had come back because he didn't think that model with the loft was such a good guy after all and he was worried about her getting home safely, which turned into her telling him that she had no home, and no one who loved or cared about her anyway, so he should just leave her here on this sidewalk grate to die, which turned into him taking her back to his place and tucking her into his bed with a glass of water and her phone charging next to her on the nightstand, which turned into her crying into his pillow while apologizing again and again saying *I never cry, I never cry,* which turned into him saying that it was okay and she probably just needed some sleep and it would all feel better in the morning.

It did not. Lucky woke up in Riley's bed and immediately wished she was dead. Sunlight pierced the dark curtains with pinpricks of light; even the slightest brightness felt like an assault on her eyes. On the bedside table, next to a stack of books that included *Sapiens* and *The Power of Now,* her phone was fully charged. She checked the cracked screen to find it was almost midday, then lay back on the pillow with a quiet groan, pressing her palms to her eyes. What had she done? How could she have drunk after all that she and Bonnie had been through together the past week? She'd ruined everything. Worst of all, she had proven Avery right. She *was* a fuckup. The shame wave that followed this thought was so violent, she involuntarily brought her hands to her mouth to stop herself from crying out as it washed over her.

She'd heard once that guilt was for something you'd done—you could feel guilty for a certain behavior or action but still fundamentally know you were a good person—but shame was deeper, shame was for who you were. Lucky didn't simply do bad things, she *was* bad, she saw that now. If the real her came out when she drank, then the real her was clearly a nightmare. She was like some vicious, snarling animal caught in a trap, swiping at the hand that tried to help. No one who had seen her last night, or on any of the hundreds of nights she'd been drunk the past few years, would want anything to do with her. And now not even her sisters would either. Avery already hated her, and after last night, Bonnie would too. She had no one.

She couldn't hide in Riley's bedroom forever, much as she longed to, so she unplugged her phone—three missed calls from Bonnie, none from Avery—and crept out of the room, wincing at the light as she entered the living room. Riley lived in a loft apartment in Williamsburg with floor-to-ceiling windows and the kind of functional, soulless furniture in stain-concealing neutrals found in fully furnished rentals. The open-plan kitchen had a whiteboard magnet on the fridge on which someone had written *Be More, IRL!* Definitely a model apartment, Lucky noted.

Riley was sitting at the dining table, shirtless, bent over his laptop. He looked up as Lucky entered without smiling. She was struck for the first time by what a beautiful man he was; golden-haired and golden-toned all over, with cinnamon freckles scattered from his cheeks to his shoulder blades. With an unfamiliar self-consciousness, it occurred to her that she must look like absolute shit.

"Hey," he said, his voice registering neither warmth nor coolness. "You want coffee?"

Lucky shook her head. The only thing she wanted was to get out of there as quickly as possible and then, preferably, curl up somewhere and expire.

"I should be going." Her voice came out in a raspy croak. She swallowed. "I'm really sorry about last night."

Riley shook his head.

"It's okay . . ." He paused. "Actually, it *wasn't* okay, Lucky."

There it was again, that shame wave, so alarming in its physicality that Lucky had to dig her nails into her palms and wait for it to pass like a contraction.

"I know——" she began.

"But," he interrupted her, "I get the sense maybe *you're* not okay." He looked at her and his face softened with concern. "So . . . are you okay?"

Lucky had not expected that, this kindness in the face of her badness. She didn't deserve it, yet here it was, simple as the offer of morning coffee. It was so surprising, it didn't even occur to her to make up a plausible lie.

"No," she blurted. "I'm not okay. I'm . . ." She may as well just say it, she figured; at this point, she had nothing left to lose. "I'm an alcoholic, Riley. And an addict. And I really think I need to be sober, but I have no fucking clue how."

Riley took a long gulp. Lucky instantly regretted saying it. Unvarnished like that, it didn't sound great.

"I'm not sure I've met too many of those," he said eventually.

Lucky gave him a thin smile.

"Give it another few years in fashion." She gestured to the door. "I'm gonna go. Thanks again and, um, sorry for burdening you with all this. Please just forget about it."

She made it to the front door, which for some inexplicable reason had three different types of locks on it. She attempted one combination, then another, but could not get it to open. She was trying, unsuccessfully, to remember which bolts she had already turned, when she felt Riley's arm reach around her.

"Let me help you with that."

He flicked the locks with practiced efficiency and pulled the door open. Lucky gave him an embarrassed smile.

"Everybody thinks they're a genius until they try to open someone else's front door," she said.

Riley laughed.

"Or use their shower," he added. "The hot water is never the direction it should be."

"True." Lucky gave him an awkward wave. "Okay. Bye then."

She was about to slip out the door when Riley caught her and pressed her to his chest in a hug. He smelled of soap and something vaguely sweet, too, like honeysuckle. Lucky was rarely shorter than anyone, but her crown fit snugly under his chin.

"You got this, Lucky," he murmured into her hair. "Ain't nothin' to it but to do it."

She looked up at him.

"Is that a southern saying?"

Riley smiled and shook his head.

"Maya Angelou." He let her go. "My mom's a high school English teacher. And Miss Angelou? *That* lady knew what she was talking about."

LUCKY HEADED TO THE MARCY Avenue station, then changed her mind and kept walking toward the entrance of the Williamsburg Bridge. She was too shaky and hungover to be enclosed on a moving train and, anyway, she was in no hurry to return to the apartment and face her sisters. The sun was high in a cloudless, chlorine-blue sky, and a stultifying heat had settled over the streets. Outside a coffee shop, a stout bulldog lay spread on its belly on the hot asphalt, lazily lifting its jowls to follow Lucky with half-hooded eyes as she passed. Lucky reached the entrance of the bridge and was relieved to feel a light breeze lift off the water. The familiar red railings and graffiti-scarred path stretched before her like time; a cyclist whooshed past, then the bridge was empty.

She set off across the water, metal balustrades swooping and criss-crossing overhead. With no headphones to allow her to escape into music, she was left with her thoughts. Her mind darted through the same closed circuit of memories, as a bee trapped indoors will pound again and again at the same windowpane, looking for escape. Nicky's wish scribbled on a strip of paper in her palm. *No more pills.* Why hadn't Lucky pushed her when she denied writing it? Why hadn't she told someone? Their last phone call. *Find out what makes you happy, then go fucking do it.* The final pane that stopped her was always Nicky's funeral. Lucky replayed it again and again, as if returning could somehow change it, could fling a closed window open.

They had retreated to a stuffy side room for the wake with thick spongy carpets and too-cold air-conditioning. They'd served tea and coffee and dry finger sandwiches, none of which would have excited Nicky. She would have wanted one of those cakes you cut open to release rainbow sprinkles, or trays of pastel-colored Magnolia cupcakes, or a white chocolate fountain, something decadent and silly to lighten the mood. The mourners milled around, chatting in somber tones, as Lucky and her sisters huddled in the corner like the three witches of Eastwick. Soon, the clinking of a glass cut through the din and their father shakily got to his feet. There was no alcohol served, so he was holding sparkling water, but they knew he would have had something before to get him through the morning. Blond and blue-eyed, he had always been a handsome man in the style of Frank Sinatra, but Lucky saw his age that day. His cheeks were red and veined and his eyes, once so pellucid, had a cloudy quality. He cleared his throat and looked down at his hand, which was shaking, and placed his glass on the side table next to him.

*I wanted to say a few words about Nicky, our angel, our darling girl,* he began, looking around the room. *Now her mother's not going to like that I tell you this, but when she was born, I wanted to call her Holly. I got the idea because, a few months before Nicky was born, I read* Breakfast at Tiffany's.

He paused for a laugh that never came.

*Most of you probably only know the film with Audrey Hepburn, which is a chick flick, really, it's not serious stuff.*

*Can we make it stop?* whispered Lucky to Avery.

*Not unless you know where to find the fire alarm,* she whispered back.

*But it's actually based on a book by Truman Capote,* their father continued. *Well, not even a full book. What's it called when it's longer than a short story but shorter than a regular book?*

*A novella, Dad!* called Avery, clearly exasperated, and a few people did laugh.

Their father raised a shaky hand and pointed at Avery.

*See, that's my eldest for you. Photographic memory. Mind like a steel trap. Don't cross her, she'll never forget it. Never forgets, never forgives . . .* He gave Avery a hard look and Lucky's heart sank. Was he really going to criticize her in front of all these people? At Nicky's funeral? But, thankfully, he released Avery from his stare and turned back to the assembled guests. *Now, where was I? Oh yeah, the nov-ell-a, thank you, Avery.* He pronounced the word with a skeptical flourish, as though suggesting she might have made it up. *Capote's story is much darker than the film, much more sinister. She's essentially a prostitute in the book, though she doesn't call herself one. A high-class escort if you will.*

Lucky could feel herself bending forward as if she could flip herself inside out and somehow disappear.

*But she's charming, you know, charismatic. Holly Golightly. Great name. So, I said to my wife, let's call her Holly!* Here, he affected a high-pitched caricature of their mother's English accent. *After a prostitute, my darling? I should think not!* Again, he paused for a laugh that did not come. *So, well, we kept looking for a name, and luckily Nicky was almost two weeks late, so we got some extra time. The week before she was born, I read* Tender Is the Night *by F. Scott Fitzgerald, what I consider to be his greatest book. And there's a character in that story, Nicole Diver her name is, who starts the novel in a psych ward. She's very beautiful, but she's mad, you see, a real mental patient.*

*He somehow retains this shit,* Avery muttered. *But none of our birthdays.*

*Now, I know what you're thinking,* their father continued, smiling to himself at his own joke. *First a prostitute, now a madwoman? This guy really must not want another daughter!*

Beside Lucky, Bonnie let out a little groan, the first noise she'd made since their father started speaking.

*But by the end of the story, Nicole is a different woman. Unlike Fitzgerald's own wife, Zelda, who died in a fire while locked in a mental institution, Nicole does get better. And by the end of the novel, she's happy, you see, and she's free.* He looked around the room, making sure each person was listening. *And I wanted that for all my daughters, that whatever life threw at them—because one thing I knew was that life would throw things at them—they would survive, and they'd find a way to be happy and free.*

The silence deepened in the room, that curious quality of quiet when you can feel the attention from every person present deepen.

*Of course, now I think I made a mistake,* he said. *Maybe if I had named her Holly, things might have been different. Maybe she wouldn't have—* He stopped himself. Lucky thought for a moment he was choking, but he was gasping back tears. Their mother stood up and rushed to his side, but he waved her away. *Sit down,* he barked, and their mother, chastened, returned to her seat. *Go lightly, that's what I wish for her now. Nicky's life was made hard, too hard, and I pray that now, wherever she is, that she may go lightly.* He swung around and caught Lucky, Bonnie, and Avery in his cloudy blue gaze. *And for my remaining daughters, as you live on after this loss, that is what I wish for you.* He grabbed shakily for his glass again. *So, if you will join me in raising a glass, to our beloved daughter, our precious girl, Nicole Blue.* He lifted the drink above his head, tears streaming unchecked down his face. *Wherever you are, Nicky, go lightly. Go lightly.*

*Nicky, go lightly,* chanted the mourners. It sounded like a song, Lucky thought, but really it was a prayer. *Nicky, go lightly.*


LUCKY WAS ALMOST TO THE other side of the bridge. *Go lightly, go lightly, go lightly.* She repeated the words to herself with each footfall. The city spread before her with no destination in sight. She couldn't go back uptown in this state, but she had nowhere to go. She stood on Delancey and watched the city rush around her, its oblivious and unbridled business, which stopped for no one. Without even consciously admitting to herself she was doing it, she pulled out her phone and googled AA meetings nearby. She scanned the list, stepping aside for a bike delivery guy hurtling obliviously down the sidewalk, quietly amazed by the sheer volume of meetings happening in the city at any given hour. There was one in the East Village on Twelfth Street that was starting soon. She looked up how long it would take to walk there—twenty minutes it said, but it would be less with Lucky's long legs—and began heading north.

As she walked, her heart ran. She would just try one, she told herself, not for Avery or Bonnie or her parents or even Nicky, but for herself. She needed to know who she really was. She reached the East

Village and passed the address several times before doubling back to find a beat-up metal door covered with stickers and peeling paint. It was just below street level, down a short flight of brick steps. Lucky descended and attempted to push it open, but the door would not budge. She pulled. Nothing. She shook the metal handle and heaved her shoulder against it. Locked. Lucky walked back up the steps, then turned quickly back in case the door magically opened now she had stopped trying. It remained as impenetrable as before. She couldn't believe it, after she had psyched herself up to come and everything.

"Well, fuck you too," she mumbled.

A perky-looking woman in neon running gear raced past, did a double take, and slowed to jog on the spot.

"Workshop's flooded!" she called to Lucky. "Try around the corner on Saint Marks." She checked her Apple watch. "There should be a meeting starting on the hour."

"Thanks," Lucky called after her as the woman set off again at a brisk clip.

Lucky watched her disappear around the corner in perplexed wonder. How many ordinary-looking New Yorkers were secretly sober? She checked the list on her phone and saw the woman was right, there was another meeting just a few blocks away starting in twenty minutes. She walked toward Saint Marks, then, deciding she couldn't face being early and making small talk, sat on a shady stoop nearby, wishing for a cigarette. Across the street, a couple packed up their convertible car for a weekend trip, kissing briskly as they closed the trunk. On the sun-dappled stoop next to her, a white-haired man combed his golden retriever, releasing tufts of hair like dandelion seeds into the breeze. He caught her eye and smiled. Despite everything, she was happy to be back in New York, the hometown she had not planned on returning to, which somehow always welcomed her back.

Nicky's funeral had been Lucky's last day in the city. After the wake finished, their parents had retreated immediately back upstate, unable to bring themselves to enter the apartment again. Without saying it aloud, the sisters felt the same. Avery had quietly paid for the three of them and Chiti to stay in a hotel nearby, a situation they all knew couldn't last. The night of the funeral, the three of them met in the hotel's bland restaurant as Chiti slept upstairs. Usually, when all the sisters were together, it was a battle to get a word in, but that night the three of them sat in glum silence. The menu had many variations of hummus on it, which was, incidentally, also the color scheme for the decor, as well as the complexion of the server hovering over them.

*I'll just have a mint tea,* said Avery, snapping her menu shut.

*Me too,* said Bonnie. *And . . . the hummus starter.*

*Which one?* asked the server. *We have several.*

Bonnie gave him a panicked look. Her right eye was still swollen shut and an angry purple color. Ever since finding Nicky and losing the fight, she had barely managed to speak a full sentence aloud.

*I-I don't know,* she stammered.

*She'll have the first one and a side of bread,* declared Avery, and Bonnie gave her a grateful look.

*I'll just get a vodka soda,* said Lucky. Avery glanced at her and raised her eyebrows. *Don't,* Lucky added.

*I didn't say anything,* said Avery.

*Your eyebrows did.*

Avery waved this off.

*Oh, you know they have a mind of their own,* she said lightly, and the tension was momentarily dispelled.

But, as it dragged on, the meal became unbearable. They didn't work as the three of them; they were *meant* to be four, and being together without Nicky only made it worse. Bonnie was the first to crack, admitting that she had decided to take a break from training to go to L.A. Lucky claimed she had to get back to Paris the very next day for an (imaginary) job she simply couldn't turn down. And Avery, of course, had a life in London with Chiti to return to.

*Go lightly,* their father had implored them. But they had never been shown how, so they had simply gone. Well, Lucky thought, leaving the stoop to make her way to the meeting on Saint Marks Place, maybe she could change that now.

She reached the address, squinting up at a faded red awning with the name of a theater written on it. Steep, crumbling stone steps led to an open door. Lucky remained planted at the bottom, as though assessing a mountain she was not sure she could scale. A bald man dressed in a glittery purple neck scarf and round Hockney-esque glasses strolled up. He looked her up and down.

"You going in, honey?"

Lucky glanced at him, panicked.

"I don't know."

He smiled, his glasses flashing in the sunlight.

"First time?"

Lucky tentatively nodded.

"You know what happens every time someone goes to their first meeting?"

"An angel gets its wings?" she said gloomily.

"A person is restored to dignity," he said.

*And they never have fun again,* she thought. She hated the platitudes, hated this weird language everyone in AA seemed to use. Avery was the worst culprit. *Fellowshipping. In program.* What did that even mean? It made it sound like some elite college course, not a free self-help group for people stupid enough to destroy their lives.

"I don't believe in God," she said suddenly. "And I'm not going to."

"Oh, that's not a prerequisite." He gave her a little wink. "But the fact you're here tells me that something sure as hell believes in you."

And with that, Lucky followed him up the stairs.

Inside, the room was small and shabby. A stained gray carpet covered the floor; a circle of old wooden chairs had been set up in the center of it. To the left was a small kitchen with a coffeepot and paper cups set out next to the sink. Lucky turned back to the door longingly. They may as well have hung a sign above it that said THE END OF FUN.

A man came toward them from the far end of the room, carrying a stack of blue books in his hands. He looked to be in his early thirties with a swoop of thick, dark hair and wire glasses. He wasn't bad looking, she observed, in a nerdy Harry Potter way. She immediately felt relieved—attractive people went to AA too!—then like an asshole for caring.

"Hey, good to see you, man," he said to the bespectacled man who had walked her in.

"Cooper, this is— What's your name, honey?"

Lucky told him.

"It's her first meeting."

"Wow," Cooper said, dropping the books on a chair and rubbing his hands on his jeans. "Welcome. That's so cool. Welcome. I just said that."

Cooper twisted his head suddenly toward his right shoulder and produced a rapid-fire series of clicks between his tongue and teeth. He turned back to her and blinked exaggeratedly.

"Thanks," said Lucky, glancing toward the door again.

"You want to read How It Works?" he asked, picking up a laminated sheet of paper and handing it to her. Lucky turned it over in her hands; it was printed densely with text on both sides.

"I'm good," she said, passing it back to him.

Another head twist and series of loud clicks. He turned back to her.

"I have Tourette's," he said, between blinks. "And no worries about reading. It's just great you're here."

Lucky took a seat and stared at her feet as Cooper and Hockney Glasses busied themselves opening packets of cookies to accompany the coffee and placing a book on each seat. Cooper handed one to Lucky and she opened it, pretending to read. She could feel a sinking inside of her, like a plug had been pulled at the bottom of her stomach, her insides circling down it. It was such a familiar sensation, though one she had not felt for years. It was the feeling of being back at school.

Unlike brilliant Avery and naturally academic Nicky, Lucky had not been good at school. Even Bonnie, who raced through the school day like a meal she did not enjoy in order to get to the dessert of boxing, had been better than her. Lucky never raised her hand to participate, never called attention to herself in any way that she could help. The worst part was when they would go around the class reading aloud. Usually, she found a way to go to the bathroom to avoid it, but one time the teacher had forced her to stay. Her heart racing, she counted the students in front of her, trying to work out which section would be hers to read. When it came to her turn, her voice came out small and shaking. She kept her eyes on the page, but she could hear students swivel around to look at her. She read as quickly as she could, trying to get it over with, but that only caused her to lose her breath. Her heart hammered inside her chest as she realized with mounting panic that she couldn't catch it again. She sat there gasping for air like some monstrous sea creature suddenly expelled onto land. A couple of students began to titter and whisper. *Lucky can't read!* More heads turned to stare at her.

No one expected her to be shy, looking the way she did. They didn't expect her to be particularly smart either. And there she was proving them right. Eventually, the teacher gave her a perturbed look and asked the next student to pick up where she had left off, and the class continued. Lucky kept her burning face close to the page as other voices filled the room one by one. The only relief she could find was the knowledge that Nicky was somewhere down the hall in her own class. Just the thought of her sister was like slipping an ice cube under her tongue. She found her between periods and told her what had happened as students rushed past them in the hallway.

*Of course you can read,* said Nicky hotly. *You just refuse to do it on command.*

*They think I'm stupid,* whispered Lucky.

She turned her face toward the locker, trying to hold back tears. Nicky pulled her in for a tight hug.

*Don't,* said Lucky, afraid people would see. But Nicky just squeezed harder.

*You are not stupid,* Nicky whispered fiercely in her ear. *You're a rebel. And rebels are always misunderstood by their peers.*

Lucky pulled away and rubbed her palms roughly over her wet face.

*It didn't feel very rebellious,* she said in a small voice. It felt like drowning, but in air instead of water. Nicky paused to think.

*Well, fuck 'em,* she said eventually. *Who cares what they think? Myopic provincials.* Nicky was studying for the SAT and was using the vocabulary words every chance she got. *Just call them that if they try to mess with you.*

*Myopic provincials.* Lucky had repeated the phrase to herself for the rest of the school day and, somehow, she survived until the final bell. The following year, Nicky went off to college and Lucky started modeling full-time. It was a relief to be able to study for her GED alone while doing a job that rarely expected her to open her mouth. Except for one time early on in her career when she'd had to read lines for that sleazy photographer, which she tried hard never to think of again, she'd spent the remainder of her life avoiding public speaking or reading. And now here she was sitting in this dingy little room, preparing to be humiliated all over again. *No,* thought Lucky. *No, thank you.*

She stood up to leave, but the door was blocked by people arriving. An elderly woman, spindly as a tree in winter, came in, helped by a young man in a suit. A long-haired skateboarder holding the trucks of his board with one hand and a bottle of seltzer in the other followed them.

"Is someone sitting there?" he asked, pointing to the chair she had just vacated.

"Lucky is," called Hockney Glasses from behind her. "It's her first meeting."

Lucky turned to glare at him, but the boy's face lit up.

"Sick," he said, offering his fist for her to bump. "Welcome."

He took a seat a few spots to the right of her and Lucky sat back down, staring into her lap. Why was everyone so pleased she was there? Couldn't they see this was punishment for her? The low hum of chatter filled the room as more people arrived, greeting each other familiarly. She glanced up every now and again as new members entered the space, taking their place around the circle. They all looked so happy. It was fucking weird.

"All right, let's get started, shall we?" said Cooper, and the room began to hush.

A tall couple bounded in arm in arm, gamboling over each other like puppies as they fell into a pair of the last remaining seats directly across from Lucky. The woman was holding a battered guitar case covered in stickers, which she placed next to her seat. Her hair was dyed the hue of Flamin' Hot Cheetos. She wore orange-lensed glasses with thick black frames, a vintage peach silk slip dress, and baby-pink ballet slippers, the satin kind worn by real dancers. She looked like a sunset. Her companion, by contrast, was the sea. He was wearing suede flares the color of the deepest part of the ocean and a periwinkle mesh shirt, beneath which Lucky could see the outline of his heavily tattooed torso. His hair, like Lucky's, was bleached the white of surf spray.

Lucky couldn't stop staring at them. They were so *cool*. The woman looked up and caught Lucky's eye, her face cracking into a wide grin. *Hi,* she mouthed. Lucky averted her eyes quickly to Cooper, who was reading from a binder fanned open in his lap.

"Welcome to a Big Book Study meeting of Alcoholics Anonymous. My name is Cooper and I'm an alcoholic."

"Hi, Cooper," the room chimed back cheerily.

He kept reading as Lucky's heart began to thump in her throat. Big Book Study? What did that even mean? At Cooper's prompting, the skateboarder read from the laminated card Lucky had refused earlier, but Lucky couldn't focus on what he was saying. She thought meetings were just people sitting around complaining about how they'd messed up their lives and couldn't drink anymore. This was so organized; just like school, but worse, because they were all *choosing* to be there. She wished Avery was with her to explain what the hell was happening.

"Thanks for your service," said Cooper once the skater was finished. "In this meeting, we read a portion of the Big Book, each reading a paragraph at a time, starting on page—" Cooper checked his notes. "Page eighty-one. Who would like to begin?"

"I will," said the orange-haired woman brightly.

She introduced herself as Butter and began reading loudly in a cheerful British voice. Her accent was very different from either Chiti or Troll Doll's, Lucky noted. She pronounced "think" as "fink." Definitely not posh. It was a nice voice, but Lucky couldn't listen to it too closely, because she was now having to count the number of people between her and this eager flame-haired British woman named after a dairy product, then scan the pages to see what passage would be hers to read. Butter was sitting directly across from her, so no matter which way they went around the circle, Lucky was fucked.

As each person read, Lucky begged herself to get up and leave. These people didn't matter. She would never have to see them again; she could extricate herself just like she'd extricated herself from the chanting volleyball circle.

"Pass," said the man next to her after reading his passage.

She willed herself to leave, but something—embarrassment or grace or some combination of the two—kept her in the chair. She stared down at the book clutched between her hands. The words looked like lines of tiny black ants ready to march off the page. *Ain't nothin' to it but to do it,* she reminded herself, and took a deep breath.

"The alcoholic is like a tornado roaring its way through the lives of others," she began in a low, shaky voice.

Then she took another breath and kept reading. Thankfully, her passage was on the shorter side, ending, for reasons inexplicable to her, with a description of a farmer coming out of a cyclone cellar to find his house ruined, then pretending nothing was the matter. She heard a low murmur of agreement rustle around the room, punctuated by a few knowing chuckles. Lucky glanced up. Were they laughing at *her*? But their faces showed only encouragement. She let out a long exhale.

"Pass," she said.

As the next person read, Lucky kept her gaze on the page, not daring to look at anyone. But if someone had been watching closely, they would have noticed a new light in her eyes, some kindling warmth of confidence in a corner of her that had previously been dark. It was nothing, she told herself. Who cares that she had read one measly paragraph? But there was another, softer voice inside of her that was saying one word: *miracle*. A small one, granted, imperceptible to anyone but her, but a miracle nonetheless.

# CHAPTER ELEVEN

# Bonnie

"I'M WRAPPING YOU MEXICAN STYLE," SAID FELIX.

He spun the strip of fabric between her fingers and around her palm in the shape of an X, humming under his breath. Bonnie cast her eyes behind his head. Word had gotten around in the gym that Danya and Bonnie would finally be sparring, and a cluster of fighters, done with their own workouts, had already gathered to mill around the ropes. Everyone, apparently, wanted to see what would happen.

Bonnie had left that awful argument with Avery and Lucky and gone straight to the gym. It was hard for her to acknowledge being angry with her sisters, even to herself, but she was. It pained her to admit it, but they were assholes. There, she'd said it. She loved them, but they were not always good people. The admission brought her no comfort. She missed Nicky, whose nature as the fellow middle child was closer to her own. They were both mild-tempered and even-keeled, endowed by birth order with a diplomacy that their fiery eldest and youngest sisters did not share. Lucky and Avery couldn't see it, but they were too similar. At their worst, they were selfish, stubborn, and self-destructive. At their best, they both possessed a fearless surety that demanded the most from themselves and everyone around them, invigorating their lives with the potency of destiny. It was easier to be furious with Avery, who was robust enough to take it, but until Lucky was safe—committed to some kind of sobriety and happy, or at least happier—Bonnie's concern for her would always outweigh her anger. And yet, what Bonnie longed for most as she barreled down Central Park West toward the gym was to be free of this love, just for a day. It was too sticky, too consuming, what she felt for her sisters. She craved the simplicity of the boxing ring, for a fight that had rules she could understand.

Avery should never have said what she said, but she was right about one thing: Bonnie *was* running out of time. Being an athlete was not like other careers. You didn't get decades to grow into yourself. There was a brief window in which your skill, experience, and fitness were all at their apex; just a few more years and Bonnie's speed and stamina would inevitably wane. She had already wasted one year of this golden window in L.A.; she couldn't lose another.

She cannonballed into the gym on the fumes of the argument with her sisters and marched straight up to Pavel, who turned to her with a look of mild surprise. She paused before him and took a breath. He crossed his arms without speaking.

"You gave me a chance letting me spar," said Bonnie. "And I didn't show up for it. I won't give you an excuse because that's not who I am. There is no excuse. But you always told me, you can't change the last round. The only round that matters is the next one. I'm here to say that the next round is *my* round. I was a champion for a reason, and I will be again. If you give me this chance, I will not waste it. I will not falter. This is where I'm meant to be, and I know that now. I'm here."

She let out a shaky breath. It was probably the most she'd spoken at one time in years, and she felt a little winded from the effort. Pavel blinked slowly. Anyone else, and he would have told them to get out of his gym; he had already given her a second chance, and you didn't

get third chances in boxing. But Bonnie was not anyone. He un-
crossed his arms and gave her a long look. She knew what he would
say before he said it. She could see it in his eyes.

"Go warm up," he said and walked away from her to the ring.


THE OTHER FIGHTERS WERE LOLLING on the ropes, towels around their
necks, sweat-soaked and spent from their own workouts. A hum of
anticipation hovered over them.

"Give 'im hell, GG!" one yelled, followed by a smattering of
laughter.

Golden Girl, that's what they'd called her. Bonnie had always kept
to herself during training, but she was not unpopular. Too shy, too
serious to engage in the kind of fast-talking banter that made a fighter
really liked, she was respected nonetheless. Her IBA Women's World
Boxing Championship pedigree and reputation for relentless hard
work had ensured that. And while there was a handful of other female fighters who cycled in and out, she was the first to have been
trained from start to finish at Golden Ring. Her success brought a
pride to the gym they all shared. Until, of course, she left.

"Don't worry about them," murmured Felix. "You just do like we
practiced."

Danya was in the other corner, talking to Pavel in low, intimate
tones. Bonnie knew Pavel wasn't worried about her hurting Danya,
otherwise he wouldn't have asked her. Danya's third professional fight
had been pushed to the following week; she knew that the week prior
to a fight a trainer wanted sparring partners who will work their
fighter hard but not beat him up. And, though the more experienced
fighter, she was out of practice. Aside from what happened outside of
Peachy's, she hadn't hit a person in over a year.

But she was trying to not think about what happened at Peachy's.
In fact, the list of things Bonnie was actively not thinking about before stepping back into the ring kept growing: her humiliating loss to
the South African last year, Pavel's ever-deepening coldness toward
her, and, of course, her asshole sisters. And always, underneath all

that, there was Nicky. Ever since returning to the apartment Bonnie had started dreaming again of that long, pointless pilgrimage to the elevator. She could still sometimes feel her sister's body in her arms, see the pale blue lips making her face strangely unfamiliar. She didn't want to think about that doomed, desperate struggle to save a life that was already gone, so she gave the thought to God. *You take care of Nicky,* she prayed. *And I'll take care of this.* Immediately, she felt calmer.

"Spread fingers more. Now grip. Too tight or okay?"

The human hand is not designed for destruction. Twenty-seven bones in each one, most of which are no thicker than a Virginia Slims cigarette. A good hand wrap is essential, which is where the trainer comes in. The cosmic transformation every fighter must undergo before stepping into the ring, the revolution from mortal to fighter, begins the moment a trainer starts to wrap.

Bonnie nodded to show Felix it was good. She had already been strapped into her headguard; she would prefer to fight without it, but the ever-cautious Pavel had insisted.

"We ready for gloves?" Felix asked.

Bonnie smiled faintly. People don't realize it, but with a good trainer a boxer is always a *we*.

"We're ready," said Bonnie.

Round one, they felt each other out. Danya had the confidence of a man who had not yet been truly tested. His body was sparse and economical, lean muscle cleaving tight to the bone. Bonnie pawed him with her jab, testing his reflexes. She left herself open a fraction too long and he flicked a jab to her forehead, without much power, but enough to jolt her. She had seen the punch coming and parried in her mind, but her hands had not cooperated. She exhaled through her nose.

*Ring rust.* Those two words were dreaded by all fighters. They meant the loss of speed and acuity that can come after a break from the ring. But Bonnie's mind was sharp as ever. In fact, she felt more acutely tuned in to Danya's movements than she had to anything in months. She could see his heartbeat pulsing in his throat like a butterfly trapped beneath the surface of his skin. She could practically hear the whirring machinations of his thoughts. But her body was slower than she was used to, as though the air around it had grown thick with resistance. Just as she was thinking this, Danya caught her at the end of a blistering double jab. He stretched his lips into a satisfied smile, and she noticed his mouthguard was painted with the daggered teeth of a shark. His movements were sharklike too; he swam through their first round in a smooth, constant motion punctuated by vicious, darting attacks. She withstood a flurry of punches to the body, then another, before pivoting out of range. Right before the bell, they both released their right at the same time, but while he jerked his head to avoid her blow, she caught his fist clean below her eye.

She headed back to the corner with electricity fizzing behind her eye socket. Felix's gaze darted quickly over her face with concern. She would have a black eye by nightfall.

"How you feeling?" he asked softly.

She gulped at the short stream of water he spurted into her mouth. She was only allowed a sip to avoid the liquid sloshing in her belly. Hard and thirsty, that's how a fighter needed to be.

"He's quick," she gasped.

He swiped the back of her neck with a flannel.

"You're just warming up."

Bonnie gave him an imploring look.

"What do I do?"

"You do like we practiced. Three-punch combinations and get out."

"I can't get close to him."

She had never felt this before, this doubt in her own abilities. Unlike Danya, she knew what defeat was like now. And every time she glanced over, she could see Pavel watching her like she was some stranger who had stumbled into the ring.

"Hey." Felix put a hand on her shoulder and lowered his lips to beside her headgear. "He ain't all that, Bonnie."

Whether he was talking about Danya or Pavel, she could not tell.

Round two. Bonnie dragged herself back into the ring. Boxing is composed of only four punches—jab, right, hook, uppercut—which, like the four distinct layers of Earth, combine to create something infinitely more beautiful and complex than its parts. But Bonnie could find no beauty in it today. Her combinations felt wasteful, uninspired. There was no sting behind her jab, no snap in her hips. It was just sparring, she reminded herself; the goal was to practice technique, not to win. But it was personal between these two, anyone could see that. The former favorite and the rising star. Danya was covetously defending what was newly his; since Bonnie left he had been the center of Pavel's cool, life-sustaining attention. Bonnie, meanwhile, was just trying to prove she still belonged there. She did not, she told herself, care what Pavel thought of her performance. The only person Bonnie needed to prove herself to was Bonnie.

But Danya was out for blood. He shot for her nose, her temple, her throat, her jaw, whatever vulnerable part of her was not covered by her headgear. By the end of the second round, she felt as though she had been battling a swarm of bees.

Felix grabbed her wrists and shook her arms out.

"You need to relax out there," he murmured. "Breathe. *Breathe.* He's not working the body much, so keep those hands up."

"I got . . . ring rust," she managed to say between great heavy breaths.

Felix twisted his dark eyebrows into a frown.

"Ring rust? I don't believe in ring rust. That kind of talk's for losers, Bonnie. And you're a champion."

"Former . . . champion."

"Nah, Bonnie. I mean you're a *champ.* You move like no one I've ever seen."

With great effort, Bonnie raised an eyebrow.

"We talkin' recently?"

"I'm talking last week."

He slipped her mouthguard back into place and gave her head a rough shake.

"Don't forget who you are, Bonnie Blue."

Round three. Boxing, as any fighter would tell you, is ninety percent mental. The other ten percent is sweat. Danya and Bonnie traded uninspired blows for the first minute and a half, each managing to avoid the worst of what the other had to offer. Until Bonnie realized something important: Danya was momentarily flagging. He'd get his energy back, but he had tired himself out early beating up on her in the second round. Finally, something stirred deep inside Bonnie. She caught Danya's eye. *You think you're it? Well, you ain't shit.* Bonnie managed to feint with the jab, rip an uppercut through the middle, then deliver a beautiful straight right to his face. She followed up with a stomach-busting hook off the jab. "Boom, boom, baby!" yelled someone from ringside. For the first time so far, Bonnie was disappointed to hear the bell.

Felix was grinning when she got back to her corner.

"You like that?"

Bonnie nodded, trying not to smile.

"Then go get some more!"

Round four. Bonnie went on the offensive and launched toward Danya right after the bell. She momentarily shook him with another well-timed hook to the body. Danya backed up and switched from an orthodox to a southpaw stance, trying to confuse her. The first time it worked; she got clipped in the cheek by his jab. But, over the course of the round, he did it once too often and eventually Bonnie timed it, catching him with his arms spread too wide to defend himself. She thought of Psalm 18, the hours and hours she'd spent staring at that faded piece of paper during training, preparing for moments exactly like this. *The feet of a deer.* She leapt forward. *My hands for battle.* Her cross slammed under his rib cage. *Right hand sustains me.* She could hear the air explode out of Danya's lungs like a valve busting open. He staggered backward, a look of keen surprise on his face. *That's right, motherfucker.* Her right was as dangerous, if not more so, than any male fighter's her size. Before he could get his feet back under himself, she pounced forward. *My ankles do not give way.* He managed to tuck his elbows into himself and get his hands up as she pummeled him from the inside. Bell. Bonnie bounced back to her corner with fireworks in her heels.

"When you go for the right, swing from your hips and your heart," said Felix. "It's got to land in your *heart* first."

Bonnie nodded. Love and pain, those were the only disciplinarians she knew in the ring and in life. But love had died when Nicky did, then again when her sisters turned on each other, and again when Pavel looked at her as though she were a stranger. Which left her with pain. That, she could deliver from the heart.

Round five. Bonnie stayed on her toes the whole time, bouncing a tad wastefully, but her legs were strong and sure. She danced in and out of range, pricking Danya with jabs as straight and accurate as a sewing machine's needle. She was back. She leaned forward, hands down, goading Danya to lunge at her. Quick as a kite turning directions in the wind, she pivoted backward and slammed him with a left hook. After landing a clean blow, she backed off, moving to the side to reset. It was a tactic she had learned early from Pavel that served the dual purpose of infuriating the other corner and giving her the chance to breathe between attacks. But it was hard with an opponent as quick as Danya. The next time she tried, he caught her with a skull-rattling uppercut. It happened so fast, an ill-timed blink would have missed it. Bonnie shook her head, as if shaking away a bad dream, but she didn't drop her hands.

Back in her corner after the bell, she glanced over to see Pavel leaning with his face close to Danya's, intoning seriously. *How do you like your boy now?* she wanted to yell. But it would be false bravado. She had always secretly feared that Pavel would prefer a male champ anyway. More money, more opportunity. Pavel had never made her feel like anything other than a prize, but now, seeing him with Danya, she felt like the unwanted first daughter of a king.

Round six. She was tired. She was thirsty. She was starting to see black spots in front of her eyes. "Man up," she muttered to herself. "Man up, Bonnie." Danya, meanwhile, was getting his second wind. For the first minute, he launched himself at her with vicious speed, never letting her get her bearings. She managed to pivot out of the corner just in time.

"Ground your feet!"

It was the first time Pavel had spoken in the whole six rounds. Bonnie looked over instinctively to see who he was addressing. Pavel had been telling Bonnie to ground her feet for fifteen years. Danya hit her with a jab to the temple the moment she turned her head. It's the punches fighters don't see coming that really rock them, and Bonnie did not see this one. Because her eyes were on Pavel. For a long moment they looked at each other and it was as if they were both suspended high above the ring, each watching the other through a multitude of fluttering, tugging currents in the air. They resisted their pull for another second. Then another. His eyes did not leave hers. At last, she fell. She landed on her knees, a momentary prayer, then pinged back up. She managed not to get rocked again for the rest of the round, even landing a couple of nice clean jabs, but the light had gone out in her.

"You did great, Bonnie."

Felix took a towel and rubbed her neck and shoulders down roughly. He picked up her wrist and began unlacing her gloves.

"He got me off my feet. No one's ever done that."

"Lucky shot. You gotta keep your eyes open."

She shook her head as her hands were freed. Her wraps were drenched in sweat. She looked for Pavel, but she couldn't see him.

"That wasn't luck," she said.

Felix kneeled in front of her and shook out her arms, peering closer at her eye.

"Let's get some ice on that." He grinned. "You've got a party to go to tonight, muchacha!"

*IF YOU CAN'T DANCE, YOU can't box.*

Pavel had repeated this ad infinitum to every boxer he ever trained. You need rhythm. You need timing. You need footwork. You need to be able to *move your hips*. Bonnie had found, over the years, that this came naturally to a lot of boxers, but she had struggled. She was stiff. Her hips were more like ice than water. And she was still a teen-ager when she started to train, embarrassed by her own body.

She particularly hated shadowboxing, dreaded the eyes of the others on her as she flailed around the ring fighting her imaginary opponent, feeling foolish. But Pavel found a way to help her. After everyone had left for the day, he would turn off all the lights in the gym. Outside, the streetlights cast their amber glow through the window, silhouetting the two of them. He would put on music with rhythm—salsa, Afrobeat, disco—and turn it all the way up on the speakers. Then, they would move.

This was how Bonnie learned to shadowbox: alone in a ring with Pavel, mirroring his movements, no eyes on her but his. Slowly, as if moving through oil, they flowed through combinations. Bonnie would start off rigid, shy as a middle schooler at her first dance, but gradually the music would melt her. Then he would let her go, stepping aside so she could follow her own trancelike rhythm as he followed his. In the gloam, they flitted around the ring like large moths. For the first time in her life, she could feel each part of her body moving as one; her uppercut sprang forward without effort when she bent her knees, her straight right extended farther when she turned her wrist down, her hook hit the mark when she shot from the hip instead of the shoulder. They circled and pivoted around each other, their arms twisting like ribbons of ink in water, and she learned to dance like a boxer.

In honor of this essential tenet of his training regime, Pavel had introduced a yearly tradition where the entire gym would go dancing together for one night every summer. The venue was always the same, a club uptown owned by Pavel's friend, a former cruiserweight who, upon retiring, pulled a LaMotta and opened his own place, this time without the underage girls. Every year, the mostly male fighters at Golden Ring descended on this small club in Harlem with their friends, families, wives, and girlfriends for a night of music and peacocking on the dance floor. It was a beloved tradition, particularly Pavel's solo performance every year, which he performed with great gusto to a traditional Russian folk song.

And yet, this year, Bonnie was dreading it.

She returned to the apartment, hoping one of her sisters would be there so they could just make up already, but both Lucky and Avery were out. She tried Lucky, mostly to surreptitiously check she wasn't at a bar, but she didn't answer, then thought about calling Avery but decided she was still too mad. Instead, she went to her room and flipped open her small suitcase, staring at its unremarkable contents. She only owned one pair of jeans, and the remainder was workout gear. She pulled the jeans on, wincing as she zipped the fly over the tender parts of her stomach that had been hit by Danya. She would feel even worse tomorrow, she knew, when the delayed onset muscle soreness really kicked in, achy as with any bad bout of flu. But that was tomorrow's problem; tonight's was what to wear. What else did she have? She picked up a T-shirt, sniffed its pits, and dropped it back in the pile. Not a lot, it turned out. In the corner of the room were the bags of Nicky's clothes for donation. Bonnie opened one and rifled through it, pulling out a simple black collared shirt made of silk. She slipped it on, fumbling with the buttons, and looked in the mirror. She looked like her sister.

Nicky was not like the rest of them; she loved makeup and scented candles and bubble baths and beauty treatments. Nothing made her happier than when she got to share these enchantments with her often skeptical sisters. She was the one who took Bonnie for her first pedicure, an experience Bonnie had not repeated since. But she had gladly endured the discomfort of having her feet touched by strangers for the pleasure of being there with Nicky. Bonnie loved witnessing the friendly way she talked with the nail technicians, all of whom knew her by name, the confidence with which she selected her color and advised Bonnie on hers. *I'm classic Ballet Slippers but you're definitely something more fun, like Electric Slide.* Bonnie had left the salon with her toes painted a bright cobalt; she didn't own nail polish remover, so flecks of blue had remained on her big toes for months afterward, a reminder of her younger sister every time she stripped off her socks.

Next, she needed to do something about her eye, which was beginning to turn a deep crimson purple. She sifted through the discard pile until she found Nicky's makeup bag, stuffed with more lipsticks and eye shadow palettes than any single person could reasonably wear. She found a concealer and dabbed the wand gently under her eye. She had the same coloring as her sister, she noted sadly. She poked the wand too close to the bruise and inhaled sharply. Yes, it hurt. It all hurt. But the physical pain was a relief from its invisible counterpart. That pain had become even more pronounced with her other sisters home, their presence outlining the sheer vastness of Nicky's absence. Now, the two sensations had started to mingle, the ache of Nicky's death and the ache in her body, and she found herself sitting before the mirror doubling over with longing.

It was Nicky who helped her hide her first black eye.

*I don't know why you're looking so pleased with yourself.*

She was kneeling in front of Bonnie, dabbing makeup over the fresh bruise so their parents wouldn't see it. Bonnie was back from a tournament and proud of the shiner, a souvenir from her most recent win, but not proud enough to risk their mother clocking it and banning her from competing. Nicky tutted.

*What is it the ref says? Protect yourself at all costs?*

*It's not ballroom dancing,* said Bonnie. *I'm going to get hit.*

*I don't like it, Bon.* Nicky frowned and twisted the lid back onto the concealer, putting it carefully back inside her beauty box. It was mostly cheap drugstore stuff, but Nicky, proud of her collection, kept it as organized as a military bunk.

*Pavel's not going to let anything happen to me,* said Bonnie.

*You can't know that. I read that it's the most dangerous sport in the world.*

Bonnie thought this was pretty unfair considering that it was Nicky who had marched her up to Pavel in the first place and encouraged her to start training at Golden Ring. She couldn't chicken out now just because of one little black eye, especially since Bonnie was starting to get good. Better than good, according to Pavel. But she didn't want to pick a fight with her sister. Instead, she plucked up three tangerines she'd pilfered from the kitchen and began spinning them through the air with acrobatic grace. She'd picked up juggling as a kid, but Pavel had instructed her to start doing it regularly again

after reading research that it boosted brain development and acceler-
ated the neural connections needed to react faster. It was a skill she
prized highly, mostly because she could always make him smile by
performing it.

*Base jumping,* she said, as the orange orbs blurred in front of her.

*What?* said Nicky.

*I'm pretty sure that's the most dangerous sport in the world.*

*Is that even a sport?*

Without taking her eyes off them, Bonnie tossed the tangerines
higher until they were moving in a great looping arc around her.

*College football,* she said.

*They get helmets.* Nicky snatched for a tangerine, but Bonnie pivoted deftly away from her.

*Rugby!* she called over her shoulder. *Bullfighting.*

*All men,* said Nicky. *And animal abusers.*

*NASCAR,* said Bonnie.

*Racists and rednecks,* said Nicky.

*That's not fair.* Bonnie lifted her leg and tossed one tangerine underneath it without breaking the cycle. *Fine. Cheerleading.*

*You cannot seriously tell me that cheerleading is more dangerous than box-
ing,* said Nicky.

*Ever seen a basket throw? Those girls go flying.*

Nicky crouched like a cat, then sprang forward and plucked a tangerine from the air in front of Bonnie. The rest came toppling down.
She set about peeling her catch.

*If you die, I will kill you,* said Nicky. *That is all I'm saying.*

She offered half of the tangerine to Bonnie, who took it.

*Same goes for you.*

Nicky laughed.

*Me? I'm getting a cushy desk job and living until I'm one hundred and
five.* She popped a segment of fruit in her mouth. *You don't need to
worry about me.*

Bonnie packed away her sister's makeup and looked herself over in
the mirror again. What was she thinking? She couldn't go to a party.
Pavel had replaced her, her sisters weren't speaking to her, and she

looked like a clown in all this makeup. She was rummaging in Nicky's pile looking for some makeup remover to undo the last half hour's work when she heard a bang at the door.

"Bonnie! Bonnie Blue!" called a gruff man's voice. "Open up! It's the police."

Bonnie felt everything inside her seize. The man at the bar with the girlfriend who looked like Nicky. He'd pressed charges and they'd found her. Of course, because she was at her parents' place, the first address they'd check. A wave of terror washed over her, followed by a riptide of sadness. She hadn't yet had the chance to make up with Avery and Lucky.

Another bang on the door. Bonnie remained frozen. She could hear her heartbeat in her ears, then something else on the other side of the door. It sounded like . . . muffled laughter? She crept toward the peephole and peered through. There, giggling into his hands, was Peachy.

"You motherfucker!"

She threw the door open as he exploded into hoots of delight.

"Seriously, Peachy, you scared the shit out of me."

Peachy grabbed her hands in his and tried his best to stop cracking up.

"Look, look, look, I'm sorry, I am." He wiped his eyes, then started laughing again. "But your face, babe!" He slapped his palms together. "Classic bants. Classic *bants*."

Bonnie tried to look mad, but the relief was like inhaling helium. Soon, she was laughing too.

"What are you doing here?" she asked once they had both gotten ahold of themselves.

"I'm in town looking for a new space. East Coast Peachy's! I had your address, so I thought I'd pop 'round."

Bonnie raised an eyebrow.

"How come you didn't call?"

Peachy rubbed his hands together, shaking his head.

"No can do, mate. See, my phone got smashed, but it's all good. Got a replacement coming *pronto*."

Bonnie gave him a knowing look.

"What happened to your phone, Peachy?"

He leaned in conspiratorially.

"Remember that bird I told you about? The one who wanted to track my phone? Well, she followed me! Found me in a situation that was a little . . . *hot,* shall we say. So I thought I'd come here and let the sitch cool down for a minute, you feel me?"

Bonnie shook her head.

"You didn't."

Peachy looked at her seriously.

"Oh, hun, I did." His face was alive with mischief. "No regrets, though! No regrets."

Bonnie leaned against the doorframe and smiled.

"It's good to see you, Peach."

Peachy grinned back.

"It's good to see you too. Actually . . . that's the other reason I'm here. I know you were in a bad way when we left, so I wanted to give you the news myself. He's disappeared, love. Not a peep. I don't think you have to worry about him coming 'round the bar anymore."

"Oh."

Bonnie felt as though she was teetering at the top of a precipice. She balanced above it for a moment, then another, then let herself fall into relief. Seeing her wobble, Peachy caught her and held her in a tight embrace.

"You know you didn't have to come all this way to tell me," she said into his hair.

"Like I said, my bird—" he began, but Bonnie only squeezed him harder.

"But I'm really glad you did," she finished.

He grabbed her shoulders and shook her, smiling broadly.

"I missed my pal," he said. He took a step back and looked her up and down. "Hold on, what's going on here?"

He circled one long finger at her outfit. Bonnie blushed and looked down at her silk shirt.

"It looks stupid, right?"

"If by stupid you mean like a total *knockout*." Peachy gave her a little wink. "Pun intended. Where are we going tonight all dressed to the nines?"

"Nowhere." Bonnie yanked at the top uncomfortably. "I mean I was, but now I'm not."

Peachy frowned.

"Go on, tell Uncle Peach what's going on."

Bonnie thought about rebuffing this, then relented.

"There's this annual party for my boxing gym—"

"A party? You should have said!"

Peachy walked right past her into the apartment, grabbing at his Afro. Before Bonnie could say anything, he was heading down the hallway, calling to her over his shoulder.

"Point me toward the bathroom! I just need to run a comb through this barnet, and I'm good to go!"

THEY TOOK THE SUBWAY UPTOWN to 145th Street, Peachy maintaining a running commentary about all the happenings at the bar, including his and Fuzz's new business idea, which was to open a laundromat speakeasy called Fuzz 'n' Fold. Bonnie listened to this monologue without adding much; she was enjoying being with him, but also anxious to get the rest of the night over with. Just like with a fight, she figured, the anticipation was the worst part.

As they walked to the club, the sidewalk shimmered with the glitter that is inexplicably poured into the city's cement, that curious combination of glisten and grime that was simply New York. At the door, Bonnie nodded respectfully at the bouncers, with whom she now felt an unspoken kinship, and gave her name. The party was already at a raucous tempo when they entered, the dance floor packed with fighters and their friends moving with unselfconscious abandon. Bonnie instinctively looked for Pavel amid the crowd but did not find him. The scent of cocoa butter and Axe body spray rose in a fragrant wave off the dancing bodies. Women flitted like bees between men petaled with muscles, their shirts unbuttoned to their navels like buds bursting open.

"All right!" said Peachy, looking around and slapping his hands appreciatively. "These boxers know how to *party*!"

Bonnie smiled. Training required such unrelenting discipline, a tolerance not only for pain but for mind-numbing repetition, as it was only by performing the same movements over and over, year after year, that they became instinctive in the ring, that when boxers did let off steam, it was not surprising that they did so with the same full-bodied gusto they brought to training. Also, thanks to Pavel, every last one of his fighters knew how to dance.

"What can I get you?" asked Peachy. "Vodka soda? Beer? Champagne?"

Bonnie shook her head.

"Do you think they have seltzer and lime?" she asked.

"Right, right, your body is your temple, I forgot." Peachy's face lit up. "You know what we need? Suicides. None of this seltzer and lime shite!"

Bonnie looked confused.

"Suicide?"

Peachy mimed disbelief.

"Don't tell me you don't know the suicide? It's all the fountain drinks, *mixed together.*" He began counting on his fingers. "I'm talking Coke, Sprite, Dr Pepper . . . Shit, what are the others? Red Bull! Let's go turbo and add Red Bull! The sugar in that concoction alone will send you to the ceiling." He gave her a little wink. "Better than a sniff of the white stuff, any day."

Bonnie followed Peachy to the bar. As they brought the pint glasses of murky soda mix to their lips, Peachy insisted they race to see who could down theirs the fastest. As Bonnie chugged, rivulets of sticky liquid dripping down her chin, she felt an old, childish happiness bubble within her. It was a hot summer night, and she was with her friend at a party. That long-forgotten visitor had arrived: *fun*. Bonnie won the race after Peachy snorted soda through his nose, then ordered them another round. She sipped the ice-cold concoction, feeling the sugar buoy her spirits. Peachy downed his again, then released a loud belch.

"Let's fookin' dance!" he declared.

Felix and his wife were already at the center of the floor when they arrived, exercising some impressive salsa moves. They both cheered when they saw Bonnie and pulled her in to join them. Soon, she was surrounded by fighters, lithe featherweights, nimble welterweights, and imposing heavyweights, the music pulling them all together like a looping drawstring tugged tight around their waists. At one point, Bonnie looked over to see Danya seated at a cushioned banquette along the wall, handing a glass of water to his pregnant wife. The two nodded at each other in respectful acknowledgment. They both knew that in the ring, it was war, but outside, what mattered most was always family.

Bonnie danced until sweat pooled at the bottom of her spine and slicked her hair to her temples. Every few songs, she checked the mass of bodies for Pavel, but he was never there. A languorous song about summer and desire came on and Peachy pulled her into him, pushing his hips against hers. They moved with the smooth undulations of the music, Peachy's hand creeping down her waist as Bonnie let the melody rush around her like warm, fragrant water. She closed her eyes and placed her cheek on Peachy's shoulder, letting his hands knead her hips. He rocked her body in a rolling, rippling rhythm, and she abandoned herself to the pleasure of movement, of touch.

When she opened her eyes again, Pavel was at the edge of the dance floor, surveying the crowd. Only his eyes moved while his head stayed regally still, like a bird of prey. Then, he turned himself to her with a look so direct that it made her start. He held her in his pensive, avian gaze and cocked his head. Instinctively, she wanted to push Peachy off her, to go to him, but she didn't. She kept dancing, letting Peachy pivot her body away. Tentatively, she glanced over her shoulder to see Pavel leave the dance floor and disappear toward the back exit. Bonnie made it to the start of the next song before stepping away from Peachy and motioning that she was getting some air. He gave her a momentary look of disappointment before noticing a ring girl who was smiling at him from near the DJ booth and setting off optimistically in her direction.

WITHOUT STOPPING TO LET HERSELF think, Bonnie slipped off the dance floor and headed toward the exit. She climbed the metal stairs, the music retreating to a distant bass note, and opened the back door of the club. There in the alley was Pavel. He was pulling on a cigar, its smoke pluming around his head. The neon light of the club's sign above him melted around his feet and formed slick pools in the hollows of his face. If he was surprised to see her, he didn't show it.

"Is you," he said mildly as she stepped onto the shimmering sidewalk next to him.

"Is me," she said.

He looked away from her, his head haloed in neon light.

"Having fun?" he asked.

"I am," she said, more pointedly than she'd intended. "You?"

"You know me." He shrugged. "I have good time if everyone else has good time."

Bonnie nodded and they were quiet again. She did know him. Pavel looked down at the glistening pavement. The neon lights formed molten puddles of brash blue and orange around his shoes.

"I didn't know you smoked cigars," she said.

Pavel snorted softly and made a self-mocking face.

"I don't."

He took another pull and blew smoke toward his feet.

"I saw you inside dancing," he said without looking at her. "That man you came with . . . is the reason you went to L.A.?"

"*Peachy?*" Bonnie scoffed.

"Why funny?" asked Pavel. "He is handsome man."

Bonnie laughed again.

"I guess he is. It's just . . . It's not like that with him. He owns the bar I was bouncing at. And I'm pretty sure he's taking home a ring girl tonight."

She looked up at him, and in the shadows of his face, she saw neither relief nor concern.

"Is good to see you enjoying yourself," he said eventually. "Has been long time."

"Yeah, well, I haven't been in New York since . . ."

Pavel shifted and cleared his throat. Bonnie noticed, with a strained feeling in her chest, that he seemed uncomfortable alone in her presence now.

"And you okay at gym?" he asked. "You happy with Felix?"

"You threw in the towel," said Bonnie suddenly. "How could you do that to me? *Me?*"

For the first time, his eyes met hers.

"I should never have let you in that ring," he said. "I will live with that shame for the rest of my life."

Bonnie shook her head.

"I *wanted* to fight."

"But it's *my* job to protect you. I failed at that."

Bonnie searched his face for some understanding.

"Is that why you avoid me at the gym?" she asked. "Because you feel guilty?"

"With you," he said softly, "I don't think clearly. You're safer with Felix."

Bonnie cast her eyes down.

"You know I would rather have died in the ring than have you do what you did," she said in a low voice. Then she looked at him, unable to contain herself. "So would you! So would any real fighter!"

Pavel dug his gaze into her like a jab. When he spoke, his voice was fierce.

"I *know* you wanted to die that night," he said. "But not because you are boxer. Because of your sister. And no, I did not let you. I regret that you fought, but I do not regret ending the fight, even though you will never forgive me. You do not owe anyone your life."

"It was Nicky," Bonnie said. "*Nicky.*"

"And you are *you,*" he said.

"She brought me to you. She's the reason I'm here."

Pavel looked away, pained.

"She was . . . very precious," he said eventually.

"She was more than that," said Bonnie. "She was—" But there was no word for what Nicky had been. "Everything," she settled on.

Pavel turned back to her and smiled sadly. He tapped his temple.

"She always taking notes," he said.

Bonnie could see Nicky sitting on the wooden bench by the ring, watching her train with that intelligent curiosity she brought to so much of her life. Even as a twelve-year-old, she was uncannily perceptive. She knew Bonnie was a boxer before Bonnie did.

"I needed you, Pavel," said Bonnie. "This year, I needed you."

Pavel raised his hands to his chest, as if protecting his heart. She knew he was not used to talking so directly with her, with anyone. In all the years they had known each other, he had remained stoic in the face of victory and defeat. He showed his feelings through actions, not words. Like Bonnie.

"But you left me, Bonnie." He gave a pained smile. "You, who was everything to *me*."

Bonnie's eyes darted around his face, trying to understand.

"You knew how I felt," she said quietly.

She had never acknowledged it aloud before, but she knew he knew. There was a joke at the gym that she was Pavel's little wife. They did everything together. Everyone knew how she felt about him.

"It would not . . . It is not correct. You are so young. You have big career ahead."

"Had," said Bonnie.

Pavel shook his head.

"One defeat, one year, does not end career like yours. You don't want to yoke yourself to old man like me."

*Yoke.* For years, Bonnie had laughed at these little mannerisms of Pavel's, the odd phrases he used that no native English speaker would. He collected these unwanted words and made them beautiful again, like a child gathering pieces of sea glass along the shore. But, this time, Bonnie did not smile. She was thirty-one and Pavel was forty-four. Their thirteen-year age gap, which had seemed so momentous when she was fifteen, was no longer an issue. Surely, he could see that? He obviously did not love her; he was simply making an excuse to spare her feelings. Bonnie nodded, defeated.

"I should go find my friend."

She turned to open the club door, but a hot gust of wind encircled her in its fluttering, batting folds, urging her backward. It was the same wind that had blown through the city the night of Nicky's funeral and scattered her sisters to their various corners of the world. Now, it was bringing her home. Bonnie let the swirling air nudge and bully her around until she was facing Pavel again. The most vulnerable fighter is the one who, behind on points in the last round, will do anything for the knockout. They have nothing to lose. Bonnie inhaled the hot night and looked at him.

"What if I do?" she said. "Want to yoke myself to you?"

Pavel shook his head softly.

"Bonnie . . ." he murmured.

She raised a hand.

"Don't say what you think you should say. What would you say if you weren't . . . If you weren't afraid?"

She gazed up at him imploringly. His face was alive with shadow and light, like the sea. He dropped his cigar at his feet and his gaze went dark, the tide of his eyes tossing and fretful. For fifteen years, Bonnie had followed his moods. They had sculpted the shape of her life, as waves carve cliffs of limestone rocks, harassing and caressing them into extraordinary forms. That is what a trainer does. Her body bore the marks of his attention; its beauty, or deformity, was of his making. He held her in his still, cool gaze.

"Close eyes," he said softly.

Without hesitating, she closed them. No longer able to see him, she could feel him. For a moment, they were back on solid ground. They were like two animals snuffling in the dark, feeling their way toward each other. She felt him move closer, then pause before her. She could sense the weight of his hesitation, but she kept her eyes closed. She forgot to exhale. Then, she felt his breath on her face. He pressed his lips to her eyelid, the one that was bruised. His lips were dry and cool. He kissed the thin skin above one eye, then the other. It was so tender, she shivered.

"Is okay?" he whispered.

"Yes," she said, or maybe just thought, knowing he would hear her. *Yes.*

She kept her eyes closed and felt his lips fumble across her brow, her temples, her cheekbones, her throat.

"Bonnie," he said, his voice barely above a breath.

He tried to say her name again, but she stopped his mouth with hers. He had swallowed her sweat, blown her nose, mopped her blood, sunk his fingers into her jaw, oiled her skin—but never this. She could taste the smoke of his cigar and beyond that something cool and oceanic that was simply him. He kissed her and it felt like trying to stand still in a great, billowing wave as it crashed over her head. Pavel wrapped himself around her, and Bonnie, who had been taught all her life to ground her feet, lost her balance and surrendered to his arms.

# CHAPTER TWELVE

# Avery

AVERY WOKE UP THE MORNING AFTER THE FIGHT WITH HER SISTERS with the worst emotional hangover of her life. She'd checked into a soulless Midtown hotel the night before to avoid seeing anyone and woken up, jet-lagged, at five A.M. with a relentless headache and a palpable sense of shame. She'd spent the early morning mindlessly watching television in bed, disassociating for hours at a time as she flicked between channels. She remembered an anecdote she'd heard about David Foster Wallace, who had considered television, not drugs, to be his primary addiction; during book tours, he apparently had the staff remove the TV from his hotel rooms before he entered, the same way, in early recovery, Avery would request the minibar be emptied ahead of time. Avery rarely watched television at home and had forgotten what a remarkably effective opiate it was. When she finally forced herself to turn it off, it was still only midmorning and the empty day yawned ahead of her. She could not go home, not to

London, not the apartment. From her window, she stared up Lexington Avenue to the familiar sight of Grand Central Station. It was then that it occurred to her what she should do with her day: She would visit their mother.

She opened her phone and drafted a text. *Hey, Mom, have a free day in New York. Can I come visit you upstate?* She read it over, then slowly deleted each word. Why was she asking permission? If her mother was too cowardly to interact with her daughters when she knew they were in the city, she didn't deserve the dignity of a request. *Coming upstate,* she typed instead. *Will text ETA once on train.* She pressed send and watched. Almost immediately, the three dots to indicate her mother was typing appeared on the screen, then disappeared, appeared, then disappeared again. Finally, a single thumbs-up appeared on her message. Avery knew better than to go before lunch, the hours in which her father was most active; by the afternoon he was usually asleep, which was how Avery preferred him. Her best chance of getting uninterrupted time with her mother was to wait until midafternoon at least. Avery turned the television back on and let her mind return to comforting blankness.

AT GRAND CENTRAL STATION, AVERY crossed the main floor and stepped into the Hudson News. She picked up *Vogue,* a magazine she had only ever looked at to see if Lucky was in it, and flicked through its pages, keeping one eye on the woman behind the register who was ringing someone up. She could feel her heart rate quickening, that glorious rush of adrenaline that eclipsed every other feeling. It occurred to her briefly that the only times she felt truly present in her body were when she was smoking or stealing, the exhilaration of transgression enlivening her every breath, making her aware of every pump of blood from her heart. With practiced nonchalance, she wandered over to a shelf farther from the checkout and placed a chocolate almond bar and a packet of spearmint gum inside the magazine. Then, without looking at the register again, she ambled toward the exit at an unconcerned pace.

Only then did she notice the little girl staring at her. Her mother was fussing with her younger brother, so the girl was momentarily unattended, her gaze fixed on Avery with eerie stillness. Avery was never good at guessing children's ages—a six-year-old was indistinguishable from a ten-year-old to her—but she'd estimate the girl was closer to ten. Despite the fact it was midsummer, she wore a pink T-shirt with an illustration of a kitten above the words MEOW-Y CHRISTMAS! Avery knew she had been clocked, but it was too late now. She was almost at the door. Would the girl say something? Call out to her mom that the bad lady over there had taken the magazine without paying? The blood was roaring in Avery's ears by the time she made it to the exit. *Don't look back,* she told herself, but, like Orpheus, she couldn't resist. The girl had not moved or taken her eyes from Avery.

Avery made it to her platform and took a seat in the first car, her heart still hammering, and looked down at the magazine in her lap. She still had ten minutes until the train departed. She was about to rip open the almond bar—she hadn't eaten dinner or breakfast and, combined with the jet lag, she was hungry—when she stopped. What kind of person steals in front of a child? Is that who she was, who she was meant to be? A hypocrite, Lucky had called her, and she was right. *Enough,* she muttered to herself. *Enough.* She stood up and propelled herself off the train, hurrying toward the newsstand. The child and her mother were gone. There was no one else checking out, so Avery marched herself to the counter before she could change her mind and placed the magazine, gum, and nut bar on the counter.

"I stole these," she said. "And I'd like to pay for them."

The young woman behind the counter had dyed jet-black hair and the glazed expression of someone who would rather be in bed. At Avery's confession, her eyebrows shot up in mute surprise. Avery fumbled a twenty-dollar bill out of her stolen Chanel wallet and placed it on the counter.

"Actually." She slid her credit cards and receipts out of their leather holders and dropped them in her bag, placing the now empty wallet on the counter. "If you wouldn't mind taking this too."

"You really don't—" began the woman, but Avery dismissed this with a flustered wave. A couple had come up behind her and were waiting to pay; she glanced back to see them watching this interaction with astonishment. Avery could feel her cheeks burning.

"I have a problem," she said. "I'm sorry." If she was speaking to the woman behind the counter, the couple behind her, the little girl from earlier, or to an invisible God above her, Avery didn't know; she only knew it felt good to say it out loud. She gathered up the magazine, nut bar, and gum, shoving them into her bag, and left the wallet and a twenty on the counter. The woman opened her mouth to protest but Avery had already turned, sidestepping the couple behind her, and hurried away.

Back on the train, Avery took a seat by the window and devoured the almond bar, licking melted chocolate off her fingertips. As they pulled out of the station, she tried to think of what she was going to say to her mother, but her mind kept pulling her back home, back to London and to Chiti. In that week of silence between them before she came to New York, she had phoned Charlie and told him she couldn't see him again, news he took with game equanimity. That was one benefit of having slept with a young, newly sober poet on the brink of literary acclaim, she thought. He was, rightfully so, too involved with his own burgeoning life to give much thought to Avery's predictably middle-aged and middle-class crises. She had tried at first to apologize again to Chiti, but her fumbling attempts at contrition were instantly rebuffed. She'd bought bunches of snapdragons, Chiti's favorite flowers, and arranged them in sprays of sunset hues—fuchsia, yellow, and peach—all over the house. She'd written notes and left them in her shoes. *Please forgive me* in her right heel. *I'm a fucking idiot* in her left. She'd attempted to cook one of Chiti's favorite dishes, coq "no" vin (coq au vin, without the wine) for dinner, but Chiti had walked in on her before she could finish.

*Please get out of my kitchen,* Chiti said, raising a hand as if to protect herself. Her expression was anguished. *No more apologies. No more notes. It's not helping, Avery.*

After that, Avery had stayed away from the house as much as possible, pouring herself into the endless pit of her work. When she was home, she skulked like a shadow, trying not to upset Chiti with her presence. On the seventh night of this purgatory, Chiti had knocked on their bedroom door while Avery lay sleepless in bed, watching the shadows move slow as time across the ceiling.

*You don't have to knock.* Avery sat up as Chiti opened the door. *This is your room. I keep saying I should be the one in the guest bedroom.*

Chiti didn't venture farther into the room.

*I think you should go to New York,* she said from the doorway. *Go be with your sisters.*

*But I want to stay with you,* pleaded Avery. *We have . . . stuff to deal with.*

Chiti shook her head.

*I don't need you here like a dog that's crapped on the rug and is trying to get back into its owner's good graces.*

Avery winced, since this was exactly how she felt.

*But I want to make things better,* she said.

Chiti shook her head.

*You don't know what you want,* she said.

Before Avery could answer, Chiti had retreated into the hallway, the door clicking softly behind her.

So, Avery had left, determined to at least help her sisters tackle the grief pit that was Nicky's belongings and keep the apartment safe from a sale, though it turned out she'd messed that up too. For the first time in a long time, no one needed her. She should feel free, but she only felt lost.

Bonnie was right that it had been hard to be back in the New York apartment after so long, a place so small and yet so full. The first thing Avery did when they'd bought their house in London was check if there were locks on the bedroom doors. Even after all these years. When Chiti asked her what her favorite part of the house was after they put in the offer, she had said, without thinking, that she liked that in addition to the front door, it had a back door that led through to the garden. As always, Chiti had understood the heart of the matter immediately. *Your father doesn't live here,* she'd reassured her gently.

*You won't need to escape.* But Avery's father lived inside of Avery, the one home she could never leave. She had once heard a man in an AA meeting talk about how his father used to grab his neck from behind when drunk; even as an adult, he couldn't sit in the middle of the dining room in restaurants without jumping every time a server moved behind him. The only thing that had ever quelled that edginess was to have a drink himself. In the back of the meeting, unnoticed by anyone, Avery had surprised herself by bursting into tears; she hadn't known, until she listened to him, why she always sat with her back to the wall.

Avery closed her eyes. She didn't want to remember, but the memories came, steady and relentless as the river outside. *Bang.* Her father slamming the front door. *Bang.* A kitchen cupboard. *Bang.* The wedding china. There was the Christmas that the oven broke yet again. Her father yanked down the tree in the living room in a rage. Pine needles everywhere; they would still find them in the carpet long into the spring. Her parents were screaming at each other in the kitchen; they heard the thud of someone pushing the other against the sink. Her mother had run to the bedroom where Avery and her sisters were huddled and pushed her slender wallet into Avery's hands. *Take them and go,* she'd mouthed. Avery had dutifully hurried them all out of the building, leading them single file like ducklings down Columbus Avenue, the wind sinking its teeth through their woolen coats. Her sisters did not know that Avery had no idea where she was taking them. They trusted her to have a plan. They walked for blocks past shuttered storefronts and empty restaurants; it seemed the entire Upper West Side was inside celebrating with their families. Eventually, they found a dim sum restaurant and feasted on round after round of dumplings, making a game of playing with the spinning top in the center of the table. When they returned home, the oven was back on, and the tree was upright. Their mother had roasted a chicken and potatoes and that evening they all sat down without mentioning what had happened. Even though they were full, Avery and her sisters ate everything their mother cooked.

She had done what she needed to do, Avery reminded herself now.

She had stayed until her last sister moved out, a deadline made easier by Lucky's modeling career taking off so young. She left that apartment, and did not come back, not that year or for many years after. Only now did she realize how rarely she thought of her father, of her whole childhood. She had built another life, far away and untouched on its own island, one that, until recently, she had done anything to protect. She could not have known that she would one day build the dream she longed for, a home where she never used the locks on the doors. She could not have expected that freedom would look like that, a forgetting that was so close to, but not, forgiveness.

SINCE HER MOTHER HADN'T OFFERED to pick her up, Avery took a taxi from the station. Their parents had moved upstate half a decade earlier, citing their father's health as the reason. Avery had visited over the years, not as much as Nicky but far more than Bonnie or Lucky had ever bothered to, but the place wasn't home, and she had no particular connection to it. The taxi pulled up to a small wooden cabin with a wraparound porch. The house was in a worse state than she remembered. Clusters of shingles had fallen off the roof like bald patches on a head and one side of the wooden banisters lining the porch steps had rotted away. An assortment of rusty wind chimes offered their conflicting cacophony of notes, one as large as a grandfather clock, another no longer than a watch strap. Avery watched a handful of golden chickens peck warily at the ground around the porch. Then the door flung open, and her mother appeared.

Avery was taken aback. None of them had seen their mother since the funeral, but she looked markedly changed. Had she always looked like this? So *witchy*? Her hair, thick and kinked as a metal scrubbing brush, was piled on top of her head. She wore layers of black diaphanous fabric, a poncho-style top that could either have been an extortionately priced item from Eileen Fisher or an old rag with a hole cut in the top; Avery couldn't tell. Her lined face was bare and she wore no jewelry except a large silver men's watch. The overall effect was severe and, in the city, could have been quite stylish but, in this context, lent her mother a hermitlike quality. When Avery got closer, she saw there was noticeable black dirt around and under her fingernails.

"I always wanted chickens!" her mother declared in lieu of a greeting. "And now I have them."

Avery had practiced the line she'd planned to open with on the train: *What the fuck is wrong with you, you fucking cunt?* But now she was standing in front of her, the words felt ridiculous. What had she expected coming up here? That she would confront their mother . . . and what? She'd hop on a train back to the city with her, broker peace between the sisters, shower them in the maternal love they'd been deprived of for the past thirty years and everything would magically be okay? They all had their roles, and they weren't going to change them now. Their mother wasn't really a mother, and Avery covered for her; their father wasn't really a father, and their mother covered for him. Trying to change them now would be needlessly painful for everyone.

Avery looked toward the patch of dirt her mother was pointing at, where a cluster of birds were clucking around a chipped xylophone. She recognized it as one of their old toys, its painted rainbow hues since faded by time and rain. There was something unbearably sad about seeing it there, but she tried to nod enthusiastically.

"They lay eggs and everything?" she asked.

Her mother guffawed.

"What a question! No, they shit chocolate. Yes, they lay eggs! Why else do you think I got them?"

"I was kidding, Mom. They're cool."

Only her mother could make her feel so stupid, so adolescent. For Avery, a person whose intelligence was the hook upon which she hung her entire identity, the feeling was catastrophic. Her mother wiped her hands on the front of her dress-sack-thing and blew hair out of her face.

"I've been busy with what is euphemistically called 'putting the garden to bed,' which is like saying Herod's Massacre of the Innocents was childcare." She barked a laugh. "The compost bins are heaving with all the cuttings, and I spend my days slashing everything back with great enthusiasm. As you can see, the abundance of summer will not be tamed."

Avery had no idea what to say to this. The garden was indeed wild looking. Beyond the house, waist-length grass dotted with pink clouds of milkweed and other wildflowers Avery couldn't name stretched forth in a ramshackle profusion. Her mother looked at her expectantly, hoping, perhaps, for some shared sense of admiration, then gave up. Avery remained looking around in silence.

"Well," said her mother, with a hint of disappointment.

"Why do the chickens have a xylophone?" attempted Avery, but her mother had moved on.

"How was the ride up?" she asked briskly. "Did you sit on the left side so you could see the river?"

Avery had, in fact, and enjoyed the sight of the fat, dark ribbon of water rushing past, but she hated being told what to do by anyone, especially her mother.

"I was working," she said. "I worked the whole ride."

"You're too busy working to look at a river?"

"I'm in the middle of a case."

Avery, who had been falling behind at work the past week, had done nothing of the sort, but the urge to make it clear to her mother that she was *busy and important* was immediate.

"Well, you'll see it on the way back if it's not too dark. You should have come earlier."

Avery bristled instantly.

"I had some work to finish up in the city, Mom."

"You're always busy, always rushing, that's your problem."

Her mother's idea of being helpful was unsolicited criticism delivered swiftly, seemingly from nowhere, like getting hit by a dart in the dark. By the time you realized you were punctured, the next one had usually been thrown.

"Let me look at you," she continued. "You didn't have to get dressed up for me."

Avery looked down at her linen trousers and light cotton shirt.

"I didn't," she murmured.

Her mother was already marching inside, gesturing for her to follow. Inside, the house was dark and cluttered with objects, some precious, many not. The kitchen was the center of the house, the largest room, with space for a large farmhouse-style dining table and eight mismatched chairs. A large abstract expressionist painting hung on the wall, contrasting with the yellowing old newspapers and damp-curled books that were scattered on every available surface. Avery glanced into the living room, where she recognized an African ram's skull her mother claimed to have belonged to Hemingway with a plastic shopping bag hanging from its spiraled horn. On a chipped credenza by the door was a flash of hot pink. Avery saw it was a picture frame containing a photo of the four sisters and their mother squeezed around a restaurant booth, grinning over plates of profiteroles and melting sorbet. Their mother was in the middle, one arm encircling Nicky and Lucky on her right and the other around Bonnie and Avery on her left.

She knew instantly that it was from Nicky's college graduation dinner, one of the rare happy memories they shared as a family, in part because their father had stopped drinking for that summer after a brief stint in the hospital with jaundice. Avery was also sober by that point; out of solidarity with her and him, they had all ordered Shirley Temples, laughing as the saccharine concoctions arrived garnished with swirly straws and maraschino cherries. Avery vaguely remembered that Lucky and Nicky had not been speaking at the start of that dinner because of some skirmish at Nicky's graduation party with her sorority sisters but, without fanfare or explanation, had forgiven each other by dessert. In the picture they were wedged close to each other like two daffodils in the same pot, Nicky's golden hoop earring resting against Lucky's cheek. It was their father who had taken the photo, *Let me get one of all my Shirleys together,* and Avery remembered how his hands were steady when he took it, how proud she had felt that they seemed, for one moment, like a regular family. Inscribed on the picture frame in the curly font usually found on posters declaring *Live Laugh Love* or *Keep Calm and Carry Prosecco* was the phrase *Mothers & Daughters Are Forever.* Avery could imagine Nicky picking it out at the store, without a hint of irony, her childish belief that good things really could last forever, even in their family.

"Come sit, come sit," beckoned her mother, pointing to the dining table. She was rustling over the sink, washing her hands. Avery wondered if she'd noticed her looking at the dirt under her nails when she arrived. She plunked herself down at the large wooden table; at its center, in a small clearing of papers, was a blue painted jug filled with irises.

"I picked these this morning when I heard you were coming," said her mother. "They're lovely, aren't they? Van Gogh's favorite. They always remind me of you." She turned and touched an indigo petal with the tip of one soapy finger.

"They are," agreed Avery, though it hurt her to think of her mother trying to please her in this small way after disappointing her in such big ones for so long. She wished she would just be a good mother or a bad one; this vacillating in between was unbearable.

"How are the girls?" her mother asked.

Anyone overhearing this would have thought she was asking about Avery's children, but, of course, she was inquiring after her own. If her mother knew that Avery was aware she had been in the city yesterday, she wasn't going to let on. *Fine,* Avery thought, *you want denial? Let's do denial.*

"They're great," she said with a bright smile. "It's so good to see them."

No need to mention they were currently not speaking; out of loyalty, Avery preferred to present a united front to their mother.

"What are they up to back in New York?"

*Why don't you ask them yourself?*

"Lucky's just taking a break," Avery said vaguely. "Bonnie's back at Pavel's training."

Her mother sniffed.

"I'll never understand her obsession with that barbaric sport. We have your father to thank for that."

"She's incredible, Mom. You should have come to one of her fights."

"What mother wants to watch that? The amateurs, that was one thing. At least they wear their headguards. But this pro stuff? It's masochistic." She shook her head and turned to lift the kettle. "Tea?"

"It's not masochism," said Avery, the old defensiveness of her sisters rising quickly to the surface. "It's a respected sport. And I'm good on the tea."

"It's a blood circus and should be illegal. You sure? I have the strong British stuff you're probably used to now."

"Sure, fine, sure." Avery waved her hand in a gesture of surrender. She had just escaped a country that held tea to be the solution to all things, a fact that, she realized now, probably annoyed her so much because it was her mother's attitude too.

"You should talk to Bonnie about doing something else. Why can't she coach? She'd be a wonderful coach."

"Because she wants to fight, Mom. I can't talk her out of it. None of us can."

"That Pavel better protect her," she said. "It's his job to keep her safe."

And then Avery saw it, the raw, almost animal fear guarded beneath her mother's querulousness. She was scared for Bonnie, scared for all her children. Had she been this way before losing Nicky? Avery never remembered her mother seeming so concerned before. The fear appeared between them, unspoken but startling in its frankness, and then it was gone.

"She'll be okay," Avery said softly. "Pavel knows how to take care of her."

"I can never get more than a grunt out of her on the phone," she continued. "Any of you! I might as well have had sons. I thought girls were meant to be verbal."

Avery chose to ignore this. Her mother had a long list of all the ways her children had disappointed her, topped forever by the fact that not one of them had had the magnanimity to be born a boy.

"Where's Dad?" Avery asked instead. "Is he sleeping?"

Her father usually fell asleep in the living room or somewhere equally central to family life; even unconscious, he found a way to dominate every space he was in.

"That's something I wanted to talk to you about. He's not here."

"I see that."

Her mother turned so her back was to the kettle she'd been fussing over and looked at Avery.

"He's back in treatment."

"What? When? For how long?"

"A few weeks ago. They want him to stay for six months this time."

"Six? Why so long?"

"Oh, it's the usual palaver of American prurience. He had a few spots of gout last year—"

"*Gout?*"

Her mother gave an exasperated sigh.

"He's getting on, darling. That's what happens to old men. And they're saying he's got some trouble with his liver, though I must say I haven't seen any real proof of that."

"Proof?" repeated Avery. "The doctor telling you, *that's* your proof."

Her mother gave her a tired look.

"Anyway, they say he needs longer supervision."

"Jesus, Mom, why didn't you tell us?"

"None of you ever called to ask!"

"Does your insurance cover it?"

"About half, but the other half is expensive. That's why we're selling the apartment. I appreciate your help with the mortgage, but no one lives there now, and we could use the money." She picked up a dishcloth and ran it through her hands distractedly. "Though God knows, we've borrowed against it enough times it won't be worth much to us now."

Avery gave her an incredulous look.

"What do you mean no one lives there?" she asked. "I just told you Bonnie and Lucky are there right now."

Her mother pulled the dishcloth in her hands taut.

"For how long? Lucky can't be relied on to stay anywhere for long and Bonnie will be at some training camp or another within the year. And they're adults! If they want to live in the city, they can find their own place."

"You can't do that to them, Mom!"

"Do what? Sell the home I own? I can't live according to your wishes, darling. I have to do what's right for me and your father."

Avery pulled at the loose threads of the faded Moroccan table-cloth.

"First Nicky and now this," she mumbled.

Her mother's attention snapped to her.

"We let Nicky stay in the place for a fraction of the rent for as long as she needed," she said. "We knew she was struggling with pain management on her teacher's salary and—"

"But you didn't see what was really going on. Just like you won't with Dad."

Her mother rolled her eyes.

"Oh, it must be hard for you," she said.

"What?" asked Avery wearily.

"To be the only person in the world whose mother isn't perfect."

Avery snorted in annoyance.

"Aren't you going to learn anything from what happened to her? Aren't any of us? This family is so fucking . . ." She tried to think of a word that could capture the disastrous jumble of recrimination, addiction, and denial that lay at her family's core. "*Fucked!*" she settled on.

"What happened to Nicky has nothing to do with this."

Avery began to count on her fingers.

"Dad's in rehab. I can't drink. Bonnie wisely never started. Lucky is . . . Well, it's a miracle she's alive. And Nicky *overdosed*. Our family has a problem, Mom. A really serious problem."

Her mother crossed her arms and paused. Avery could practically see the cogs of her brain whirring as she decided which tack to take between denial, delusion, or defensiveness.

"You want to be called an alcoholic so badly?" she began evenly.

"I don't *want*—" Avery interjected but her mother kept going.

"I can't stop you if that's what you want to call yourself. You were a very brilliant and sensitive adolescent who got into some trouble with drugs. Does that make you an addict?"

"Yes. That's exactly what that makes me."

"I can't say." Her mother was speaking with slow, affected reasonableness. "That's for you to say. But your father has *gout,* not to mention old age. Bonnie is a pillar of health. Lucky is young and a bit reckless, I'll admit, but fine. And Nicky had *endometriosis.* She got on those drugs because none of the doctors knew how to treat her pain, the result of a medical system that does not prioritize research funding for women's health. I hardly need to tell you this, Avery."

So she had gone with good old straightforward denial. Classic. Avery had her rebuttal already prepared.

"There are plenty of women living with endometriosis who didn't do what Nicky did."

"So you're blaming her?" her mother countered. "How can you talk about your sister this way? If you want to blame something, blame the androcentric medical field. What have I been telling you all these years?"

"I do not need lessons about the patriarchy from you! Only one of us is married to the fucking patriarchy and it's not me!"

Avery was losing her cool, a feeling she hated more than anything. Her mother curled her lip into something between a snarl and a smile.

"I'm not blaming her," Avery continued before she lost the thread of her argument completely. "She was *suffering.* And none of us knew how to help her. We have to talk about this stuff or it's going to keep killing us one by one."

Her mother narrowed her eyes.

"You never used to be this histrionic. Is it Chiti who tells you this?"

Her mother had always been suspicious of therapists, a class of professionals she lumped with psychics and healers as created to exploit the desperate and foolish. Avery suspected she was afraid of her children seeing one because she thought the therapist would fault her for whatever was wrong with Avery and her sisters. *I don't blame my mother for how I turned out. Why should you get to?* Avery suspected that her choice to marry a therapist was regarded by her mother as not merely a betrayal of common sense, but of her mother too.

Every part of her wanted to scream, but with the greatest largesse imaginable, she decided to ignore this jab at her wife and try a softer approach.

"Can you at least acknowledge that he drinks a little too much?" she asked.

Her mother cast tensely around the room as if looking for a trap, then conceded with a slight drop of her shoulders.

"Yes, I can admit that."

"Thank you. I'm not trying to criticize you and Dad. I'm just worried. It's worrying that he should need to be in treatment for so long."

"I appreciate that."

Her voice was wary, but there was a relaxing of her jaw. Avery proceeded with caution.

"Have you thought about ever going to an Al-Anon meeting?"

Wrong move. Her mother's voice shot up half an octave.

"And sit around listening to a gaggle of sad saps who blame everyone else for their problems tell me I should leave my husband? I'm quite all right, thank you!"

Avery folded her hands on the table and placed her forehead on them in defeat. How had she ended up here again? No matter what line of reasoning she chose, she ended up in the same futile place. If this was a case, she would have dropped it long ago. She wasn't going to change her mother, not now, not ever.

"That's not what it's like," she said in an exhausted voice.

"Don't tell me what it's like. I've been."

Avery lifted her face from her hands. This was new.

"You went? When?"

"They judged me, Avery. Those women judged me. They told me to *keep coming back*. Sanctimonious twats."

Avery almost laughed.

"That's just a slogan. They say that to everyone who's new."

"I don't need to be treated like some naughty schoolchild. I'm a grown woman with four grown children. I don't need to be told to *keep doing* anything."

"Three."

"What?"

"You have three grown children."

Her mother twisted the dishcloth in her hands. When she spoke her voice was cold, devoid of whatever emotion was roiling within her.

"I'm sure this streak of pedantry is put to good use in your chosen profession, but it is quite irritating in general conversation, Avery."

Avery scowled.

"But why couldn't you?" she asked.

"Why couldn't I what?"

"*Keep coming back?*"

"I just told you—"

"Not for you, for *us*. Who was going to teach us how to be okay if you and Dad didn't? How else were we meant to learn?"

Her mother looked at her in surprise.

"But look at you. You *are* okay. Better than okay! You've got a great career. A huge house, from what I hear. A beautiful wife. Bonnie was a world champion, for Christ's sake. Lucky's been on billboards all over the world. And Nicky was loved by those kids before . . ." She stopped herself. "How bad of a job could we have done if this is how you all ended up?"

Avery shook her head.

"You don't get to do that."

"What? What am I doing?"

"Take our accomplishments as proof of your competence as a parent. They're ours, not yours."

"I'm *saying* they're yours, darling!"

"And you don't get to tell me how my childhood was. *I* know how it was."

"Oh god, this again. Were you beaten? Were you starved? Did you sleep in the garden shed?"

"We didn't have a garden."

"You *know* what I mean. Do you know how good you girls had it in comparison to so many others? To me? And now you come here to tell me all the ways we let you down? No, I'm sorry, darling. You're too old to be blaming your parents for your problems. That get-out-of-jail-free card has expired."

But Avery was not ready to back down. All the resentment, all the recrimination, everything she had spent years trying to work on and move through came rushing back. *Clean house, trust God, help others.* That's what she'd been taught in program. But she looked around herself now and she was surrounded by filth.

"Where were you when *I* went to detox?" she demanded. "Where were you then? Why do you always support him? Why not us?"

"You didn't tell us you went to detox! You didn't want us to know. We didn't know where you were for over a year, Avery!"

"You could have tried to find me!"

"I did! I went to the police! But you were twenty-one years old and you'd left of your own free will. We didn't have any legal rights. You, of all people, should understand that."

Avery had not known this, and the pain this knowledge brought now was far worse than the self-righteous fury she had felt for years. For her mother never to have looked for her was maddening, but for her to have tried and failed was heartbreaking, too heartbreaking for Avery to bear. She wanted to press her palms into her eyes and cry like a child. She wanted to shrink until she was small enough for her mother to pick up and cradle against her chest. She wanted to be a baby again, to go back to the beginning, to the time when she was her mother's only child and there were no sisters to let down or lose. Before she found drugs, before she left home, before she met Chiti, before she ruined her life. But she couldn't, none of them could, so she set her jaw and glared straight ahead.

"How could you not come upstairs?" she asked.

"What?"

"Yesterday. You knew we were all there, why would you not wait to see us? They know you came by the apartment. How do you think that made Bonnie and Lucky feel?"

*And me,* she thought but did not add. Her mother hung her head.

"I wanted to," she said quietly.

"Then why didn't you?"

"I know it must seem weak to you, but that apartment, all Nicky's things . . . I can't go in there, Avery."

She came and sat across from her at the table, resting an open palm between them.

"She was my girl," she whispered.

Avery nodded. Nicky was her mother's favorite; it wasn't right, but it was true. She was the only one of them who had managed to penetrate her mother's heart, not with force but with a gentle and persistent attention. Avery thought of Aesop's fable of the sun and the wind competing to make a man remove his jacket to prove who was stronger; the wind blew and blew, but it only made the man wrap himself tighter in his coat. Then the sun gently shone down upon him, warming him until he willingly slipped it off. Bonnie and Lucky had known better than to even try, but Avery had always approached their mother like the wind, willing and wanting her to change through force. Only Nicky had been the sun.

"I know she was," said Avery.

Her mother knotted her hands in front of her.

"What happened to her," she said, "was too much. For all of us. But please understand that I cannot accept what you're suggesting: that it was all my fault." Avery tried to interject but her mother raised her hand. "I can't, I couldn't . . . I couldn't live with myself if that were true."

Avery looked at her across the table. She looked small in all that black fabric, smaller than she had ever seen her.

"Did you want to be a mom?" Avery asked.

She had not planned to ask it; the question was plaintive rather than accusatory. Her mother cast her eyes to the ceiling as though the words could be found up there.

"Honestly?" she said eventually. "I wanted to be a wife. I'm no
sure if I wanted to be a mother." She smiled ruefully. "But one sor
of came with the other."

Avery looked at her. She realized, with a jolt of fear, that her
mother was describing her own feelings.

"Then why did you have four kids?"

Her mother shrugged.

"Catholic."

"That's it? One word to explain our family's entire existence?
You're not even religious."

"Well, *I'm* not Catholic, darling. My family's Church of England,
which hardly counts, as you know. It was your father's thing."

"We barely went to church!"

"I'm speaking culturally as opposed to denominationally."

"So you just let him knock you up? That's insane."

"It was a very different time. I got married when I was twenty-
three. Ten years younger than you are now. You can't imagine what
it was like."

"But it wasn't the Middle Ages, Mom. You could have said you
didn't want children."

Her mother sighed.

"I didn't know how hard it would be. Becoming a mother is a
shocking thing, Avery. Like landing on the moon. Everything
changes." She looked at her from under her wiry eyebrows. "It was
the worst with you."

"Right," said Avery. "Sorry."

What could she say to that? *She* didn't ask to be born.

"It got a little better with the others, but I knew I didn't bond with
any of you the way I was meant to. After each birth I just went . . .
flat." She shook her head. "There's language today for what I had, but
back then the doctors just told you to get on with it. It was seen as
pretty shameful. What kind of mother—" She stopped herself. "Anyway, there's no use dredging all that up now."

Avery searched her mother's face.

"Did you talk to Dad about it?"

Her mother dismissed this instantly with a wave.

"Oh, men don't understand these things. He was competitive with you lot anyway. You all wanted more of me than I could give." She exhaled a dry laugh. "Not like now!"

Avery tried to keep her voice neutral as she spoke.

"Did you ever think about divorcing him?"

Her mother looked up at the ceiling.

"Sometimes," she said eventually.

Avery tried not to look shocked. She had not actually expected her mother to answer honestly.

"You *did*?"

Her mother leaned back with a tired sigh, as though being forced to repeat something for the hundredth time, rather than revealing a totally novel side of her inner life.

"I could never come up with a good enough plan," she said. "What could I do? Take you all out of school and back to England? And live where? My parents were both dead by then. Split custody and leave you alone with him? I knew what it was to have to deal with . . . You think your dad's drinking was bad? My dad's was worse." She looked into the distance. "Father was vicious," she said quietly.

"I didn't know you'd ever considered it."

Her mother slapped her palms down on the table.

"And I love him! I felt for him! He tried his best to control it and I could protect you girls better that way. I kept us separate from you. You see, I knew you would have one another. And the younger ones would have *you*. I thought that way you could at least grow into your own women. And you did. Look at you."

Avery's voice, when she did speak, was barely a whisper.

"But I wasn't ready. I couldn't even look after myself."

Her mother made a gesture to dismiss this.

"But you *did* it."

"Not Nicky. I lost . . . I lost her."

Her mother reached across the table and clasped Avery's hand with the fierceness of a falcon clutching a field mouse in its talon. The intensity of her gaze frightened Avery.

"Is that what you think?" she asked. "That it was *your* fault?"

"You said it yourself, they were meant to have me."

"To walk them home from school, not to babysit them for the rest of their lives!"

Avery shook her head.

"But I left them. Twice. First for California and then for London. I was so happy with Chiti and my big job. It was selfish. I should have known what was going on with her. I should have come back."

"You think you moving back to New York could have saved her?"

"I don't know," Avery said, and it was a child's keen. "Wouldn't it?"

Then her mother did something highly unusual; she scooted around the table and took Avery in her arms. She rocked with Avery's head against her chest, making little gentle shushing noises and smoothing down Avery's dark hair.

"Listen to me," she said. "I want you to really listen." She put her mouth next to Avery's ear to speak in a fierce whisper. "*You are not that important.*"

HER MOTHER INSISTED AVERY COULD not visit the country without collecting some fresh eggs, which was how she found herself kneeling in the dirt by the chicken coop, her hand grasping blindly into the still, dusty darkness within. Finally, her hand settled on the familiar shape.

"They're still warm!" she exclaimed.

"You can put them in here." Her mother proffered her a shoebox filled with straw. "I used to only collect them once a day in the morning, but then some of the eggs broke and the chickens began to eat the yolks. They got a taste for the stuff, apparently it can happen, and now I have to check a couple of times a day to make sure they're not pecking them open themselves for a snack."

"Eating their own eggs? That's disgusting."

Her mother snorted roughly through her nose.

"You girls are such city kids. I should have raised you around the brutalities of nature, that would have toughened you up."

"You think growing up in New York didn't make us tough? A homeless man jerked off in his sleeping bag in front of our entire field trip outside the Natural History Museum. Trust me, we didn't need the chickens."

Her mother gave a sharp laugh and Avery felt the unbidden pleasure of saying something she found funny. Avery passed her another egg, and she grabbed her hand before Avery could retrieve it.

"Do you want to tell me what's wrong now? Why you look so sad?"

Avery glanced at her in surprise, then yanked her hand away.

"What do you mean? If I look sad, it's probably just because I've been thinking about Nicky."

Her mother leaned back on her heels to inspect her, frowning.

"That's not it."

How could her mother see her clearly now, after all she had missed for so long? *You're too late,* she thought. But the tug to be known, to be seen by her mother at long last, pulled her back to meet her gaze.

"I cheated on Chiti," she said.

Her mother nodded. Around them, the chickens clucked in witness.

"With a man," she added.

Her mother nodded again.

"And she found out and now she's sleeping in the guest bedroom and I'm here," she finished with.

A final nod. Avery waited for a response, but her mother only sat on her heels like an ancient apostle, blinking calmly. Avery gave an exasperated little cry.

"*Say* something," she said. "I'm burning down my fucking life over here."

Her mother picked up a piece of hay and twirled it between her fingers.

"Once you get to my age, you will learn that you can take a lot of wrong turns and still end up in the right place."

"I don't know what the fuck that means," said Avery.

Her mother looked at her evenly.

"Yes, you do."

Avery sighed.

"She wants to have a baby."

"And you?"

"Don't." As soon as the word left her mouth, it felt like a betrayal. "Know," she added quickly. "I don't know."

"You never wanted one when you were little."

"How do you know?"

"You told me! You were always saying it. I thought it was a bit of an indictment. Your way of telling me you wished you'd never been born."

"It probably was. Doesn't mean I feel that way now."

"Well, do you?"

Avery let out a dry laugh.

"Wish I'd never been born? All the time."

"I meant want children." Her mother gave a thin smile. "But join the club."

All Avery wanted was someone to tell her what to do. She wished her mother could give her the answers, but of course she couldn't. She hadn't known the right way to live her own life, let alone her daughters'. Her family was so lacking in guidance, Avery realized. At least Charlie's mother had a God, and he could believe she believed, even if he didn't. What did Avery's mother put her faith in? Her father. And what did her father have faith in? Alcohol. Her mother had taught her to believe in nothing but a woman's capacity to survive disappointment. And yet, despite all this, all Avery wanted was her advice.

"What should I do?" she asked. "What would *you* do?"

Her mother twirled a piece of straw between her fingers pensively.

"Do you love this other man?"

"Charlie? No! God no. He's . . . It's not like that. I don't want to be with any man. I'm a lesbian, Mom."

"Then you commit to Chiti. Show her she's the only one for you."

Avery watched a chicken strut behind her mother, its head turning in tiny jolts like a glitching robot.

"And how do I do that?" she asked.

Her mother smiled and opened her hands.

"You give her what she wants."

Avery hung her head.

"And if I can't?"

Her mother dropped the piece of straw and brushed off her palms.

"Then you're allowed to stop looking for penance and move on with your life."

Avery looked up at the ash tree whose shade they were seated under. Ribbons of light fell between its leaves. A warm breeze gathered momentum and was met by a chorus of wind chimes.

"Are you okay out here, Mom?" she asked suddenly. "All on your own?"

Her mother kept her eyes on the egg in her hand.

"It's not your job to worry about me, darling."

How many times had Avery said that to her sisters? She moved so she was sitting next to her mother on the ground. When she was younger, she used to fantasize about taking her mother and sisters away somewhere, far from her father, someplace where they could live together unafraid. A world of only women and girls, that was what she dreamed of.

"Why don't you come stay in the apartment with Bonnie and Lucky for a bit?" she asked. "Just while Dad's gone. I'll be there too." She smiled. "It could be fun."

Her mother put her hand on top of Avery's and gave it a firm shake.

"We're selling it, my love. It's time to move on."

Avery's face crumpled.

"No, Mom. It's too much loss so soon after Nicky. Please—" Her mother tried to say something, but Avery raised a hand. "I'll pay for his rehab. I'll cover the mortgage. Please."

Her mother shot her a bemused glance from under a wiry eyebrow.

"How much money do you make?"

"A shit ton."

This was an exaggeration, but she would make it work, and she needed to convince her. Her mother stood up and dusted off her swaths of black fabric, then offered a hand to help Avery up.

"No," she said. "I don't want you bailing everyone out anymore. Your sisters have to grow up. We all do."

Avery took her hand and heaved herself to standing.

"But what am I meant to do?" she asked in a small voice.

Her mother raised a hand to Avery's cheek and stroked it softly with the back of her knuckle. Avery had never seen herself in her mother, but she saw her sisters in her. Lucky had her sharp canines. Bonnie had her narrow nose. Nicky had her tulip-shaped face. She had planted pieces of herself in all her children. Avery was wondering which part was hidden inside her when she heard the tinkling sound of music notes. She looked down to find a cluster of chickens pecking at the colorful bars of the xylophone. They appeared to be playing together, each plucking in time with the others. It was a surprising, joyful sound.

"That is why chickens have a xylophone," her mother said.


AVERY SURPRISED BOTH HERSELF AND her mother by wanting to stay upstate longer, sleeping for two nights in the large wrought-iron bed beside her in one of her mother's old nightgowns. She spent the days helping her in the garden, tending to the chickens, and reading from her father's yellowing collection of Penguin paperback classics. They did not speak again with the directness they had when Avery first arrived; they had said what they needed to and could now spend time together in companionable quiet. It was the most time Avery had shared alone with her mother since before Bonnie was born, and she was surprised by how easeful it felt. She had always marveled at women who appeared to *want* to spend time with their mothers, planning weekend trips and mother-daughter days with evident delight, and she had secretly suspected that neither party could actually enjoy that time. Now, Avery thought with mild astonishment, she could perhaps be one of them, or at the very least understand the impulse. Her time with her mother had softened her all over, as a warm hand softens clay, and by the end of the second day she found herself longing to return to Bonnie and Lucky, to mold around them again and make peace. She only hoped they would let her.

ON THE THIRD MORNING AVERY woke up before the sun rose and took the earliest possible express train back to the city, letting herself into the apartment just as the sun was beginning to rise over the serrated skyline. She assumed her sisters would still be asleep—she was hoping to drop her stuff, then head out to buy breakfast from the diner on the corner as a peace offering—but, as she crept down the hallway, she heard a low strumming sound coming from the bathroom. Beneath the closed door was a bar of yellow light. Avery pushed it open to find Lucky sitting on the lid of the toilet, a cherry-red Gibson guitar in her lap. She glanced up and stopped playing as Avery entered.

"What are you doing?" Avery whispered.

"You're back," said Lucky, her expression momentarily opening, then closing again, like a fan. "Don't you knock?"

"Is that your guitar?" asked Avery.

Lucky dropped the instrument between her legs with a hint of self-consciousness.

"No, I stole it," she deadpanned. "Isn't that what entitled messes do?"

Avery turned and carefully clicked the door shut behind her so they wouldn't wake Bonnie. Lucky could have no idea how close to the bone that retort was; but she wasn't stealing anymore, Avery reminded herself, she was done with all that. She'd had such clear intentions returning here, yet as soon as she was back in the presence of her sister, the waters muddied. Lucky evidently wasn't ready to make up and, seeing this, Avery's own resolve faltered. Why was it so much easier to love her youngest sister from afar?

"I don't know," she said, turning back to Lucky. "Let me just put my judgmental cunt hat on and try to figure that out."

"I called you a judgmental bitch, not a cunt," said Lucky.

"Oh right, no offense taken then. Glad we cleared that up."

At the corner of Lucky's mouth, Avery saw the tiniest twitch of a smile.

"Do you need to pee?" Lucky asked, beginning to get up. "I'll leave."

"No." Avery gestured for her to stay put. "You keep doing what you were doing. I'll go."

Lucky didn't say anything to stop her, so Avery turned back to the door. With her fingers on the handle, she paused. What was she doing? She was the older sister; who was going to be the bigger person if not her?

"It sounded good, by the way," she said. "What you were playing. I liked it."

Lucky remained silent and Avery opened the door and slipped back out into the hall. Then she heard Lucky's voice, low but earnest.

"Do you really think so?"

Avery pivoted and reentered the bathroom, closing the door behind her again.

"I do." She nodded. "It's been ages since I've heard you play anything."

Lucky set the guitar beside her and gave Avery a long look, deciding if she wanted to explain.

"My new sponsor lent it to me," she said eventually.

Avery could feel Lucky's eyes alert on her, watching for her reaction. She had such a beautiful face, twitching and intelligent, like some lissome deer that must be coaxed, ever so gently, to eat from her palm.

"Your sponsor," Avery repeated slowly, buying herself time. If this meant what she thought it meant, it was a delicate situation, and she didn't want to mess it up.

"I met her at this meeting downtown," Lucky said, trying to appear nonchalant, but Avery could see the effort it took. "I told her I used to play, and she said it might help my recovery to write how I'm feeling on it."

Avery swallowed slowly. She could feel tears pricking her eyes.

"And has it?" she asked quietly.

Lucky shrugged. Avery stepped forward, trying to keep her voice level.

"Lucky, I'm so—" she began.

"Look, I don't want to make a big deal out of it," Lucky interrupted. "And I know you think I'm a fuckup and it's probably too late or whatever. But I'm trying, okay? I'm trying."

In England there was a saying used by football fans: *It's the hope that kills you.* A loss is always more bitter if you let yourself dream of victory first. Low expectations, that's how the Brits liked to live. Protectiveness dressed up as pragmatism. It was how their mother always operated. But Avery was American. She believed in hope, had eaten it for breakfast along with Frosted Flakes and local news segments about everyday people who jumped onto subway tracks to save perfect strangers. And nothing was more hopeful than sobriety.

But she was a realist too. She knew the facts: Addiction was a chronic disease for which there was no cure, only a daily reprieve, et cetera et cetera. Most people did not stay sober. Every AA anniversary meeting, she saw it: dozens of people taking chips for ninety days, a handful celebrating one to five years, a few for five to ten, and then a wasteland of double-digit anniversaries you'd be lucky to find one or two people celebrating. Where did they all go? Some got busy with careers and family and simply stopped going to meetings. Most drank again. Many overdosed or developed chronic conditions. Some died. Why Avery was one of the lucky few who'd gotten to stay this long, she didn't know. She couldn't quite believe she would be celebrating her own anniversary of a decade next week. Ten years. Ten had seemed about as attainable as one hundred when she was new. What she'd learned in that time was that few people stay. And most people never even make it into the room.

But some did. She had. By some miracle, Lucky had. And if addiction ran in families, maybe recovery could too. Oh, there it was again, ballooning inside of her, that great, childish, colorful, American thing: optimism. *Maybe it will work for Lucky,* she thought. *Maybe she'll be okay.* She couldn't help it; the *maybes* bloomed bright and strong like dandelions, those lovely and uninvited weeds that always find the cracks. She hoped and hoped and hoped.

"Lucky, stand up," she said.

Lucky looked at her warily.

"Why?"

Avery tried to look serious, but she couldn't stop smiling. She noticed suddenly that tears were rushing down her cheeks, hot and unchecked.

"Because I am about to squeeze the shit out of you."

Lucky maintained her guard for a moment, then let her face break into her brilliant, lupine smile.

"But I didn't do anything," she said, standing up.

Avery wrapped her youngest sister in her arms and held her still against her.

"In my experience," she whispered into the soft whorl of her ear, "the *not* doing is the hardest part."

AVERY AND LUCKY WERE STILL sitting in the bathroom discussing all things recovery—Had she started the steps yet? Was her sponsor really a British punk singer called Butter? Yes, the slogans were cheesy, but they came in surprisingly handy—when Bonnie padded into the bathroom wearing a pair of men's boxer shorts and a Golden Ring tee. She saw them and started.

"You're both here," she said dazedly.

Avery let go of Lucky's hand and smiled at Bonnie.

"Did we wake you?"

"It's past five," said Bonnie. "This is when my day starts. What are you doing?"

Lucky offered a happy little shrug. Avery could see from the ease between them that they had already recovered from their part of the fight without her.

"We're making up," she said.

"Oh, thank god," said Bonnie. "Can I get in on this?"

She launched toward them with a bear hug and the three of them held one another, swaying and laughing, squeezing one another tighter then laughing some more. After they'd disentangled, Bonnie went to the sink and started brushing her teeth.

"What's that doing in here?" she asked, spotting the guitar propped against the toilet in the mirror.

Avery pointed at Lucky.

"She's written a song."

"That's great, Lucky!" exclaimed Bonnie, toothbrush dangling from her mouth. "Can we hear it?"

Lucky grabbed the guitar and clutched it to her chest.

"No!"

"Come on, pleeeeease," wheedled Avery.

"I can't do it with you two watching me!"

"We'll close our eyes," said Bonnie.

"I don't trust you. You'll open them."

"Here—" Avery pulled back the shower curtain and motioned toward the tub. "Get in there. We'll close this so we can't see you."

With a little more cajoling, Avery and Bonnie managed to hustle Lucky into the bath and pull the curtain shut to conceal her.

"You good?" Avery called.

Lucky's voice came tentatively from the other side.

"You promise you won't laugh at me?"

Avery gave Bonnie a look to show her heart was melting, which Bonnie promptly returned.

"Promise!" they called.

Bonnie spat in the sink and rinsed her toothbrush, then they both settled down on the bathroom floor. Lucky plucked two notes over and over in plaintive succession. Then, very softly, she began to sing.

Soft, low, and just a little raspy, her voice was not what Avery had expected. It was caught somewhere between a growl and a purr, a sound made for expressing the pain hidden at the heart of pleasure. She was singing about Nicky, about loving someone without fully knowing them. *If you had been my twin,* intoned Lucky, *could I have shared the pain you were in?* Avery closed her eyes. She wished she could have taken a share too. Maybe then she could have protected her. But they were sisters, not twins. They came from the same place, but not the same time. And as close as she felt to each of her sisters, there would always be so much she didn't know. Avery opened her eyes. No, they would never have that, but they had a choice to have something else. This song, it was like Lucky was finally offering them a key to her, and Avery could do the same; she could let them see her. Lucky finished singing, and Avery and Bonnie pulled back the shower curtain with a flurry of whoops and cheers, piling on top of her so all three were squished in the tub together. Lucky let out a yowl of protest, but they held on tight and, eventually, Lucky let herself be held.

A lot was written about romantic love, Avery thought, about the profundity of that embrace. But this, too, was deserving of rapture, of song. Before she ever knew a lover's body, she knew her sisters', could see herself in their long feet and light eyes, their sleek limbs and curled ears. And, before life became big and difficult, there were moments with them when it was simply good: an early morning, still dark out, their parents asleep. Her younger sisters arriving one by one at her bedside, hair tangled, exuding their sour and sweet morning musk. She'd lifted the covers for each of them, letting them crowd into her bottom bunk, bodies pressed tight against one another, and they'd fallen asleep again like that, dropping off like puppies curled around a mother's warm belly. She'd slept, too, safe in the center of her sisters, not knowing or needing to know where she ended and the next began. Squeezed beside Bonnie and Lucky now, it was superfluous to describe what she felt for them as love. They *were* love, beautiful and unbearable and hers.

A WEEK LATER, AVERY GOT the call to come home.

"I'm ready to talk," Chiti had said simply on the phone, and Avery booked her ticket for the next day.

Since her flight wasn't until the afternoon, Bonnie came back early from the gym and Lucky stuck around uptown so they could have a final lunch together. They got bagels from the deli on the corner and took them to the park, sitting side by side on the benches near the playground under the shade of the elm trees. It was a bright summer day, and the sky between the crisscross of branches was swimming pool blue. The scent of caramelized peanuts drifted down the path from the Nuts 4 Nuts cart, mingling with that unique combination of mowed grass, garbage, horse manure, and car exhaust that could only be found in Central Park. Avery closed her eyes.

It had been a happy handful of days, packing up the last of Nicky's stuff together and chatting for hours about their lives. Avery had told them about their father's return to rehab and her time with their mother upstate. Lucky wasn't ready to see either of them, which Avery understood, but Bonnie had offered to join their mother to visit their father that month. Lucky and Avery had watched Bonnie training at the gym with Pavel, marveling at her speed and power, and gone to AA meetings together. Since Bonnie was often training, the eldest and youngest sisters spent a surprising amount of time together and, miraculously, managed to only bicker what Avery considered a regular sibling amount. They all had dinner together every night and Avery felt the pleasure of being a sister among sisters again after so long. They were not four, and they never would be again, but they were starting to find the symmetry in three.

"It's weird that in a few weeks it will be gone forever," said Lucky, looking across the park to where their apartment was hidden. She wrapped her arm around Avery and rested her head on her shoulder. "I'm sad," she said. "But I'm also relieved, you know?"

Bonnie and Avery both nodded. Somehow, Avery thought, in the process of disassembling their home, New York had finally begun to feel like one to them again.

"The real question is . . ." said Bonnie. "Who gets to keep the bunk beds?"

Avery laughed.

"I think it's time to officially say goodbye. Only took thirty years. And anyway"—she nudged Bonnie with her shoulder—"I don't see Pavel as a bunk bed man."

She turned to her sister, who gazed back at her sanguinely. The sun had bathed her face in yellow and in that honeyed light she looked like something cast in gold. Avery waited for her to blush or change the subject, but she remained serene.

"I like his bed as it is," said Bonnie.

She smiled widely. There was nothing more to say. Bonnie had informed them with characteristic equanimity that she would be moving in with Pavel after the apartment was sold and, while they had both grilled her mercilessly, Bonnie, true to form, had not offered much in the way of exciting details. She did tell them that it turned out Pavel had been in love with her for years too. Since this revelation Avery had never seen her sister look more at home in herself.

Avery took a bite of her bagel and turned her face to the sky. They were sitting near the playground, the sharp cries of the children lobbed like shining arrows toward the bench where they sat. Avery dropped the remainder of her bagel into its foil.

"Do you guys want kids?" she asked suddenly.

Bonnie wiped a glob of cream cheese from her lip and gave her a funny look.

"Me and Pavel? I think it's a bit soon, don't you?"

"I meant generally," said Avery. She turned to include Lucky too. "Both of you. Growing up, did you want kids? Do you now?"

Bonnie thought about this.

"I love kids, but with my career . . . I can't imagine it." She smiled. "Maybe when I retire."

Avery looked at Lucky.

"What about you?"

Lucky grimaced as she swallowed a hunk of her everything bagel.

"Dude, I'm just trying to keep myself alive right now."

"But you do, right?" Bonnie asked Avery. "Didn't Chiti freeze her eggs?"

Avery glanced toward the playground.

"Nicky really wanted children," she said. "She was made for it."

Bonnie nodded. "She would have been the best mom."

"Mm-hmm," murmured Lucky in agreement. "Much better than ours."

"Not exactly a high bar to vault," said Avery. Then, feeling guilty, she added, "But she did her best."

"Fair." Lucky sniffed, then suddenly laughed. "Oh god, remember when we all thought Nicky was going to get knocked up by that vegan trumpet player?"

"He was nice, wasn't he?" asked Bonnie.

"He was *very* vegan," said Avery.

"So?" said Bonnie.

"He had a tattoo sleeve of endangered species on his arm," said Avery.

"The skinny polar bear!" cried Lucky, and they all laughed.

"He was such a weird choice for her after all those frat guys she dated in college," said Lucky.

"Chad!" said Avery, and they all laughed again.

"I think she was trying to connect to her creative side," said Bonnie.

"The vegan came to the funeral," said Avery.

"I don't remember him there," said Lucky.

"You didn't hear him?" said Avery. "He was the one crying loudly in the back. Totally lost his shit."

"But they weren't even together anymore," said Lucky. "Nicky broke up with him for that hot hedge funder with the ball fetish. What did she used to call him?"

"Lick-and-Handle-My-Balls," said Bonnie, and she and Lucky laughed.

"I hated that funeral," said Avery, staring ahead.

Lucky stopped laughing and looked at her.

"Well, yeah, Aves, we all did. Obviously."

"All those other people loudly grieving," continued Avery, her voice flinty. "What did they know? What the fuck did they know what it was like to lose her?"

"People were sad," murmured Bonnie. "It was a sad thing."

"But it wasn't *their* sadness," said Avery. "It was ours."

"Sometimes I wish she'd just had a baby," said Lucky suddenly. "With anyone, you know, Chad, the vegan, Lick-and-Handle-My-Balls, who cares? Then she could have had the surgery earlier."

Avery winced. It was too painful to consider.

"She was so young," she said. "And she didn't love those guys."

"But if she had," continued Lucky. "Even if she'd still . . . At least we'd have someone, you know? Someone left who was partly her that we could look after."

"*We're* partly her," said Avery.

"I know," said Lucky quietly. "But with a baby, we'd get a new chance. With a baby, we'd . . ." Lucky paused to think what she was trying to say. "Do better," she settled on forlornly.

Bonnie placed the remainder of her bagel carefully in the foil and turned to them, her face twisted with worry.

"There's something I've never told you," she said.

Avery and Lucky looked at her in surprise.

"What is it?" Lucky asked.

Bonnie swallowed slowly.

"The day before she died, she asked me . . . She asked if I could get painkillers for her at the gym and I said no." Bonnie dropped her head into her hands. "I didn't know. I didn't know she was going to buy them."

"Oh, Bonnie," said Avery, reaching for her sister instinctively, "no one could have known. Why didn't you tell us?"

"I wanted to protect her," she said. "Or me. I don't know." She looked at them both with a pleading look in her eyes. "Do you think I should have done it?"

"Absolutely not," said Avery decisively. She couldn't bear for Bonnie to think that for even one second. "You did the right thing."

"I never thought she would . . . What she did," said Bonnie.

They sat in silence, staring ahead. It was still hard to even name what had happened to Nicky. *Overdose* always sounded like they were talking about someone else, someone who was nothing like their confident, capable sister.

"You weren't the only one," said Lucky quietly. "I knew she was struggling, that she wanted to get off the pain meds."

"You did?" asked Bonnie.

"There was this wishing tree at her school," Lucky explained. "Where we wrote our wishes on pieces of paper and tied them to it. I looked at hers without her knowing and that's what she wished for. *No more pills*. I saw it, but she denied it afterward and I didn't push it. I didn't want to make it worse . . . Or I was too self-involved to try, I don't know."

Lucky hung her head. Avery placed a hand on her back.

"I knew too," said Avery. "Deep down. It was her eyes."

More and more frequently, Nicky's pupils had been tiny black dots. Avery had noticed because it reminded her of how Freja's pupils used to shrink to pinpricks after they shot up, a mirror of what Avery's own eyes must have looked like. But Avery had convinced herself it wasn't the same thing.

"I want you both to listen to me," she said, turning now to Bonnie and Lucky. "I know we want to make sense of what she did, and blaming ourselves for not doing more is one way to do that, but none of us could have changed what happened to her." She thought of what their mother had said. "None of us are that important."

They watched as a knot of pigeons corkscrewed into the sky and disappeared into the blue.

"But how do we live with it?" Lucky asked softly.

It was the question they had all been asking themselves in one form or another for the past year. How to live with this grief. How to love a life without their sister in it. Avery sighed.

"I think Dad told us," Avery said. "At the funeral."

Lucky looked up.

"The *Breakfast at Tiffany's* thing," she murmured. "*Go lightly*. But how?"

"You're doing it already," said Avery. "Not drinking anymore, taking care of yourself, that's going lightly."

"She's right," said Bonnie, nodding.

"What about you two?" Lucky asked. "How are you *going lightly*?"

Avery looked at Bonnie.

"Well," Bonnie began. "Don't make fun of me . . . but, sometimes, I talk to God."

"God?" repeated Avery.

Bonnie may as well have said Ronald McDonald for all the comfort the idea of God brought Avery.

"Not Jesus Christ or anything like that," clarified Bonnie quickly. "It's a different kind of God, one I kind of made up. It, or She, or I don't know what to call it, is someone for me to talk to. And I think they're looking after Nicky until we get to see her again."

"Do you really think something's looking after her?" asked Lucky, her voice high with hope.

Bonnie nodded.

"I do."

"Good," said Lucky softly.

"I want to believe that, Bon . . ." said Avery. "But honestly, I'm not sure that I can."

"Can you just believe that I believe it?" asked Bonnie. "Does that help?"

Avery considered this. The idea of anything helping Bonnie brought her comfort too—that she knew to be true.

"Maybe," she said. "Maybe it could."

They fell silent and listened to the sound of the children playing, which contained all the ecstasy and terror of youth. Avery's thoughts, as always, returned to her life with Chiti. Bonnie had told them the truth; now she must as well. She turned to her sisters.

"I fucked up, guys," she said. "I really fucked up."

"I told you not to get poppy seed," said Lucky, pointing to her bagel.

Bonnie gave Lucky a look to shush.

"What is it?" Bonnie asked, leaning toward Avery.

Avery took a deep breath.

"I slept with someone else." Avery exhaled. "And I lied about it. And then I promised Chiti a baby and I . . . I can't. I can't do it. I want to want it, but I don't. It's not . . . It's not who I am."

"Oh shit," murmured Bonnie.

Avery glanced up at them. Bonnie, clearly taken aback, let out a long exhale. Lucky, meanwhile, appeared unfazed.

"So *that's* what happened," she said.

Avery gave her an incredulous look.

"You knew?"

"About the sleeping with someone part, not the baby stuff. Well, I had my suspicions."

"How?" asked Bonnie.

"Chiti showed me the Plan B. She thought it was mine."

"And that's why you called me a hypocrite," said Avery, finally putting together that piece of their fight. "I thought it was just because of the stealing."

"What stealing?" asked Lucky.

"I've been having a bit of an issue with the five-finger discount," said Avery. "But I've stopped that now."

"Avery!" exclaimed Bonnie, looking shocked. "What the hell?"

Avery gave her a desperate shrug.

"I have impulse control issues."

"Join the club," said Lucky with a dry laugh.

"You two . . ." Bonnie shook her head, then turned to Lucky. "Why didn't you tell me about the Plan B?"

"Or *me*?" added Avery.

Lucky turned to Avery.

"We've been in a good place, and I didn't want to ruin it. And—" She turned to face Bonnie. "It's not my shit to tell."

Bonnie made a face to show this was fair, then looked at Avery.

"Does Chiti know?" she asked.

Avery nodded.

"About the sleeping with someone else, not the baby," she said. "She needed some space after she found out and that's, in part, why I came here."

They sat in stunned silence. Eventually, Lucky let out a low whistle.

"I'd heard a rumor," she said. "But now I know it's true."

Avery glanced at her with a look of panic.

"A rumor? About me?"

"Yeah." Lucky nodded. "That you are not, in fact, perfect."

Avery snorted with relief.

"When have I ever claimed to be perfect?"

Now it was Bonnie's and Lucky's turn to roll their eyes.

"Okay," conceded Avery. "I may have tried to give you that impression once or twice. But that's just because I wanted . . . I don't know, after our parents, I wanted you guys to have one solid person in your lives. And I fucked up so badly when I was younger, leaving you all like I did, I may have overcompensated a little as an adult."

"Well, apparently you're not overcompensating anymore," said Lucky. Avery gave her a pained look. "Sorry," she said. "I'll shut up."

Avery leaned on her knees and clasped her hands in front of her, like a coach watching a particularly grueling game she can do nothing to change. Her jaw twitched as she stared ahead.

"It's all my fault," she said.

"Do you think you and Chiti will split up?" Bonnie asked.

"I don't know. She'd have every right. Every right," she repeated quietly.

"I love Chiti . . ." said Bonnie.

Avery felt a sinking sensation in her chest. She was breaking her sisters' hearts too. She had spent so long trying to be an example for them, trying to prove that marriage—life!—could be different, better, than the model they were offered by their parents. She had wanted to give them hope, but she had been another disappointment instead. Bonnie placed a hand on her back. It felt soft and heavy, like the paw of some friendly bear.

"But you have to be who you are," Bonnie said.

Avery let herself lean into Bonnie.

"Thank you," she whispered.

She dropped her head into her hands and let out a shuddering sigh.

"It's okay for you to be angry with me," she said between her fingers. "I understand you're disappointed."

Lucky got off the bench and knelt in front of Avery. She took

Avery's hands away from her face and held them. Her bony grip was surprisingly strong.

"Look," said Lucky. "We're your sisters. Whatever you do, we're ultimately on your side. You could kill someone, and I'd help you sneak the body back to us and fill a bathtub with hydrochloric acid so we could dispose of it discreetly."

Avery tried to suppress a smile.

"That's weirdly specific," she said.

"I wouldn't *like* it and I don't *like* this," said Lucky. "But I'd do it."

Bonnie scooched over so she was nearer both of them.

"Me too," Bonnie said. "Fill that tub."

AVERY ARRIVED BACK IN LONDON just as the sun was rising. She took a taxi from Heathrow through the slowly awakening streets, past the bread delivery vans idling by the restaurants and early-rising shop owners flinging up the latticed metal gates to reveal their window displays. A peach sun smeared across the sky, scattering violet and blue clouds. She arrived at their address in Hampstead and looked up at the beautiful, crumbling brick house they had spent the last eight years making a home together. Letting herself in quietly, she headed straight upstairs. Chiti was asleep in their bed, her dark hair coiled in its bedtime bun on the cream pillowcase. She noticed with a pang that Chiti was wearing a pair of Avery's blue cotton pajamas, something they always used to do when the other traveled and they missed the other. Chiti stirred at the sound of Avery entering.

"Is it you?" she murmured.

Avery nodded, her eyes already filling with tears. Chiti had been the home she wanted to return to for so many years.

"It's early," said Avery.

She reached for her suitcase and extended and retracted the handle nervously, then stopped and went to sit on the bed.

"I have to talk to you about something," she said softly.

She knew if she waited even one minute there was a chance she would talk herself out of it, prolonging the inevitable even further.

Chiti sat up and wrapped her arms around her knees under the covers. Her gaze, which before had been sleep softened and warm, turned cold.

"I've been waiting," she said.

"Chiti," she said quietly. "There's more I haven't told you. And I'm sorry I didn't before I went to New York, but I needed to know it was true."

She saw Chiti brace herself. Avery took a deep breath.

"I don't want to have a baby."

It was as though the last invisible thread holding Chiti upright had been snipped. She crumpled back against the headboard and dropped her head into her hands. Immediately, Avery wanted to take it back, tell her she'd been wrong, pull Chiti's hands from her face, smooth her brow, kiss her temples, get into bed beside her and stay there all day with this woman she loved, who had loved her so well and for so long. Chiti's voice, when she did speak, was small with defeat, empty of recrimination.

"Then why did you say you did?" she whispered.

"I wanted to want one," said Avery. "I'd hoped that was enough."

Chiti shook her head and clasped her hands together in front of her.

"I should have listened to my mother," she said.

Avery felt a twinge quicken her pulse. Ganishka had never warmed to her, it was true, but her coldness seemed less to do with Avery as a person than the fact she was an American. It wasn't fair to act as though Ganishka had been right all along now; she had been a good partner to Chiti for seven of eight years—that should still count for something.

"She never liked me," Avery said.

Chiti shook her head.

"Oh, it's not that. Or not *only* that," she said. "She said you were not cut out for motherhood."

Avery frowned. *Fucking Ganishka,* she thought. She resented her for talking about Avery as if she knew her. She resented her even more for being right. What Ganishka didn't understand was that

Avery had already *been* a mother. She'd raised her sisters; for her, that was enough.

"How would she know?" she asked, trying not to let the defensiveness she felt creep into her voice. Chiti sighed and let go of her clasped hands.

"Because *she* was not," she said. "And I imagine she thinks you are more alike than she lets on."

Avery saw it then, the color of Chiti's grief. It was the deepest indigo, dark enough to be almost black, like the farthest parts of the ocean. It was an ancient grief, old as indigo itself, and like that age-old dye, its origin was in India. Chiti's mother was not a loving mother. Chiti had talked many times over the years to Avery about her wish to raise a child differently, to lavish her baby with all the attention, wonder, and affection of which she had been deprived. Now Chiti had chosen the very thing she had been trying to escape, a partner who did not want to be a mother in the place of a mother who had not wanted to be one. The realization weighed heavy as a stillborn in her arms.

Avery stayed on the bed next to her wife. There was no anger in them anymore; they were left with the sadness that always lay in wait beneath it. Avery would have preferred shouting to this leaden, heartbroken silence. She took Chiti's hand.

"You will be a mother," she said. "You will."

She was saying it, she knew, in part to ease her own guilt, but she also believed it, she had to. Chiti squeezed her hand.

"I wanted to do it with you," she said.

"I know."

Chiti raised her head hopefully.

"And you're sure you can't?"

Avery nodded.

"I'm sure."

Chiti also nodded slowly.

"I always felt that the way we started . . . It was a hard foundation to build a relationship on. The shame has never left me."

Avery looked at her in surprise.

"You have nothing to be ashamed of. Therapists date clients. Shit happens."

Chiti shook her head sadly.

"You can't take away my shame, just as I can't yours."

They sat together as the home they had created released its sundry moans. The floorboards beneath the bed creaked. The curtains sighed. A pipe downstairs clanged. Outside, someone walked past chatting loudly into their phone. They never had gotten around to getting the windows up here double glazed, Avery thought.

"I'm sorry," said Avery. "About Charlie. About everything. You never deserved that."

"You're right," said Chiti. "I didn't." She shifted slightly to face Avery. "And I'm sorry for what I said about Nicky. You couldn't have saved her. No one could have. You know that?"

Avery nodded. It was time to speak, to find a way to communicate with Chiti what she had been feeling, not because it would change anything, but because it was what Chiti had asked for.

"I miss her and I miss her and I miss her," she began. "And I wait for the feeling to end because every other feeling has ended, no matter how intense, no matter how hard—but this won't. There's just no end to the missing. There was life before and there's life now. And I can't seem to accept it. I can't accept that I'll have to miss her forever. There will never be relief. There will never be a reunion. And I wish I had a God. I wish I believed in an afterlife or something, anything. But when I try to talk to her in my head, there's no response. I can't hear her. And I can't feel her. All I have is this missing. And part of me is glad it won't end because it's all I have to connect me to her now."

Avery rubbed a hand over her face. She had been waiting a long time to say this, and now she was here there was no point holding back.

"But I'm not strong enough, Chiti," she said. "I thought I would be, but I'm not. So I keep trying to cut the missing off. And, yes, I've been smoking and I've been stealing. I betrayed our marriage and I lied to you and I . . . I ruined our life together. I know I should have handled everything differently. I can't understand why I didn't. I thought I was one person before Nicky died, but it turns out I'm not. I know you said you have been losing me for a year, but I have too. I lost her *and* I lost myself. I don't know who the fuck I am anymore."

Chiti put her hand on Avery's and looked into her eyes. Avery searched for forgiveness, but she saw only resignation.

"Maybe that's because you are becoming someone new," she said.

An hour later, Vish came to pick Chiti up in his beat-up Mini Cooper. Avery stood on the top step as a bright sun climbed the morning sky and watched as he and Chiti packed his car with her bags. Vish shot Avery a look full of confusion and hurt. She swallowed the lump in her throat and resisted the urge to call out to him. She was losing him, too, she realized.

After they left, Avery wandered around the large empty house. She glanced into the bedroom, where the bed was still imprinted with the shape of Chiti's sleeping body, then retreated to the kitchen. She plugged in the kettle to make tea, smiling ruefully to herself; it was exactly what her mother would have done. But before the water boiled, Avery decided to leave. She couldn't stand the silence. She pulled on her swimsuit and a pair of sweatpants, then flung open the front door, heading toward the Heath. Ever since moving to London, she had always wanted to swim in the Hampstead Ladies' Pond. Today, she would do it.

As she entered the park, a handful of emerald-green parakeets shot out from the trees above. They called to one another in an excited chatter, filling the air with their squawks. When she first moved to the city, Avery had marveled at the sight of these bright birds flying free in the heart of gray, muted London. It was Chiti who told her the urban legend that Jimi Hendrix was responsible for their outlandish presence; allegedly, he had carried a birdcage to Carnaby Street and, without fanfare, unleashed a breeding pair of ring-necked parakeets named Adam and Eve. Now, they could be spotted anywhere from Croydon to Crouch End, but many favored the wild abundance of the Heath. Avery watched as the birds flew north. She watched until they were nothing but a tiny spot of green in the pale blue sky, until they were nothing at all.

It had just gone seven, early enough that the pond was empty save for a cluster of gliding mallards and a lone elderly woman swimming slowly, her neck jutting forward like a determined turtle. Avery left her things in the changing room and padded out onto the wooden dock. The cool air whispered around her skin. Around the pond, a leafy canopy of trees sighed and rustled as if politely rearranging themselves. She grasped the metal handrails and descended into the water beneath. A sharp, involuntary exhale escaped her as coldness encased her to her neck. She bobbed, her hair fanning around her, and caught her breath. Then she slipped beneath the surface of the water, of the world itself.

Down below, everything was quiet. Pond water, silken and thick as oil, slid over her skin. Liquid gulps and hisses curled around her ears. Tiny glistening bubbles pearled her skin, then drifted away like thoughts. Cones of light pierced the water above her head. She propelled herself deeper, the light retreating behind her. Swaying reeds brushed her toes as she pushed toward the cooler depths. Below was a dark floor of mud, a place the sun reached for but could not touch. She laid herself horizontal and let her body sink to the coolest depths. Mud sucked at the back of her legs and spine as she fell softly onto the bed of the pond. She closed her eyes and exhaled air.

Avery had taught all three of her sisters to swim. Stood in the shallow end, hand under their bellies holding their thrashing bodies aloft. Even as they gulped and spluttered, eyes red with chlorine and tears, she had not let them stop. She needed to know they could keep themselves safe. Of all of them, Nicky had become the best swimmer. Avery could see her now, streaking beneath the water's glistening surface, a pale blur of limbs, her hair a serpentine thread. She could hold her breath longer than any of them, disappearing for such lengths that Avery would feel her heart squeeze with panic. But always, after that long stretch of silence, would come the sound of her sucking in breath, the exultant sight of her slick head bursting forth. She saw her sister now, far away across a glittering expanse, smiling and waving, amazed at herself, turning to see if Avery was amazed too.

What had Nicky thought in her final moments? Had she known? Was it a relief not to have to fight anymore? Not to feel? The water pressed around Avery, insistent and beckoning. Up above, Bonnie and Lucky were safe. Could she leave them now? Could she be free? Avery opened her eyes. Pale light danced far ahead. Her lungs ached. It was too much, this love. Then she felt it, her legs kicking out beneath her, turning her upright. Her soles sank into the mud, then pushed off. A thousand dark tugging tides pulled her back as she propelled herself, but she did not stop. Her palms thrust water aside, as though flinging open heavy curtains to let in the day. It grew warmer as she drew closer. She kept swimming. She was almost there. Light broke over her head like applause. She breached the surface, gasping for air.

# Epilogue

TEN YEARS LATER, THE SISTERS CAME FROM NORTH AND SOUTH. IN Morningside Heights, a few streets from the Columbia University campus where she was now teaching, Avery slipped out of bed and kissed the sleeping figure beside her. The woman stirred and murmured.

"Is it happening?" she asked, her voice thick with sleep.

"I'm going to see her now," whispered Avery. "Keep sleeping."

The woman lifted her cheek from the pillow.

"Give her every ounce of my love," she said.

Avery stroked the woman's braided head and bumped her lips against her temple. She turned to grab clothes from the chair beside the bed and padded softly out of the room, closing the door before turning on the light in the living room and kitchen. She dressed quickly, leaving her pajamas in a crumpled pile, then splashed water on her face from the kitchen tap. Beside the sink was a large pink

Smeg fridge. Before leaving, she picked up a gold wedding band from the counter and slid it on.

A HUNDRED AND TWENTY BLOCKS south in Tribeca, Lucky was attempting to check out. The lobby she was standing in could have belonged in a midlevel hotel, except for the fact the young man behind the front desk was refusing to let her leave.

"But it's after curfew," he repeated again.

"I know." She flashed him a smile. "But I think this constitutes extenuating circumstances."

The man, who was still in his early twenties, cast around nervously. His hair was in a floppy bun, and he was wearing, unironically Lucky presumed, a T-shirt with the D.A.R.E. logo on it.

"I don't think I'm authorized to do that," he said. "I, like, just started here."

Lucky leaned across the desk and flicked her eyes up at him. Her long hair, recently dyed a deep crimson, fell forward around her shoulders.

"But, see, this is kind of a once-in-a-lifetime thing," she said, twirling her finger in front of her on the desk. "You wouldn't want to be the reason I missed it, would you?"

The man blushed and looked down at his lap.

"I don't know, man . . ."

"Please?" she purred. "You'd be my hero."

He glanced up at her face, a little more lined than it was in her twenties, but still irresistible, still lovely, then blushed some more.

"Look, I didn't see you, okay?" he said.

Lucky clapped her hands in delight from her side of the desk, then turned on her heel.

"You're a legend!" she called over her shoulder.

Clearly delighted, he called something after her, but she was already propelling herself through the revolving door.

———

IN THE TAXI HEADING DOWNTOWN, Avery scrolled through her emails without reading the words, then checked her app of international clocks. It was nine-thirty in the morning in Delhi. Perfect. She called Chiti, who answered on the second ring.

"Is it happening?" asked Chiti.

"I'm heading to the hospital," said Avery.

"Oh goodness! How are you feeling?"

"Nervous!"

"That's normal, but it will all be okay. Bonnie's an ox."

"I thought after she retired, I'd never have to visit her in the hospital again."

"That's your sister, full of surprises. And Pavel?"

"He started speaking Russian halfway through calling me, but the gist of it was to come now."

Chiti hummed down the phone.

"It's good you're there," she said.

Avery nodded.

"How's Azad?" she asked.

She could not believe he was eight years old now. It had been a decade since Avery and Chiti divorced; Chiti had conceived him using a donor the year after Avery returned to New York. In Hindi, *Azad* means *free and independent*.

"He and Ganishka are still thick as thieves. She's teaching him to use her old Bolex camera as we speak. He doesn't want us to go home next week. How's Fatima?"

"Tired from touring, but the book's doing well."

"I got tickets for her reading in London, by the way."

"You didn't have to do that."

"I wanted to."

Avery smiled.

"Look, I'm almost at the hospital, I just wanted to let you know."

"I'm glad you did. Tell her she is in my heart."

Avery hung up and looked out the window at the dark New York streets streaking past. It was after midnight, but the bars were all still open, people chatting outside of doorways and milling on street corners smoking. Avery taught an Advanced Corporate Law seminar at eight A.M. twice a week that ensured she was rarely up this late, but it was comforting to see the city's nightlife was still thriving. There would always, she thought contentedly, be young people who did not need eight hours of sleep.

LUCKY DIPPED INTO A BODEGA by the subway entrance to pick up a pack of Marlboros. She'd quit, again, a couple of months before, but tonight was a special occasion, and she figured she deserved a little treat. She was relieved that the store still sold them; everyone vaped now, and with all the taxes, cigarettes were hard to come by. She smiled to herself as the man behind the counter slid the pack to her; she hadn't been out and about on her own, without chaperones or a gaggle of other recovering addicts, in weeks. She was about to pay, then picked up a bar of milk chocolate at the last moment. Bonnie might want the sugar. A group of college-aged students toppled through the door, heading toward the frosted fridges of beer. Of course, Lucky thought, it was Friday night. She'd forgotten, and that was a good thing.

She stood outside the bodega, turned one cigarette in the pack upside for luck—a habit she'd had for over twenty years now—then lit another, inhaling with a spine-tingling sensation of pleasure. The college students were tumbling back out with their beer, yelling excitedly to one another, when one of them spotted her.

"Wait a minute, aren't you Lucky Blue?" He slapped his friend. "Oh shit, I thought she died or something!"

Lucky raised her hands like an apostle.

"And yet, I am reborn."

"Yo, can I get a picture?"

Lucky relented and let two young men sandwich either side of her to take a selfie. She thought about removing it, then let the cigarette dangle from her lips. Fuck it; she was nobody's role model.

"Yo, my girlfriend's obsessed with you," one of them said as he wrapped a beefy arm around her shoulders. "She's going to freak when she sees this. That video of you falling off the stage at Glaston-bury? *Wild*."

Lucky squeezed herself out of their embrace as soon as the picture was taken.

"Not my finest hour," she said. "But I live to serve. Now, gentle-men, if you'll excuse me."

She saluted them with one hand, flicked her cigarette away with the other, and disappeared down the subway stairs.

AVERY WAS WAITING IN THE hospital lobby when Lucky strutted in. All these years, Avery thought, and she'd still never managed to erad-icate that model walk. She stood up and hugged her sister.

"How was this week? Did you pick up your chip?"

Lucky gave her a sharp-toothed grin.

"Sixty days at the Monday meeting."

Avery patted her back, holding on a little longer.

"Proud of you." She sniffed Lucky's hair. "But you're smoking again."

"We tackle our addictions in the order they'll kill us!" recited Lucky cheerily, pivoting away on her heel, and her sister, to her relief, laughed.

"Did you speak to your tour guy about pushing back your dates so you can stay for the full ninety days?" Avery asked.

Lucky let out a groan.

"Can we not talk about that now?"

Avery narrowed her eyes.

"Okay, but your case manager said—"

"Aves, please!" Lucky cut her off. "Let's just focus on Bonnie and give this a break for, like, one day? Please?"

Avery flared immediately.

"It's only been two months," she barked. "And you almost *died*. Apologies if the fact I'm still concerned about you isn't convenient."

Lucky raised her hands and shook her head without a response, pleading with her eyes for Avery to drop it. Avery gave her a long look, then relented. She turned and picked up a large bouquet of hot-pink roses from the chair behind her, pointing them toward the elevators. They set off across the lobby.

"They're pretty." Lucky touched a coiled petal with her fingertip, offering peace. "When did you get them?"

"While I was waiting for you. The gift shop's open all night here. Not exactly Bonnie's color, but I figured it's the thought that counts."

"They're Nicky's color," said Lucky.

Avery smiled sadly.

"That's true."

Lucky linked her arm in Avery's.

"From both of us?" she wheedled, using her best youngest-sister voice.

Avery laughed in spite of herself and leaned closer to her as she pressed the elevator button.

"That goes without saying."

BONNIE WAS RESTING WHEN HER sisters appeared in the doorway. Pavel was by her bedside, alert as a hound, watching her with anxious attentiveness while continually offering apple juice, which he seemed to be convinced, apropos of nothing, had magical restorative properties. Not even when Bonnie became the undisputed lightweight world champion, becoming the first woman fighter to unify the belts by defeating her opponent via unanimous decision in a grueling ten-round battle that is still lauded as one of the toughest fights of all time, had he been so wired. Bonnie had retired a few years later to become one of the most in-demand trainers for women fighters, so it had been some time since Pavel had worried for her physical safety. But it had been a long labor, not made easier by the reminder from the doctor that at forty, Bonnie was considered both a geriatric and a high-risk pregnancy. She had, however, managed to deliver as she'd hoped, without medication or intervention, leaning into the pain, as a lifetime of combat had her trained to do, and now she was both satisfied and spent.

Bonnie had been privately concerned that she wouldn't feel whatever she was meant to when her daughter was placed in her arms, but she needn't have worried. She was perfect. Her eyes were blue and very bright, like Bonnie's father's. The nurse laid the baby against her chest, and the child immediately looked up at her with great curiosity and stillness. In that look, Bonnie was undone by love. The baby's face was red and creased and soft as velvet, with Pavel's thick eyelashes and square nose. But her fingers were classic Blue, long and expressive. When she cried, she stretched her hands out in front of her like tiny exploding stars. When she slept, she wrinkled her forehead and frowned as if having deep conversations in her dreams. Bonnie could not take her eyes off her.

She glanced up as her sisters entered and beamed. Pavel leapt from his chair to give each of them a kiss and offer them apple juice, which they politely declined.

"I go get some more just in case," Pavel insisted, heading to the door. "Give you girls your moment."

Avery squeezed his arm in thanks. Of course, it *was* a moment, one of the most precious they would have. They were high up in a hospital room in the middle of the night, the city stretched beneath them at a quiet remove, the headlights of cars gliding up and down the avenues like shooting stars, and before them, safe as a hatchling in a nest, was their very own miracle. Lucky bounded to one side of the bed while Avery approached reverentially, staring at the bundle in Bonnie's arms in awe.

"She's here," declared Lucky, her voice already full of love.

Bonnie nodded.

"She's here."

"I can't believe we were all born in this hospital," said Avery. "And now all these years later she's joined us."

"Not Lucky," Bonnie reminded her. "She basically fell out of Mom at home, remember."

Lucky made the rock-and-roll sign and grinned.

"Speed freak from birth," she said.

"How could I forget; sorry, Lucky." Avery smiled and turned back to the baby, marveling at her. "Have you called Mom?"

Bonnie nodded.

"Pavel did. She's coming in the morning."

Their father had been dead for four years now from liver failure. Their mother insisted on remaining alone upstate with her garden and chickens, but she visited the city more now that all three of her daughters lived there again. Avery had a guest bedroom for this exact purpose, though she wished their mother would make more use of it.

"Have you decided on a name?" asked Lucky.

Bonnie looked up at her sisters.

"We had one picked out, but then . . . it didn't feel right. She came with her name, I think."

"What is it?" Lucky asked.

Bonnie swallowed and placed a hand on the baby's crown.

"Nicole," said Bonnie. "Nicole Petrovich Blue."

Lucky tried to say something but found she could not speak. As always, Avery had the words for both of them. She leaned forward and kissed first Bonnie, then the baby, on the forehead.

"Welcome to the great, wide world, Nicole," she said.

The baby stirred and looked up at the three figures above her. She could feel their attention on her like light. They had many eyes, and they were all on her. Their mouths were big and bright. Now she closed her eyes. All dark. Now she opened them. The light was back on her. She opened her mouth and made a sound. Now her mother was feeding her. Her mouth was full. Yes, she liked this. A rush of warmth and sweetness. This was good. There was plenty and she was hungry. Now, suddenly, she was full. No more. She made another sound and the figures all laughed. Everyone was delighted by her. Soon, the baby's eyes were heavy. The light went away. She tried to bring it back, but her eyes were too heavy. Now she could not see, only feel the figures around her. They felt like warmth. She was safe at their center. Something soft stroked her cheek as she drifted. That was good. She could still hear them, and she liked that. Laughter. What a good sound. She wanted to hear more, but she was drifting away. She would come back again soon. She would not be gone long. The darkness deepened. The figures circled her. This place was good. She would stay.

# ACKNOWLEDGMENTS

I dedicated this book to the two loves of my life: my sister Daisy and my husband, Henry. This story, and everything about me, has been shaped for the better by them.

Writing is an inherently solitary experience, so I'm grateful to all those who ensured the researching, editing, publishing, and just plain living parts of the process were not:

My agents, Mollie Glick and Emily Westcott, for their tenacity, graciousness, and support.

My editors, Sara Weiss and Katie Bowden, for believing so whole-heartedly in these sisters and providing me with the holy trinity for rewrites: unconditional support, sagacious suggestions, and space to find my own solutions.

My assistant editors, Sydney Collins and Lola Downes, for their enthusiasm and insights.

My boxing trainers at CMC Gym, Marcelo Crudele, Felix Martinez, and Alberto Solto, for helping me understand and inhabit Bonnie more fully, and for instilling in me the most important (and hardest for this chatty writer to follow) rule: LESS TALK, MORE ACTION!

My fellow writers in L.A. for their encouragement and feedback on the early drafts of this novel: Annabel Graham, Tess Gunty, Alexandria Hall, Zach Hines, Isabel Kaplan, Victoria Kornick, Claire Nuttall, and Jacquelyn Stolos.

My friends Albie Alexander, Frankie Carattini, Adam Eli, Lindsay Fishkin, Sean Frank, Sophia Gibber, Emily Havens, Alba Hodsoll, Kala Jerzy, Jess Jobst, Shamikah Martinez, Corey Militzok, Amanda Montell, Olivia Orley, Jonathan Parks-Ramage, Zoe Potkin, and Max Weinman for the endless walks, dinners, calls, laughs, and general loveliness that propelled me onward while writing.

My mother, always, for being my best and first reader.

My father, my sister, Holly, and my brother, George.

My therapist, Karen.

The sober communities in New York, L.A., London, and Paris for being my lighthouses.

The readers, the readers, the readers. To every person and bookseller who read, recommended, posted about, or championed my debut *Cleopatra and Frankenstein,* I am endlessly grateful for you.

As I write this, I am pregnant with my and Henry's first child, so the final thanks must go to this mysterious being inside of me, our baby—My darling, I had a different ending in mind while writing this book; then you appeared and bent the curve of this story, and my life, inexorably toward hope. Thank you for choosing me.